# CLASSICS OF THE SOUL'S QUEST

BY

## R. E. WELSH, M.A., D.D.

PROFESSOR OF APOLOGETICS AND CHURCH
HISTORY IN THE PRESBYTERIAN COLLEGE,
McGILL UNIVERSITY, MONTREAL

NEW YORK

GEORGE H. DORAN COMPANY

*First published 1922*
*Reprinted May 1923*

*Made and Printed in Great Britain. Butler & Tanner, Frome and London*

## TO

## MY COLLEAGUES

IN THE THEOLOGICAL COLLEGES, ANGLICAN, CONGREGATIONAL, METHODIST AND PRESBYTERIAN, AFFILIATED TO McGILL UNIVERSITY, MONTREAL, WHOSE CO-OPERATION IN THE TRAINING OF STUDENTS HAS SET AN EXAMPLE OF CATHOLICITY OF SPIRIT IN THE COMMONWEALTH OF CHRISTIAN KNOWLEDGE

# Preface

THE great documents of the soul in its quest of the Eternal Goodness have severally been treated in separate works. But, so far as I am aware, there is no book that offers a comprehensive and comparative survey and estimate of them in their consecutive connexion and their general significance. An attempt—confessedly all too incomplete—is here made to show, not only the influence of each upon those that came after, but the place of each in the ever-fresh, continuous movement of the Spirit of Life and Grace under changing conditions and modes of thought.

Spiritual experience, like the whole of life and as part of life, is always expanding, never finished, in each generation voiced in fresh expression and calling for fresh exposition. There are foretokens of a fresh literature of the soul with a new insight into the things of the spirit in an altered scheme of things. Yet those personal records of spiritual quest and experience which are historic will retain their value ; they are capable of generating some equivalent movement in our inner life in any diverse mode ; they are corrective of ephemeral moods and of individual aberrations ; and they afford vital material for further interpretation in the growing light of life.

Classics in literature are writings which have attained universality and permanence, appealing to the catholic mind of man, and, while bearing the imprint of the times and the personality of their writers, capable of acquiring fresh significance in later ages and under new conditions. Most of the writings herein surveyed are classic in that sense. On others entitled to rank in the same class I had proposed to write in separate chapters. But under limitations of space one is compelled to make selections from a literature that is almost inexhaustible, and I have to confine these studies to representatives of various types of the soul's enterprise and vision in successive ages.

This book is not specially engaged with mystical writings, with devotional works, or with the intellectual problems of religion, although these do enter into the subject-matter and consequently into the treatment thereof. It is concerned with the life of the spirit, more specifically (in Gladstone's words) with " that personal and experimental life of the soul with God which profits by all ordinances but is tied to none ; dwelling through all its various moods in the inner court of that sanctuary whereof the walls are not made with hands."

The book originated in a course of lectures to a College class, which have here been considerably changed and extended.

I have pleasure in making acknowledgment to Prof. A. R. Gordon, D.Litt., of McGill University, Montreal, and to Prof. W. S. Milner, of Toronto University, of their kindness in reading the MS. and offering valuable suggestions.

R. E. WELSH.

# Contents

[Over

9

# I

# Introductory Survey

AS part of our spiritual heritage, there has come to our hand a body of literature expressive of spiritual experience which has become classical and has almost attained the rank of a sacred canon. These documents of the soul have won this high rank, as Apostolic writings won their place in the canonical literature of the New Testament, by the singular service they have rendered in bringing earnest men into living touch with God, in voicing the various moods and tenses of the heart under the upward calling of the Spirit, in crystallizing Christian experience, and in generating experience kindred with that of which they are the " fair deposit."

They make a universal appeal through their penetrating insight into the conflict of the inner life, " piercing even to the dividing asunder of the soul and spirit, quick to discern the thoughts and intents of the heart." They transcend religious traditions and divisions and the conditions of time and place in which they were produced ; and they outlive the systems of theology to which they were attached. Naturally they appeal mainly to avowed Christian people. But they have called also, and still make their call, to earnest spirits holding to other systems of belief, even to those who, holding no dogmatic beliefs, yet endure the common ordeal of inward strife, respond to veracious cries of the human heart, and are wistful listeners to " the eternal voice of prophecy." It is significant that, of these, George Eliot the Positivist kept the " Imitatio Christi " of Thomas à Kempis close to her bed-head for use before sleep, and that J. A. Froude wrote a monograph on Bunyan and Edmund Gosse another on Jeremy Taylor.

1. These Christian Classics have a many-sided interest ; they bear significance and value in various directions.

(*a*) They are notable in themselves as books, as literature of a high order.  They belong fundamentally to the literature of grace and power rather than to that of knowledge, although in Dante's " Vision " these two are combined. They are commonly marked by aptitude and force of expression, by graphic description, searching insight and often rhythmic cadence.  And these qualities spring from profound feeling, keen vision, great ideas deeply rooted in human history, and life born personally out of sore struggle issuing in precarious victory.

The New Testament documents, the primary Christian classics, are richly charged with a vital air, a freshening breath of life, throbbing pulsations of joy and love and magnanimity, a sense of  dominion over dark demonic powers and sin and death, under the incommunicable thrill of felt divine, protecting Presences.  They are pitched to a lofty keynote.  The sound of singing runs through them (echoed in Pater's " Marius the Epicurean ")—Canticles at the beginning, Anthems at the end.  Often elsewhere (as in 1 Cor. xiii. on charity) they express the essential music to which the lives of their writers were attuned.  A spiritual afflatus blows through them, the winds of God animating new-begotten souls.

Herein is the source of the inspiration which gave them to us and which stirs us in response to them.  The cadence or lilt of language, in its " measured wavelike movement of sentences," reflects the rhythmic exaltation of Christian consciousness according to the measure of personal life-power.

Something of the same kind marks many portions of the classics of Christian experience reviewed in the present series of studies.  Their literary qualities are not a matter of mere style or conscious artistry.  The first thing in style —according to the saying ascribed to Longinus—is a great soul, and then real thoughts and deep feelings.  John Bunyan in writing the " Pilgrim's Progress," made the avowal that he " could have stepped into a style much higher than this, and could have adorned all more than here is done." But God did not play with him in temptation, nor did he play with hell; " wherefore I may not play in relating of them, but be plain and simple and lay down the thing as it was." Does not the pith of his skill in writing, the pith of this matter, lie just there?

Carlyle said to his wife when he finished the MS. of his " French Revolution ": " I know not what the world will do with this book, or misdo, or entirely forbear to do, as is likest; but this I could tell the world—You have not had for a hundred years any book that comes more direct and flamingly from the heart of a living man." These classics of the soul come always direct and some of them flamingly from the hearts of men wholly alive, and for this reason they belong to the literature of power. The book of power is the offspring of a man or a woman of strong personality. The strength thereof need not lie in aggressive, domineering egoism; it is often found in gentle souls of gracious charm; but the personality is at any rate definite, unitary, vital, impressing itself tellingly, because it has been caught up and swept by an ennobling interest and cleansed by a grand passion in which it has felt itself the agency of a power greater than itself.

Their power we trace to their authors' endowments; but their authors seem to themselves, like old-time prophets and men of genius, to be rather the agents and voices of a higher power possessing them. Ruskin (in " Frondes Agrestes ") put it thus: " I believe the first test of a truly great man is his humility. By humility I do not mean doubt of his own power or hesitation in speaking his opinions, but a right understanding of the relation between what he can do and say and the rest of the world's sayings and doings. All great men not only know their business but usually know that they know it, and are not only right in their main opinions but they usually know they are right in them; only they do not think much of themselves on that account. Arnolfo knows that he can build a good dome in Florence. Albert Dürer writes calmly to one who had found fault with his work: ' It cannot be done better.' Sir Isaac Newton knows that he has worked out a problem or two that would have puzzled anybody else; only they do not expect their fellowmen, therefore, to fall down and worship them." Then comes Ruskin's phrase of rare insight. " They have a curious undersense of powerlessness, feeling that the greatness is not in them, but through them ; that they could not do or be anything else than God made them ; and they see something divine and God-made in every other man they meet."

Of such are St. Augustine, Dante, Bunyan, John Woolman, William Law, John Wesley, Tolstoy, and their kindred. " See, then, what God has done," says Pascal. The power that comes through their work, enriching it with grace as well as pith and insight, is felt to be " given " them from above.

(b) These writings are specially significant for the Psychology of Religion, as exhibiting in concrete living expression the elusive phases of the soul, the deep founts of religion, the crises and stages in the spirit's quest for life-power and peace in God—that vast labour in which, pray God, we are all engaged. They and their authors have individually been the objects of much study, of analysis and comment. But not much has been done in studying them specifically from the psychological point of view, in studying the inner processes, the temperaments of the writers, the reaction upon social conditions, the relations between bodily and spiritual life, and between the different sides of human nature, emotional, intellectual and voluntaristic. Still less has been done in the way of the comparative study of these documents and their authors, in tracing kindred lines, similar processes and common laws, along with differences and individual peculiarities.

(c) These writings have also historical significance. They are usually representative historical documents more suggestive and illuminating than ecclesiastical chronicles and doctrines for an understanding of the age to which each belongs. They are the expression-points of a people and a movement, the quintessence of an epoch past or coming to birth, and at the same time the seed-bed or germinal origin of a new growth and crop of spiritual experience and moral effort. Several of them mark the point of departure introducing a new order in mental or social revolution or reconstruction. The religious ideal or type in the organic whole, the community—Church or State or Society—is realized and embodied in a signal concrete instance.

This is exemplified in St. Augustine's Confessions. The struggle in him between his duplex ancestry, pagan (in his father) and Christian (in his mother), and the triumph of the Christian element in his conversion, reflect the historical transition from Roman and Greek paganism to the Christian empire.

So Dante, c. 1300, at the watershed between the mediæval and the modern religious world, sums up the past in structural ideas, and yet in germinal conceptions and enlarged vision forecasts the new world of thought and life which is travailing towards birth and is about to emerge. Bunyan, Jeremy Taylor, Samuel Rutherford, William Penn represent British struggles for both spiritual freedom and parliamentary autonomy.

Tolstoy is individual in the traditional fight for the saving of his own soul, but also exhibits the modern social application of the Gospel, beyond his own intent paving the way for a socialist revolution.

These documents have to be interpreted in the light of historical antecedents, contemporary conditions and tendencies, the mass-sentiment in the corporate order. In turn they assist in the interpretation of the inner spirit and the point of view characteristic of the generation and the progressive forces in the Church.

They usually mark the development of fresh individualism after the reign of institutional religion and the organic system of life. The individual experience or vision is the creative and progressive factor, makes a fresh special contribution to the spiritual wealth in the common stock, and so fills out the orbit of the whole.

2. These great souls, through the records of their signal experiences which are individually their own, have sometimes set a type, established a new tradition, and even prescribed a form which has come to be imposed on others, and to which others' spiritual experiences are expected to

conform.   The preformed type enforced in the one notable case is indeed by the power of suggestion almost hypnotic in the expectation of a similar experience which it generates. Thus it is apt to lay a limiting requirement upon others, and so to restrain free individual religious life.

We can trace connexions and resemblance between St. Paul's experimental religion in his sharp revolution and St. Augustine's.   And from St. Augustine's time onwards in the West many prominent Christians, as Harnack has indicated (" History of Dogma," V, 74), have followed the same distinctive type.   "We find marked conviction of sin, complete renunciation of their own strength, and trust in grace, in the personal God who is apprehended as the Merciful One in the humility of Christ.   The variations of this frame of mind are numerous, but the fundamental type is the same. . . .   To it youthful Christians are trained and dogmatics are framed in harmony with it. . . .   He who has once come in contact with it can never forget it."   It governed the crisis in the soul of Luther, as shown in his commentary on Galatians (chapter ii.) and reproduced itself in the critical hour of Bunyan's reconciliation to God, as it has in many later cases.

Yet it is a mistake to suppose that this stereotyped form of spiritual experience has been the only type.   Another is to be observed of an ascetic form, embodied uniquely in Thomas à Kempis' " Imitatio Christi," in which the religious life is one of moral drill and spiritual exercise, in the practical management of the spirit with the guidance of principles of purity, veracity, obedience, fraternity and charity. The " Theologia Germanica " was cast in this same mould, born of the same self-oblivious monastic discipline.   And Jeremy Taylor's " Holy Living and Holy Dying," with a difference in his mental climate and conditions, is in keeping with this type, in regulating the inward life and its outward expression according to high principles and the obedience of Jesus Christ.

In the former type, which was set in St. Augustine's " Confessions," we find the vehement forces of human nature at war with the soul ; struggle of full-bodied men of warm blood, as were Luther, Bunyan and Samuel Rutherford, tempest-tossed between natural passions and conscience; and then the triumph of conscience achieved and maintained against repeated onsets of the "Old Adam." In the latter type the elemental fires appear to be extinguished, and self-possession by restraint gives a somewhat austere calm to soul-culture. The "Friends," Quakers, seemed to have most freshness in their spiritual experience, doubtless because of their withdrawal from the organized society of the Church and their appeal to the individual inner light and the freedom of the spirit. Yet they soon also established a general formal type, and their spiritual life adopted a fashion and formulated a terminology which comes under Russell Lowell's description of the "dialect of Canaan."

While the general resemblance between the spiritual histories of great souls is largely due to the sway of the preformed type, there is a deeper cause for such identity, to be found in the unity of human nature, the common psychic founts in the identity of human need and effort, and in the ideal type of the blessed life in Christ Jesus and in the Apostolic standard. Indeed the fresh experience from which a classic of the soul sprang often came from a return to the founts in the original Christian documents.

3. There are marked diversities, under a general unity, in these documents of the soul, as we see when we bring them into comparison. Each has its own individual accent, its specific tone or standpoint, just because each was born of personal experience which leaves its hall-mark on the surface and of which it is a veracious transcript. They sprang straight out of life itself, as it comes fresh to each truly living soul. Each is unique, expressing what the writer has seen and known and handled of the word of life. It is in virtue of this reality of personal experience that they afford us authentic words of eternal life, words of veracious insight, of fire, vision, power, and that they make swift appeal to that "mysterious deep life that slumbers in man," bringing a "direct impact of life upon life."

The diversities in their cast are due, not only to differences in antecedent types and individual temperaments, but to the different climates and forms of creed and ecclesiastical organization in which the authors were bred. St. Augustine's "Confessions" betrays the heat of North African blood; Sta. Teresa exhibits the hectic Spanish temperament and colour; Bunyan represents the Puritan spirit and moral standard; Lancelot Andrewes, Jeremy Taylor and William Law the fine ethical culture of the Anglicans who were nurtured on the Book of Common Prayer; Pascal the conflict between Jansenists and Port Royalists, between reason and conscience and heart; Tolstoy the sense of the wild and the unpractical Russian visionariness.

Yet in their essential spirit and prophetic messages they manifest fundamental sympathies which are closely akin in all Christian experience that is vital—the kinship of souls in common intuitions, struggles, and aspirations. They move along companionable paths, that diverge here and there, and yet keep the pilgrims in their progress within hail of each other. They transcend prescribed formularies and temporal conditions, and, like hymns from men of divided communions, they come close together when the authors pray before the one altar and when they sing the new song, the new type of song taught of the one Spirit. They meet at the top.

Great souls are said to be lonely; and they are so in that the common crowd around them are scarcely in touch with their higher thoughts or endeavours; yet they are not alone, for, like the peaks in high mountain lands, they recognize and greet each other; peak calls to peak; deep calls to deep in a divine antiphony.

4. Hence in the succession of seers and the classics which they wrote there is a fellowship of giving and receiving. St. Augustine drew from St. Paul—having a spiritual measure with which to draw from that deep well. Dante was steeped in and drew from St. Augustine and St. Bernard, as well as from Plato, Cicero and Virgil. Petrarch recognized himself in St. Augustine under stress of kindred temptations besetting his pious efforts, and addressed him (Augustine) as he appeared in a vision, "Whenever I read your 'Confessions,' I am moved by two feelings, by hope and

by fear (although not without tears at times). I seem to be reading the history of my own wanderings, and not of another's." Santa Teresa ("Autobiography," ix. 9) wrote : " When I began to read the ' Confessions ' (of St. Augustine) I thought I saw myself there described. When I came to the Conversion and read how he heard that voice in the garden, it seemed to me nothing less than that one had uttered it for me. I felt it so in my heart." So Pascal, the Augustinian Jansenist, as well as Thomas à Kempis, the Augustinian canon, read and recalled sentences from both St. Augustine and Dante. Luther, of the Augustinian order, found springs of water and green pastures beside them in the " Theologia Germanica," as did Bunyan in Luther's commentary on the Galatians. Milton's great epics bore the impress of Dante. William Law and other later lights had their lamps lit or kept burning by Thomas à Kempis. John Wesley acknowledged his obligations to both Thomas à Kempis and William Law. So has the lamp before the high altar never ceased to give its light to successive generations who waited on God.

5. These writings can be and have been classified in different ways, according to the points of view from which they are studied, the lines chosen for comparison and contrast.

One method of comparison and classification brings out the direction of personal interest or the mental note in the writers. The common note of some is emotional self-expression or mystical vision, as Tauler, Sta. Teresa, Jacob Behmen ; of others, evangelical, like Bunyan ; of others, intellectual, as Pascal and Amiel ; of others, ethical in individual practice, as Jeremy Taylor and William Law ; of a few, ecclesiastical, as Newman's " Apologia " ; and of a few the bearing is social, as in Tolstoy. The small number in the last group indicates how slowly the social claim has been felt and recognized by pious men.

On another line of comparison, i.e. form determined by purpose, we distinguish between those that come under the title of " Apologia " and those of the nature of Confessions —what is called Confessional Literature.[1] The former are

[1] Cf. Burr (A. E.), "Religious Confessions and Confessants " (Houghton Mifflin).

marked by the purely individual note, containing a vindication of the writer's course of life and conduct, or of his departures in his spiritual pilgrimage or ecclesiastical connexion.  Here Newman's " Apologia pro Vita Sua " is representative.  In the latter class the writer is engaged definitely in self-study, is introspective, analytic of his own soul, displaying his struggles, temptations, emancipation and reactions, and the processes of the work of Divine Grace—all depositing the ripe fruits of spiritual experience in golden baskets of truth and wisdom.  Here the outstanding instance is St. Augustine's " Confessions."  Others partake of the elements of different classes.

6. The impulses, the motives, leading to the production of this " confessional literature," were various, and yet were psychologically linked.

There is a natural reticence about their souls among most people ;  yet we notice sometimes a disposition to turn contrariwise and expose the secrets of the sanctum to open view.  Is privacy the more natural instinct, or publicity ? The real question, however, cannot be cast in that crude alternative.  Each is natural in different cases and conditions.

Primarily the soul suffers from shyness, seldom showing itself naked before others' eyes.  This is a form of instinctive modesty ;  it is not mere secrecy ;  it is chastity of spirit. Of the multitudes who have gone through the spiritual ordeal and pursued the quest for divine power and freedom, very few have given a faithful record of their travail or otherwise unbosomed themselves.  If men's eyes were windows through which we might see the *binnenleben*, what should stand disclosed to us of the panorama passing before their inner sight, of the ferment, the shame, the struggle, the narrow escapes from the fowler's net, the ebb and flow in their battles, the overcoming grace of Heaven that has enabled them to rise from every fall and gain the victory of just holding on, that has carried them forward through all turmoil towards the calm of unclouded vision and undivided love, and has fixed them steadfastly in the grasp of God's love and brought them the peace of Christ passing understanding ?

Surely, we think, that hidden life must be lonesome. Many have related their intellectual history, the working of their minds through doubts to some rational standing-ground. Many more have told the old yet ever-new tale of love. So far *ben* have we been admitted; but the innermost chamber has seldom been set open to view. Why? Not every one has a right to a key of admission into our private chambers; perhaps some would misunderstand us, perhaps even misuse our confidences. Ruskin speaks of "that cruel reticence in the hearts of men which makes them always hide their deepest thoughts." But Luther reached deeper in saying, "If thou feelest this in thy heart, it will be so great a thing to thee that thou wilt rather keep silence than say aught about it"—though, indeed, he generously broke this silence in abundant self-revelations, as Carlyle commended silence in some two score of volumes.

Many are reticent because their innermost experience is sacrosanct. Generally also the spiritual life of average people is inarticulate because they have not the faculty for self-analysis and for diagnosing their own case, or lack the insight into God's dealings with them that would enable them to interpret their experiences. Like Lazarus raised from the dead, according to Tennyson, what has transpired behind the veil is unspeakable, and so their lips are sealed. Others doubtless are reticent because they think their case is too peculiar, exceptional, to be recited, or again because they are ashamed to disclose the emptiness of their hearts, the poverty of their experience—though, if they but made a beginning and drew out the one root-fact that each person has in his life as the gist of the whole, they would be surprised to find how much would flow up after it from the silted springs.

But, on the other hand, there is an impulse to confession which seems instinctive in other souls in other conditions; and to appreciate them we must look for the special motives that govern them. It is not the practice of auricular confession to a priest that we have here in mind. It is the inward pressure that thrusts a man into the open with the story of his soul, that in notable instances induces him to write it down and publish it.

Sometimes the spiritual document springs from the felt need or craving for self-expression, as though the burden of one's thoughts demanded to be written out for the relief of utterance. Such is Carlyle's " Sartor Resartus." In some rare cases, again, as in that of Rousseau, confessions are made from egotism, vanity, complacent pleasure in finished self-portraiture.

More often the work springs from the motive exemplified in Nathaniel Hawthorne's " Scarlet Letter," where Hester seeks easement from her unbearable secret of sin in showing herself on the platform before all eyes as the true woman she is, as she knows herself, and as God knows her. Samuel Johnson goes back as a mature man to Lichfield to stand in the public market with bare head in reparation for his early disobedience to his father. It is an act of self-immolation on the altar set under the blue dome. Or, in addition to this public self-judgment, it is an act of sacrificial thanksgiving to God before the world for the triumph of Divine grace. Such was the impulse, such the motive, of St. Augustine, to make a penitent and cleansing confession of his errors and of the despite done to God, and to confess in praise and astonishment his sense of the unsearchable riches of grace that had redeemed him. This sort of religious document has served the needs of others, as an altar of confession for their own use, or has performed priestly functions in interpreting and voicing their souls otherwise dumb. Many have warmed their hands at these fires of life and hope.

Others have written classics of experience as a means of carrying on some form of public service or ministry which had been compulsorily arrested or silenced. Dante, driven from Florence into exile, determined to utter his vision of eternal realities for a wider public than his beloved, distracted city. So Bunyan by his " Pilgrim's Progress " meant to continue under imprisonment his ministry to those who had heard the gospel from his lips. So Jeremy Taylor, when deprived of his freedom under civil war, maintained the ministration of the word from his circumscribed retreat. So Samuel Rutherford's " Letters " from his confinement within the city of Aberdeen were missives of godly counsel to his disciples.

The "Imitatio Christi" was originally prepared by Thomas à Kempis as a body of instructions for the guidance of novitiates under his care.

The aim of some writers has been—it seems to have been the aim of Walter Pater in writing "Marius the Epicurean" —to discover their own mind, to explore and define the obscure movements of their souls.

7. When we come to characterize this class of literature, we have to consider how far it can be described as mystical. Some of it certainly partakes of mysticism rightly understood. But the term "mysticism" is often misunderstood or misapplied. Sometimes it is ignorantly taken as a term for the mysterious, or even the misty ; more often for inner spirituality in personal experience. But it is not a synonym for experimental religion or deep spirituality of mind.

Mysticism has been most diversely described and defined, and perhaps no single definition can adequately cover all the phenomena. We must make a broad distinction between its more usual, milder forms and its rare ecstatic moments exemplified in Plotinus, Jacob Behmen and Sta. Teresa. It views nature and life as inherently symbolic and sacramental—as transparencies of the Divine, eternal realms of being. It is the effort of the refined spirit to rise above the plane of the sense-world and clear self-conscious understanding into immediate perception of supersensible realities, into vision of and vital union with God. In other words, it seeks elevation above time and space and the limitations of the normal mind ; and by illumination and oblivion of all things, and even of self, the soul in its highest reach gains transcendent and direct insight into the Eternal and participation in His nature through the exercise of exalted devotion. It is more than " the consciousness of a Beyond." It has been defined in plain terms as " the sense of the presence of a being or reality through other means than the ordinary perceptive processes or the reason." [1]

[1] See Pratt, " The Religious Consciousness " ; Coe, " The Psychology of Religion " ; Evelyn Underhill, " Mysticism," and " The Mystic Way " (in the New Testament and the Early Church) ; Inge, " Christian Mysticism " ; Rufus M. Jones, " Studies in Mystical Religion " ; von Hügel, " The Mystical Element of Religion." Concrete expression is given,

Expressions of mysticism are found in some portions of St. Paul's epistles, in St. Augustine's " Confessions," especially in his parting talk with his mother at Ostia, in Ruysbroek, Tauler, " Theologia Germanica," Sta. Teresa, absolutely in Jacob Behmen, more moderately in the Quakers, Madame Guyon, and William Law. But the great body of material with which we are concerned in these studies is not strictly mystical; it is experimental religion within range of the normal Christian sphere and faculties. It has a definitely moral as distinct from a speculative quality, and as such it can be apprehended by all quickened minds. It may seem elusive to some, but that is only because their experience has not advanced so far as to make its significance plain.

These writings do show the effort of the soul to rise above the natural plane and reach its true home in personal fellowship with God. It finds itself distracted between two poles, of sense and of spirit, between two worlds, not this world and the world to come, but the passing show of things below and the permanent blessed life that already is celestial. Its quest is for self-harmony in the mastery of the one spirit—in " one whole man "—so making for peace. Sometimes peace is sought in restful quiet, sometimes in action that engages all the energies in a great dynamic undertaking. The end in view is completeness, fullness of life, with personal power through central repose. Some seek this end by entire self-surrender, consent to be " nothing "; others seek it by self-development, spiritual culture and activity in the midst of the human world. While the religious ideal of Asia is rest by repression of desire, that of the Western Christian world is life, effort, striving, and thereby rest through victory in oneself amid earthly circumstance.

In most of these writings we observe that the divine life

e.g. in art by William Blake, in essays by Maeterlinck (" Treasure of the Humble "), Coventry Patmore, and A. E. (Geo. Russell) (" The Candle of Vision "), in poetry by Wordsworth (" Tintern Abbey "), Coleridge (" Ancient Mariner "), George MacDonald (" Diary of an Old Soul "), F. W. H. Myers (" St. Paul "), in fiction by Fogazzaro (" The Saint "), in Bible exposition by Christina Rossetti (" The Face of the Deep," Bk. of Revelation).

is a task as well as a gift. The position won is contested
repeatedly from fresh points of danger ; the great adventure
is never finished ; the godly have to keep sentinel watch
to the very last. Holiness, more than art, is a long and
arduous task. In its pursuit men seem to be saying, "We
see not yet all things put under . . . *but*—BUT—we see
Jesus," and that sight wields an endless drawing power and
gives pledges of final attainment.

These products of experience display the higher reaches
of power and vision attained by men and women specially
graced and gifted ; yet in common Christian life undis-
tinguished souls find in them a community of aim, a kinship
of spirit, which stimulates them to give themselves to " the
utmost for the highest."

8. The estimates of these books among Christian people,
we must acknowledge, do seriously vary. While to many
the study of them is attractive, their introspective character
repels others, who dislike self-analysis, so much in vogue
to-day, and even much exercise of self-consciousness. To
have the mental eye long turned in upon personal states is
felt to be unwholesome, if not destructive of serenity and
practical efficiency. Some classics, again, have a penitential
note that is absent from the New Testament scriptures,
where the dominant notes are joy, peace, the sense of
dominion, liberation from self through absorption in the
cause of the Kingdom of God among men. The study of
them accordingly should not be continuous, lest they
obsess the mind. The healthiest life is in the main objective.

Further, there is a certain stringency and hardness in the
saints and in their writings which is apt to chill and discourage modest and tender natures. They may seem to
demand too much of human beings, the air they breathe too
rare for those unaccustomed to high altitudes. There are
passages in Thomas à Kempis of diamond brilliance and
hardness. Sta. Teresa, so competent in her organization
of devout women, imposes action repressive of the milk
of human kindness. In Newman there is an austere
stringency kindred with that of Calvin.

Some of these writings, for example those of Jeremy

Taylor and William Law, prescribe regulations for the exercise and conduct of the Christian life. They are found to be of great value for the direction of conscience. They take over into the Reformed Church the functions of priestly directors in the Roman Church. But we must not look to legislative rules for the reform or the sanctification of ourselves or others : from the enforcement of rules and absolute standards sprang the hardness of the saints. A good rule serves as a guide, but also sometimes as a substitute, for a good impulse. What we need is inspiration. The impact of Jesus Christ on the soul is creative and inspirational. The Christian character is not built to architectural specifications. It is built to music, to ideals, to hope, love and enthusiasm surmounting discrepant appearances.

With all limiting qualifications, however, these books remain permanent treasures of the purest wisdom and stores of personal power. As instruments of soul-culture they are profitable for correction and instruction in righteousness. They are companions of the devout heart, prophets of its yearning foregleams, priests assisting it to interpret and express itself and offer spiritual sacrifice to God. This literature is particularly valuable for those who have the " cure of souls."

We must add, in opposition to a common assumption to the contrary, that spiritual self-culture reflected in these writings is quite consistent with practical work and has often been combined with active service. In some cases quietist reflection has been maintained in a life withdrawn from the human arena, though the sacrificial spirit which they expressed has incited others to a practical life. But most of those who figure in these chapters have been men of action. St. Augustine, like St. Ambrose and St. Bernard, and in later days John Bunyan, Jeremy Taylor, Samuel Rutherford and Tolstoy, were active in public causes in Church and State. Social reform or benevolent humanitarianism was undertaken by mediæval mystics, like Tauler and Henry Suso, by Madame Guyon in visiting hospital patients, by Fénelon among the poor, and by Quaker quietists like William Penn and the Gurney family.

If some of these classics are deficient in the social conscience, it is not because of mystical interests or spiritual detachment; it is only because the Church in general has been slow to apply Christian principles to the social organism in its corporate action, not to the betterment of mankind, but to the reconstruction of the community life. Dante rightly placed men of action among the saints in the upper Paradise.

Writing of St. Vincent de Paul, Miss Edith Sichel (" New and Old," 333 ff.) has said : " A saint is an enthusiast for goodness . . . above all, one who enjoys holiness as the artist enjoys beauty. Nothing is done well, still less transmitted, without enjoyment . . . and a saint is no renouncer, ascetic, except as a means to an end. No practice of goodness in him grows stale by becoming a habit. A discipline it may be, but it is touched, often burnt, by fire from heaven." And the fire which burns in musing is calculated to become dynamic in labours of love.

## II

## St. Augustine's " Confessions "

IN the " Confessions " of St. Augustine we have the first autobiography in all literature, and the first great classic of Christian experience outside the New Testament. Through fifteen hundred years it has held its place as one of the most seizing and illuminating expositions of the human soul. While some of its contents belong only to the age in which it was written, the book is immortal, sure to retain its spell as an authentic transcript of spiritual experience so long as the heart has passions and aspirations and cares to see its secret warfare reflected in a mirror. It appeals to all who have felt deeply, and who, through much conflict, doubt and strange delusion, have striven for a positive faith and the triumph of the spirit in serene peace. It is the record of a soul's tragedy ; yet, in the sense of Dante's " Divine Comedy," it is a " comedy " in that it ends happily.

1. This book is highly significant as an historical document. It is significant both of the past and of the future, of the " decline and fall of the Roman Empire," and of the current confusion in social and religious life and philosophical thought ; and it is pregnant with forces and tendencies determining and dominating the millennium to follow. His life-story is a piece of life cut out of the very heart of his age, or rather of two ages at their junction, of two worlds, one dying, the other labouring to be born. His father a pagan till near the close of life, his mother a Christian, he personally represents the transition from the pagan Empire to the imperial Christian Church.

It was in one and the same city, Milan, that Constantine's edict of universal religious toleration was proclaimed in

313, and that in 386 Augustine's conversion was consummated. Christianity was now the professed religion of the Emperors ; pagan temples were under orders to close ; but the old cults and ground-gods kept tenacious hold upon the common people. The capital of the empire had been transferred to the city in the East named after its founder, Constantine ; although East and West were not to break asunder for a time, Rome was left to suffer under the incursion of Gothic hordes, and the Roman Church to civilise the raw races from the north ; and Augustine was yet to fashion the ideal of Church and State in the Holy Roman Empire.

Meanwhile the very elements of order and human intercourse were in the melting-pot and forming curious combinations. Religion and eclectic philosophy, ready for dissolution, were interfused. Hybrid systems, such as Manichæism, compounding superstition and intellectual notions, drew many under their shelter—often half-way refuges that could not long retain earnest men in their spiritual pilgrimage.

The welter of social morals in his time and country is reflected in Augustine and his "Confessions." The city of Carthage, where he was student and teacher during his early formative years, had under Roman colonization become second only to Rome in wealth and importance. African paganism was half-Asiatic, as Pressense says ; the ancient worship of nature, the adoration of Astarte, had obtained full licence in Carthage ; the mythological Dido, the protecting divinity of that dissolute city, was really the Phœnician goddess under a local name. We can easily imagine Augustine's father enjoying the lascivious displays of the Colosseum and its gladiatorial shows with their contempt of human life, while such scenes under the ban of the Christian Church were shunned by his mother. Luxury and sensual pleasures prevailed, and the sins into which her son fell, though she had brought him up as a Christian, are intelligible in his environment.

Augustine is a representative man. He assimilates the motley wisdom of his time, passes through moral errors, scepticism, disappointment with vain shows of pleasure and sapience, finds inner rest and new life in the Church that guarantees the holy Faith with its authority, and seeks security in monastic chastity and ecclesiastical service. It was (in Harnack's words) "a course of development such as not a few of Augustine's contemporaries passed through. No other outlet, indeed, was then possible to piety and a serious scientific mind. He entered into the closest sympathy with all the great spiritual forces of the time."

2. The absorbing story and self-portraiture of a soul in spiritual travail and in pilgrimage under the guiding hand of God must be studied by the reader of these pages in the book itself. Enough to recite in outline the main course of events with explanatory comments before considering its general aspects of interest.

The book covers St. Augustine's career until he was near his forty-sixth year, and was written towards the year 400 A.D., therefore about thirteen years after the time at which the story closes, and when he had been a few years bishop of Hippo. Owing to this interval between the events and the composition of the record, and owing also to new points of view as an ecclesiastic, there are lapses of memory, a *tendenziös* setting of events which requires occasional correction of the chronicle; and there are estimates of his early life which are exaggerated.

It is not strictly an autobiography, but rather a series of impressionist sketches in a personal record. With the exception of the last three of the total thirteen books—usually omitted from modern translations because exegetical of the book of Genesis—it contains memoranda of the author's spiritual career, self-revelations, praises, reminiscences of his circle of friends, with occasional digressions into speculations about memory, time, eternity, and the Manichæan heresy into which he had wandered in his circuitous search for God.

His motive in writing his "Confessions," at the instigation of his friends who desired to have his life-recollections, was to induce them to unite with himself in sorrowing and in rejoicing over his career of sin and salvation, and to encourage others by showing the gracious Hand of God

in delivering him *de profundis* (Bk, X, iii., iv. ; XI, i.).
The work is a great act of devotion and act of penance,
a most humble confession of errors and iniquities, but also
and mainly a devout utterance of praise—for " confiteor "
peculiarly means an ascription of praise—a thankful avowal.
" Grace ! grace ! all of grace ! " as though he proclaimed
from his epispocal chair, " By the grace of God I am what
I am."

It is addressed directly to God from beginning to end ;
it is a " spread letter before the Lord." " Why do I tell
Thee so much ?  Not surely that Thou mayest know them
by me, but I waken up new affections towards Thee and
the affections of those who read these things."  To this
small extent it is obliquely addressed to men for their
profit, but over all it is his personal *Te Deum*.

Augustine was of North African ancestry—born at Thagaste, Numidia, in A.D. 354—and in his writings we remark
the hot and vehement blood of his race.  The country had
been partially Christianized—though soon to be devastated
by pagan Vandals—and he had been reared in the Christian
way and been taught the Christian scriptures by his
devout mother Monica, who stands forth as the type of
Christian motherly solicitude.  His father, Patricius, a
fiery husband whose occasional beatings she endured in
secrecy, was pagan until he became a Christian catechumen,
" seasoned with salt " previously exorcised, a year before
his death, c. 371, when Augustine was still young.  As
already indicated, this double thread in his ancestry, these
two sides in his nature, are represented in his divided heart,
both contending for his soul from his youth up.  The
father's influence " did not prevail over the power of a
mother's piety in me, that as he did not believe so neither
should I.  For it was her earnest care that Thou, my God,
rather than he, shouldest be my father ; and in this Thou
didst aid her to prevail over her husband " (I, xi.).

After some schooling at Madaura, and a year's evil
idleness, he was sent for better education to Carthage, a
gay Paris of the time, supported by his later wealthy friend
Romanianus.  He mixed with other students in its university, where (he says) " debauchery bubbled round me

like a frying-pan." He tells how here he fell into grievous clandestine sin, letting loose the rein all the more because he was not yet baptized and therefore considered free to live as he chose. He heard people say, " Let him do what he likes ; he is not yet baptized "—for sins after baptism were at that time regarded as more deadly, calling for more severe penance, than sins before baptism. He delighted in the theatre, and slaked his emotions in the mimicry of forbidden love and moving tragedies on the stage that tore his heart and left a festering sore.

He formed friendships—" ever so quick and warm in his friendships "—amongst the wildest spirits of the city, among the " wreckers," " eversores," the " fast set " as we should call them, the rowdy revellers who made raids into university class-rooms and broke up lectures, who " yet prided themselves on being good style (urbani)." Still he did not go to such extremes as the others, as perhaps he was glad to remember when in later years he suffered as a professor of rhetoric from the same intrusions !

" Among my equals," he writes with subtle insight, " I was ashamed of being less shameless than others when I heard them boast of their wickedness . . . and I took pleasure, not only in the pleasure of the deed, but in the praise. . . . I made myself worse than I was, that I might not be reproached ; and, when in anything I had not sinned as the most abandoned ones, I would say that I had done what I had not done, that I might not seem contemptible exactly in proportion as I was innocent." " I was foul and dishonourable, yet in my abounding vanity I strove to be elegant and polished."

In these self-exposures he doubtless drew the blackest possible picture of his moral disorders, mainly to glorify God for the grace that later redeemed him, but partly also from the severely ascetic standpoint he came to adopt in the monastic life. None the less his life was wild and heedless.

He won distinction in the school of the rhetoricians, and his pagan father was so ambitious for the son's future success that he was indifferent about the promising lad's moral behaviour. Monica implored him to lead a better life; yet she also was so ambitious for him that, although he had reached what was in that country a marriageable age, she did not seek to get him steadied by marriage, lest he should be hampered in his career.

Then, at the age of seventeen, no longer indulging in loose, passing dissipation, he formed an irregular union to which he and the nameless young woman remained faithful for thirteen years without formal marriage. This practice was common in pagan circles at that time, and viewed lightly, bringing no loss of social standing. "Even the Church recognized monogamous concubinage" (Glover). Then he adds with a significant touch: "I experienced in my own case what difference there is betwixt the self-restraint of the marriage-covenant for the sake of issue, and the bargain of a lustful love where children are born against their parents' will, although, once born, they constrain love" (IV, ii.). Once the little son was born—born to him when he was only eighteen—how he loved him! In an access of piety he named him "Adeodatus," "God-given." Yet he was ill at ease.

Becoming a teacher in his native city, Thagaste (375), he gained a friend in a former schoolmate of like interests in studies and games. He drew this companion astray from the true faith. Fast-bound, they wandered together in error. When that friend was taken with grave sickness, he was baptized, and on recovering consciousness he was so changed as to repel a light jest from the astounded Augustine, who, when death tore them asunder, fell under such black gloom of soul that he could find nothing but death and fear and torture in the familiar scenes. "The half of my soul," he calls him. "I fled my country, because my eyes would miss him less where they had not been accustomed to behold him" (IX, iv.–vii.).

On his return to Carthage (376) he became a teacher of rhetoric, that is, of literature and forensic oratory. "I sold the art of conquering in the strife of words in the market of verbosity" (IV, ii.).

One of his pupils and friends, a young lawyer, Alypius, whom he helped to lead astray, will appear later as his fellow-convert in his hour of restoration, and became bishop of Thagaste.

A work of Cicero, " Hortensius," most of it now lost, fell into his hands, and with its praise of philosophy it awakened a burning thirst for truth, for an immortality of wisdom, and helped to withdraw his affections from rhetoric. The gay spectacles of Carthage, with its gladiatorial shows, its idolatrous rites, and its Roman splendour, began to lose somewhat of their charm, and philosophy, as in other known instances in those times, turned his mind towards its Divine home. One thing in this book damped his enkindled interest, that the name of Christ, which " my infant heart had drunk in with my mother's milk," was not in it.

Yet, he exclaims, " I had my back to the light, and my face to the things enlightened ; whence my face was not enlightened."

He turned to the Bible in his search for wisdom. But he had not the key to the mystery of godliness ; its poor Latin—prior to Jerome's translation—" seemed far inferior to the stateliness of Tully " (Cicero) ; and he had neither the teachable child-spirit to learn its simplicity nor the will to bow to the self-restraint it demanded. At Carthage he also came under the influence of Plato, a fact the more noteworthy in that the study of Greek was going down ; but that Platonic influence had to wait for its full fruition.

In this restless state of mind, craving supernal wisdom, at the age of nineteen he fell into the meshes of that early rival of Christianity, Manichæism, named after Mani, a Persian who compounded Zoroastrian, Buddhist, and Gnostic ideas. It captured him by its pretensions to solve the riddle of the universe, and by its deceptive inclusion of the name of Jesus and the Paraclete (III, vi.–x.). According to this cosmology there were two independent warring eternal Powers or World-Principles : one, King of Light (to us, God) ; the other, King of Darkness (Satan) : each having kindred elements in the earth, in man, and in the astral spheres. The good character of the former seemed to be saved by having the responsibility for anything bad relegated to an alien Power. Evil existed of necessity; man partook of the dark and material elements in the mixed world-order of which he was a captive. This necessity of evil served Augustine, as it served others, with an excuse for their sins. Thus physical forces composed and confused moral issues. But agents of the Power of Light had at times entered into the field to deliver the elements of good imprisoned in things sensible. Like Buddha in India, Jesus was one of these agents—not, however, the historical crucified Jesus, but the teacher of the "first man;" and Mani came to complete revelation as the Paraclete. This redemption of good elements in the world and man was a semi-physical operation. The Divine Power was likewise conceived in elemental and visualized terms. Ascetic discipline followed by sequence from the material basis of evil; and to ascetic initiates immediate salvation and immortality at death were guaranteed—and to no others. All is thus elemental. And here we recall St. Paul's repudiation of the vain philosophy which dealt in the "rudiments," or rather ($\sigma\tau o\iota\chi\epsilon\tilde{\iota}\alpha$) the "elements or elemental powers of the world" that despoiled Christian faith (Col. ii. 8).

For about nine years Augustine was one of the "hearers" of this system, but never one of the elect "perfecti" initiated into the supposed secrets of the inner circle from which he had looked for Divine wisdom. No wonder that, as in many such cases to-day, revolt from such "notions" led towards scepticism of any truth anywhere.

Meanwhile his mother, Monica, had been broken-hearted over his fall into error, thought it her duty for a time to exclude him from her home, and wept over him as if he were dead, praying for his return without ceasing. She had a comforting dream, well-known (III, xi.), in which she stood sad at heart on a wooden measuring-rule—the "Rule of Faith"—when a youth with beaming face asked why she was in tears. When she told him she was bewailing her lost son, he bade her banish her distress, for "where you are there he will be."

His craving for some ideal satisfaction was expressed in the book (lost to us) he now wrote on "The Fair and the

Fit " (IV, xiv.). In his eyes, as Bertrand says (p. 32), " beauty dwells in all things, in so far forth as beauty is a reflection of the order and the thought of the Word. But also it has a moral value. Everything can be an instrument of the loss or the redemption of a soul." Yet meanwhile he, now a professor of rhetoric, was still cleaving to his concubine.

He was becoming disillusioned with Manichæism. He had met Faustus, one of its chief prophets, and found him somewhat of a vacuous windbag, lacking liberal culture and knowledge. He was weary of its baseless speculations and mythology of the universe. He had been learning the true science of astronomy from Aristotle, and lost faith in astrology ; the vanity of " science falsely so called " afflicted him. His mind was more and more being liberated from it ; he often assails it (V, iii. ff. ; VIII, x.), though even as a Christian he never quite escapes from some of its ideas of the basis of evil. In sceptical recoil, he thinks those wisest who hold that certainty in religion is unattainable (V, x.). As to Christianity, he could not think of God but as corporeal (a remainder in his mind from Manichæism), and it seemed shameful that He could " wear the form of human flesh."

He resolved to cross the Mediterranean and push his fortunes in Rome. Monica discovered his intentions, tried to intercept him, and watched the shore. Pretending that he was merely going to see a friend off to sea, he led her to a little chapel in memory of the martyr Cyprian, but by a ruse eluded her, and slipped off to catch a ship bound for Italy, and she was left alone to pray in that chapel and lift her lamentations over his departure.

But goodness and mercy would pursue him, though he might flee to the ends of the earth. She consulted a good priest of the Church and told him of her prayers unanswered, and he replied in the well-known words, " Go thy way, and God bless thee, for it is not possible that the child of these tears should perish." And Augustine writes, as to her prayer that he should stay with her, " God refused her what she prayed for then, that He might give her what she prayed for always."

In Italy he fell ill, doubtless with Roman fever, and had poor success as a teacher of rhetoric, finding that his pupils were apt to leave him unpaid, a worse misfortune than the rowdy incursions of his Carthage students.

He secured the appointment to the chair of Rhetoric in Milan, an imperial appointment, which was state-paid. He rented a villa, with a garden attached. He sent for his mistress and little son, and there came others of his African circle—Alypius " brother of his heart," his brother Navigius, and two cousins.

His mother Monica also came. She was no longer young ; she was of a delicate constitution ; but she made her way from Africa to Italy in a long and terrible voyage, in loving pursuit of her son.

The friendly company had great times of discussion upon high themes, and they even proposed forming a kind of monastic fraternity. "But what of the wives ? " Monica shrewdly asked, saying the plan was " nonsense."

As the next movement in his spiritual history, he became acquainted with the writings of the Neo-Platonists, especially with those of Plotinus, the ascetic philosopher of Rome, and probably with some of Plato's own works. The translations he used were those of the Neo-Platonic philosopher Victorinus Afer, the sensational story of whose conversion to Christianity was soon to play a part in his spiritual pilgrimage, and whose doctrines seem later to have influenced his theology.

Neo-Platonism, to give only a brief indication of its elements, combined a metaphysical theory on idealistic lines with religious experience of a mystical type.[1] The structural conceptions came from Plato, but the system developed on other lines under various influences, amongst these being Christianity, which this philosophy sought to emulate.

The spiritual Ground of all, in the supreme unity of Being underlying and including the multiform differences of existence, forms a fundamental idea. The universal Spirit that breathes through all modes of existence is not, however,

[1] Cf. Inge's " Plotinus " ; Edward Caird's " Evolution of Theology in Greek Philosophers," Vol. II ; Bigg's " Neo-Platonism."

absolute undifferentiated unity, but includes inner diversity, one as the human person is one, yet also complex as man is. This one Being is the Good, which is yet beyond all human terms of definition and intellectual comprehension, while the source of all thought and existence.

The next hypostasis is Mind (*nous*), the image of the One, and " contains the whole intelligible world, the originals of everything that exists." This eternal Intelligence is the Creator, and " all things exist in virtue of the divine thought or word,"—compare the Johannine " Logos."

The third hypostasis in this speculative trinity is the Soul, the World-Soul (*psuche*), receiving from the Mind and giving form and beauty to the existing world.

There are intermediate demonic Powers in grades between the Supreme Being and man and matter. All are an outflow from the Divine Source, having less and less worth according to their distance from the Primal Being. Evil is not, however, an independent Power (as in Manichæism), but a lack of being or reality.

All spirits, including man, are essentially immortal. There is in all of them a desire to return to the Divine Source from whom they have departed.

The process of return, which may involve successive lives by transmigration, includes contemplation, ascetic discipline, and rapt ecstatic elevation of spirit. In this process it escapes from the limits of sense and individuality, losing self-consciousness. It is " the flight of the soul towards God on whom it gazes face to face and alone."

Neo-Platonism came with emancipating effect to Augustine's mind disappointed with his previous hungry search for Truth. Through it he was delivered from scepticism, and regained confidence in the attainability of truth in these high realms. He learnt to think of God as Spirit, as against his former conception of the corporeality of God.

He became familiar with the idea of the one Supreme Deity in whom at the same time there is an inner Trinity—preparing his mind for the orthodox Christian doctrine of the Trinity.

And the difficulty about Evil, which always lay heavily on his mind, was lightened ; he came to see that it was not an independent Power, but privation of being, and lay in the perversity of the will.

Thus he, who had been conducted so far on the homeward path to God by the Roman Cicero, found Plato in new garb a schoolmaster leading him to the Father and to the light supernal in Jesus Christ.

Yet these Platonist books, he confesses, while deepening his understanding, increased his pride and did not recreate him in heart (VII, xx.).

His mind was turned again to the study of Holy Writ, especially the Epistles of St. Paul, who indeed raised stumbling blocks incidentally but revealed to him the might of Grace (VII, xxi.).

In Milan he was soon attracted by the eloquent preacher, Ambrose, " trying his eloquence," he writes, " whether it answered to the fame thereof . . . and I hung on his words attentively ; but of the matter I was as a careless and scornful looker-on ; and I was delighted with the sweetness of his discourse."

But soon it was the truth proclaimed by Ambrose that seized him.

He unlearned much that the Manichees had taught him and learnt about God as not only the Truth but as Father, about Christ as the " way," the principle of Scriptural interpretation (allegorical), the true Trinity, the Church as the sphere of grace and the divinely appointed interpreter of Scripture and authority for revelation and faith.

His intellectual difficulties were lightened if not finally dissolved ; but the weight of sinful habit clung to him ; these two, in him and in others, interplay (VII, xxi. ; VIII, v.).

His friend Simplicianus, a Neo-Platonist Christian, told him of the conversion of Victorinus, whose translations of the Neo-Platonists he had read, of his hesitation to avow openly his new life and thought, and of the triumph of his courage through grace. " I was eager to imitate him," writes Augustine.

Another friend, Pontianus, told him of St. Anthony, how grace had conquered in that Egyptian monk's experience, and how, on entering church, he heard the words " Sell that thou hast and follow me," and, taking them as a message to himself, surrendered all in favour of the monastic life.

All this acted as a " psychological preparation " for his own surrender to the holy call.

Desiring a congenial and respected place among influential citizens, as well as a higher official post, he turned his thoughts to regular marriage.  His mother, along with others in his circle of friends, encouraged the idea.  In her quest for a suitable bride she sought leadings in a vision or dream, but in vain.  His mistress was apparently not thought suitable as a wife for him ; perhaps she was not of the class to meet the situation, perhaps a freed-woman or one who could not be legally married to him (Glover, 199).  Some men in like circumstances broke off their irregular attachment under vows of celibacy.  At last a girl was found, who, however, was too young for marriage, and he should have to wait for her maturity.  His mistress in the meanwhile must go.  " When," he writes (VI, xv.), " they took from my side, as an obstacle to my marriage, her with whom I had been used for such a long time to sleep, my heart was torn, and the wound was bleeding."  She agreed to sacrifice herself and be sent back to North Africa, and she " vowed that she would never know any other man."

This was a year prior to his conversion—though his conduct in this matter has mistakenly been charged to him as a Christian ; yet there is no record of him, when a Christian, ever making amends to the discarded one.  In the confused transitional state of morals, pagan and Christian, Church rules forbade the casting-off of " those who were wives in all but name."  One defence suggested is that perhaps Augustine did not know of any such rule. His action here, in any case, is a deep and dark blot on his record.  Her going is one of the appealing things of history :

> " Into the dark she glides, a silent shame,
> And a veiled mystery, without a name,
> And the world knoweth not what words she prayed,
> With what her wail before the altar kept,
> What tale she told, what penitence she made,
> What measure by her beating heart was kept,
> Nor in what vale or mountain the earth lies
> Upon the passionate Carthaginian's eyes." [1]

---

[1] Quoted from Farrar's " Lives of the Fathers," II, 330.

A striking parallel to this case may be noted (in Virgil) in the abandonment of Dido, also of Carthage, by Æneas, of whom she was deeply enamoured, when in obedience to the command of the gods he left her city to enter upon his wanderings which, like Augustine's, landed him in Rome ; the tragic death of the forlorn queen by her own hand in her angry despair lies outside the parallel.

During the delay of two years before the youthful bride would be ready for the expected marriage, Augustine took another mistress. In this the already dark blot on his record becomes the darkest blot of all. In his " Confessions " he severely reprehends his moral obliquity as a disease of soul under slavery to lust (VI, xv.).[1] We cannot fathom his abyss. In the phrase of Burns, " What's done we partly may compute, but know not what's resisted." Yet his betrothed bride was sacrificed after all when he became a celibate under the ascetic idea of holiness then prevalent.

Augustine now enters upon the " duel " of the two wills of which he gives such a penetrating analysis (VIII, v., IX, v.). The mind commands the body and it obeys ; it commands itself to will, and its command is inoperative. " But it willeth not entirely, therefore doth it not command entirely." This " will and will not " is a " sickness of the mind " due to evil habit. " With what sharp reasons did I flog my soul to make it follow Thee."

" Convicted of the truth, I had nothing to answer but these dull and drowsy words, ' Presently, presently,' ' leave me but a little.' But my ' presently ' had no present, and my ' little while ' went on for a long while." His secret cry was, Lord, make me holy, but not yet : " I had said, ' Give me chastity and continence, only not just yet.' For I feared lest Thou shouldst hear me in a moment, and in a moment cure me of the disease of concupiscence, which I wished to have satisfied, not eradicated " (VIII, v–vii.).

It is an instance of William James's " divided self," an expansion of St. Paul's sentence, " To will is present with

---

[1] Compare the blandly acknowledged and unrepented conduct in like case of Cellini (" Memoirs." Everyman Library, pp. 132, 141.).

me, but how to perform that which is good I find not."
Here is St. Augustine's doctrine of the human will in
religion.

"Soul-sick was I, and tormented . . . rolling and writh-
ing in my chain, till it all but snapped, yet still held me
fast. And Thou, Lord, pressedst upon me in inward part
with a severe mercy, redoubling the lashes of shame, lest
I should again give way, and, not bursting that same
remaining tie, it should grow strong again and bind me
the faster. For I said, ' Be it done now, be it done
now '; and as I spake I all but enacted it : I all but did it,
and did it not ; yet sunk not back to my former state,
but kept my stand hard by, and took my breath. And I
essayed again, and wanted less of it, and somewhat less,
and all but touched and laid hold of it ; and yet came not
at it ; nor touched nor laid hold of it ; hesitating to die to
death and to live to life. . . ."

" The very vanities of vanities, my ancient mistresses,
still held me ; they plucked the garment of my flesh and
whispered softly, ' Dost thou cast us off ? and from that
moment shall not this or that be lawful for thee for ever ? '
. . . Not openly showing themselves, and confronting me,
but muttering as it were behind my back and privily
plucking at me, as I was departing, that I might look
back on them. Yet they did retard me, so that I hesi-
tated to burst and shake myself free from them, and to
spring forward whither I was called : a violent habit
saying to me, ' Thinkest thou, thou canst live without
them ? ' "

But from the side whither he had trembled to go, there
appeared to him the chaste figure of Continency, serene,
joyous, honestly alluring him to come, stretching forth
" her holy hands full of multitudes of good examples,"
and saying, " Cast thyself upon Him, and fear not ; He
will not withdraw Himself that thou shouldst fall." " And
she again seemed to say, ' Stop thine ears against those
thy unclean members.' "

He goes into the garden with his friend Alypius, taking
a codex of St. Paul's Epistle to the Romans with him :
he has recently been studying St. Paul's writings.

In order to pour forth the heaped-up storm of misery in his heart, bringing a shower of tears, he leaves Alypius, who, silent and astonished, sees his distracted state, and he withdraws to another part of the garden.

"I cast myself down I know not how, under a certain fig-tree, giving full vent to my tears; and the flood of mine eyes gushed out an 'acceptable sacrifice to Thee.' And, not, indeed, in these words, yet to this purpose, spake I much unto Thee: 'And Thou, O Lord, how long? how long, Lord, wilt Thou be angry for ever? Remember not our iniquities for ever,' for I felt that I was held by them. I sent up these sorrowful words: 'How long, how long? to-morrow, and to-morrow? Why not now? why is there not this hour an end to my uncleanness?'

"So was I speaking, and weeping in the most bitter contrition of my heart, when, lo! I heard from a neighbouring house a voice, as though of a boy or girl, I know not, chanting, and oft repeating, 'Tolle, Lege,' 'Take up and read,' 'take up and read.' Instantly . . . I began to think whether children were wont, in any kind of play, to sing such words: nor could I remember ever to have heard the like. So, checking the torrent of my tears, I arose; interpreting it to be no other than a command from God to open the Book and read the first chapter I should find. . . .

"Eagerly then I returned to the place where Alypius was sitting; for there I had laid the volume of the Apostle when I arose thence. I seized, opened, and in silence read that section on which my eyes first fell: 'Not in rioting and drunkenness, not in chambering and wantonness, not in strife and envying: but put ye on the Lord Jesus Christ, and make not provision for the flesh, in concupiscence' (Rom. xiii. 13, 14). No further would I read; nor needed I: for instantly at the end of this sentence, by a light of serenity as it were infused into my heart, all the darkness of doubt had vanished away."

He makes known to Alypius what has happened, and finds that his friend, formerly comrade in sin, is ready to cast in his lot with him as a Christian (VIII, xii.).

"Thence we go in to my mother; we tell her; she

rejoices at it ; we relate in order how it took place ; she leaps for joy, and triumphs, and blesses Thee, ' Who art able to do above that which we ask or think.' "

" Thou hast made us for Thyself, and our heart is restless until it rests in Thee," is the most notable phrase and the characteristic idea in his "Confessions." Yet full rest had still to be won.

Does a decisive conversion make an end of temptation ? Alas for the backwash after the storm, for the counter-workings of the old nature and habit, for the scars left on the soul, the blots on memory ! Still he felt the " old infernal fire," and still had inward battles to fight. The old life left a legacy of evil dreams—how he cries to God for the purification of his dreams !—as many good people alive are shamed and distressed by their dreams. His pleasant vices are still " lovingly tugging at the garments of my flesh and saying, ' Can it be, then, that we are to part for ever ? ' " He challenges his conscience on the question whether his dream-life is his real self (X, xxx.). Whether modern psycho-analysis in its one-sided emphasis on neuroses resulting from unfulfilled desire would relieve his moral anxiety may be doubted, unless we could show him that the " repressions " of desire supposed to occasion sinister dreams reveal the action of a new moral will restraining (if not yet subjugating) remainders of natural impulse. If there be two ways to happiness, one the way of nature, the other the way of conquest, the redirection of his mind to the latter must be counted for righteousness despite the clinging lure of the way of nature. (Here compare the night-serpents against which Dante in the " Purgatorio " sought and received celestial protection.)

" Am I not in my dreams the man I am, O Lord my God ? Does my reason slumber as well as the senses of my body ? [1] Cannot Thy mighty hand purify the weak-

[1] Plato, who was known to Augustine, wrote ("Republic," Bk. IX, 571 f.) of appetites controlled more or less by reason, and dealt with " those which are awake when the reasoning and human and ruling power is asleep ; then the wild beast within us, gorged with meat or drink, starts up and, having shaken off sleep, goes forth to satisfy his desires ; and there is no conceivable folly or crime . . . which at such a time, when he has parted company with all shame and sense, a man may not be ready to commit. But when a man's pulse is healthy and temperate,

ness of my soul and with richer grace exterminate the guilti-
ness of my dreams ?   Yea, Thou wilt more and more extend
to me Thy gifts, that my soul may follow Thee, and even in
my dreams may be beside Thee, full of purity."

The conversion of Augustine in the year 386 is com-
memorated in the Church of Rome by a festival on May 3,
though it probably took place two months later.   With
some scruples he allowed twenty days to pass before resigning his chair of Rhetoric in Milan and his " forensic war
in the market of verbosity " (IX, ii.).   Then, for about
six months, he is in retreat at a country house and estate
at Cassiciacum, near Lake Maggiore, lent him by his friend
Verecundus.   It is not exactly another case of St. Paul
in Arabia, for he has round him a company of choice friends
as well as his mother and his son, who enjoy a happy mental
symposium which has been compared to a university
reading party (described, not in the " Confessions," but in
his Dialogues).   This interval served as a period of intellectual and emotional readjustment.

and when before going to sleep he has awakened his rational powers,
and fed them on noble thoughts and inquiries, collecting himself in meditation ;  after having first indulged his appetites neither too much nor too
little, but just enough to lay them to sleep, and prevent them and their
enjoyments and pains from interfering with the higher principle . . . ;
when again he has allayed the passionate element, if he has a quarrel
against any :  when, after pacifying the two irrational principles, he rouses
up the third which is reason before he takes his rest, then he attains truth
most nearly, and is least likely to be the sport of fantastic and lawless
visions."   Yet he admits that " in all of us, even in good men, there is a
lawless, wild-beast nature that peers out in sleep."

Here we recall St. Paul's counsel for the hour of evening sacrifice, " Let
not the sun go down upon your wrath," and the numerous appealing hymns
of eventide.

Aristotle also said that " the good and the bad are least distinguishable
in sleep," while " in this way the visions of the good will be better than
those of the common sort."   The rise of vital warmth clogs the perceptive organ in sleep, whose object is to preserve the functions of animal
life by providing a rest for them, although nutrition goes on more during
sleep than waking—" creatures grow most during sleep."   As to prophetic
dreams he urges that, since in dreaming the moral distinctions between
men are lost, dreams cannot be sent of God, though elsewhere he connects the illusions of dreaming with personal character (cf. " The Ethics of
Aristotle," I, xiii. 13, by Sir A. Grant, Vol. II, 59, and his works on Sleep).

For a more ethereal view of dreams see " The Candle of Vision," by
A. E. (George Russell), who regards the chaos of fancies recalled as only on
the fringe of waking, beyond which in the highest dreams the spirit reaches
its apex as in the moments of self-oblivious meditation.

Returning to Milan, he is baptized at Easter, 387, along with his precocious boy Adeodatus, now 15, and Alypius, his comrade in sin and in conversion, who later forsakes the legal calling and becomes Bishop of Thagaste, Augustine's native town. "What tears did I shed over the hymns and the canticles, when the sweet sound of the music of Thy Church thrilled my soul! As the music flowed into my ears, and Thy truth trickled into my heart, the tide of devotion swelled high within me, and the tears ran down, and there was gladness in these tears " (IX, vi., vii.). Unverified tradition says that Bishop Ambrose and he sang alternate verses of the *Te Deum* (ascribed by some to Ambrose), which in the old offices of the Church of England is called " The Song of Ambrose and Augustine." (We shall find this use of the *Te Deum* in Dante's "Purgatorio.") He was then thirty-two years of age : " too late I learned to love Thee, O Thou beauty of ancient days ; I have loved Thee late."

Intending to return to North Africa to pursue a life of ascetic devotion, the little family reaches Ostia, the port of Rome at the mouth of the Tiber. Monica is resting to recruit her strength for the voyage to her old home, none of them having any premonition that for her there may be a short way Home.

In a memorable and touching scene, brought home to our imagination in Ary Scheffer's famous painting, mother and son are leaning out of a window overlooking the garden of the house where they tarry, discoursing very sweetly together and inquiring about the eternal life of the saints which eye hath not seen, etc.[1]  The transcendental descrip-

[1] To summarize the passage, too long for full quotation : " We panted after those heavenly streams of Thy fountain . . . in comparison with which the very highest delights of the earthly senses are not even worthy of mention.  With more glowing affection we raised ourselves up and did pass through all corporeal things, even the very heaven of sun and stars, soaring even beyond our own minds unto the region of never-failing plenty. We sighed at being compelled to leave the first-fruits of the Spirit, and return to the expressions of our mouth.  We were saying : If the tumult of the flesh were hushed ; hushed the images of earth and waters and air ; hushed also the poles of heaven, yea, the very soul hushed to herself and by not thinking of self surmount self ; hushed all dreams and imaginary revelations ; if, having roused only our ears to Him who made them, and He alone speak, not by them but by Himself, not through angel's voice

tion is rich with mysticism. Soaring with glowing hearts
above the ladder of the material order, and even above the
sunshine, touching things beyond their own clear minds—
the realm of Plenty and Wisdom—they descend again to
the use of words. What if all things seen around, above
and within were hushed, all dreams and symbols hushed,
if He whom our souls love were Himself to speak—not
through any voice or similitude—if without any inter-
mediary the beholder were rapt and plunged in ineffable
joy, and life were evermore like this one moment of understanding : would not this be the meaning of the vision,
" Enter Thou into the Master's joy " ?

This " one moment of understanding," as the phrase
of mystics for the rarest and highest reach of illumination
in direct vision of God Himself (*visio intuitiva*), we shall
meet again in Dante's great Vision.

After this fashion, though perhaps not in these exact
terms, had they been communing in silence and speech,
when " my mother said, ' Son, for mine own part what
do I here any longer, now that my hopes in this world are
accomplished ? One thing there was for which I desired to
linger for a while in this life, that I might see thee a catholic
Christian before I died. My God hath done this more
abundantly, that I now see thee, withal, despising earthly
happiness, become His servant ; and now what do I here ? ' "
Five days after the celestial flight of mother and son on the
wings of mystic vision, she fell sick of a fever. Recovering
consciousness, she said, " Here shall you bury your mother.
Lay my body anywhere." When asked if she were not
afraid to leave her body so far from her native city, she
replied (in words on which Matthew Arnold based his
sonnet, " Monica's Last Prayer "), " Nothing is far from
God ; nor was it to be feared lest at the end of the world
He will not know whence to summon me."

After eight days' sickness in the fifty-sixth year of her

nor sound of thunder nor in the dark riddle of a similitude, but might hear
Whom in these things we love, might hear His Very Self without these :
could this be continued on, and other inferior visions be withdrawn, and
this one alone ravish the beholder, absorb and plunge him into mystic joy,
so that life might be for ever like that one moment of understanding which
we now sighed for : were not this to ' enter into the joy of Thy Lord ' ? "

age, she " entered into the joy of her Lord," into those realms of Plenty and Wisdom of which she and her son had a week before caught a wistful glimpse, as Bunyan's Pilgrim was from the Delectable Mountains to catch through a perspective glass a gleam of the Celestial City. His sorrow first overflowed in tears, and then " mine eyes, by a violent command of my mind, drank up their fountain wholly dry ; and woe was me in such a strife." Many in such an hour involuntarily know this dry-eyed grief. He joys in her dying testimony, mingled with endearments, that she had never had any harsh word from him but many dutiful acts. " But yet, O my God, who madest us, what comparison is there betwixt that honour I paid her, and her slavery to me ? " His tributes to " that holy soul," " so reverent and serviceable to Thy saints," are incomparably rich—" such a mother . . . twice my mother, in the flesh that I might be born into this earthly light, in heart that I might be born into light eternal " (IX, viii.–xii.).[1]

So he, who had left her to weep and pray alone on the North African shore, was left alone on the northern shores of the sea to remember her by her dying wish in his hours of prayer, in the everlasting communion of the saints.

After a year's stay in Rome, writing certain of his earlier books, he returns in 388 to the old scenes in North Africa —after five years of wandering as appealing as those of Æneas that had thrilled his boyish mind. He is the leader in the formation of a small semi-monastic community. Within three years his precious son Adeodatus is dead ; he is ordained presbyter at Hippo (now the French town Bona), a sea-port within range of Mount Atlas. Much against his own wish he is made coadjutor Bishop and then (c. 396) sole Bishop of Hippo. By this time we have passed beyond the period covered by his " Confessions." For over thirty-three years he spends his ardent life in his official duties, in controversies with Manichæans, Donatists, and Pelagians, and in writing his 150 letters, his " Civitas Dei "

[1] In 1430, when Ostia had long been in ruins, the Pope saw fit to translate her ashes to Rome, to the Church of St. Agostino, and annually on April 4 to keep the feast of St. Monica.

and other works. He has the Penitential Psalms inscribed
on the walls of his chamber. The Vandals are besieging
the city ; he refuses to forsake his post ; and in the third
year of the siege, 430, at the age of seventy, he dies in that
" rest " which he had long sought and now had long enjoyed.

3. Augustine's case as thus portrayed by himself is one
of the most revealing among the records of the human soul.
It opens a window into the complexities and subtleties of
inward motions that seem to surge chaotically and yet
are working towards an appointed issue to which the diverse
lines of influence and action converge.

He is profoundly impressed by the invisible Divine Hand
providentially directing his course through devious ways to
an end unsought by himself. Sovereign mercy was making
a *cul-de-sac* of by-ways he had taken, and hemming him in
to the predetermined fold. " I was tossed about by every
wind, but yet I was steered by Thee, though very secretly."
Even things evil—which later he came to regard as having
a relative or possible good in them—were overruled to this
end. " In order that I might change my earthly abode
for the salvation of my soul, Thou wast driving me forth
from Carthage and alluring me to Rome by the agency of
men who loved this death-in-life—by their mad doings in
one place and their empty promises in the other—and to
correct my wanderings wast secretly making use both of
their perversity and of mine " (V, viii.). " By inward
goads Thou didst rouse me, that I should be ill at ease until
Thou wert manifested to my inward sight " (VII, viii.).
He had not been consciously pursuing God, but God had
been as a Divine huntsman pursuing him all the days of
his life. This idea, immortalized in Psalm cxxxix., is reproduced in Francis Thompson's " Hound of Heaven," after
R. L. Stevenson, who (" Pulvis et Umbra " in " Across the
Plains ") vividly describes people in every circumstance of
failure and error obscurely maintaining a fight for some
imaged virtue that yet miscarries, " clinging to some rag
of honour, the poor jewel of their souls." They cannot
escape this doom to seek some nobility ; " all their lives
long, the desire of good is at their heels, the implacable

hunter." From beyond himself Augustine found a push Godward in sorrow dogging sin, in disillusionment bred of fictitious satisfactions. And within himself there was a pull toward God in cravings for fullness of being, for beauty, for love. Is not part of the Divine work now as ever just this, to show errant men the real thing they are after, the true good in the specious but deceptive shadow whose glamour haunts their eyes, the something infinite and spiritual behind the plausible imitation ? So much sin or error lies in misdirected efforts after pulsing fullness of life—see, later, Dante's sins of "love distorted." God is the reality which men are blindly seeking in their wanderings, not only our creator but the native land of the soul. In Pascal's memorable sentence, " Thou wouldst not seek Me hadst thou not already found Me."

The object under study is Augustine's action ; but the chief Actor throughout is seen to be God. We need scarcely wonder that the theology constructed out of his experience is predestinarian—though the predestination at work is not so much external compulsion as it is the drawing-power of One Person over another. To use a Hindu similitude, the tiny kitten is seized at the nape of the neck and carried to safety by the mother-cat ; the baby monkey clutches its mother round the neck and depends on the grasp of its slender arms. Augustine did not rely upon the monkey-grip—he arose to fight against Pelagianism ; he had been driven to the " cat-hold theory." Evil had plucked at his skirts, but God had hold of his heart. No doubt the full case is given in the motto, " Teneo et Teneor "—I hold and I am held. But the ultimate guarantee lay in the hold of the Divine hand.

Yet, while a gracious Guide is the chief actor out of sight, St. Augustine's record enables us to see the inner processes and forces in the successive stages of the whole movement. Psychologically we can trace the steps in the development of his nature along with the inner logic of his experiences. We can see—and his case exemplifies a very common fact —the persistence of religious impressions, after giddy careless years the recurrence of Christian sentiments with which his soul has been deeply dyed in boyhood under his

mother's training and example, the lasting direction given
in the spiritual atmosphere of the family to the future of
the soul. His case illustrates the influence of the pre-formed
type of religious experience and the expectancy awakened
in correspondence thereto. It illustrates the power of
suggestion over a soul in a highly susceptible condition.
In his case the suggestion came from the writings of St.
Paul, from the stories of Simplicianus, Victorinus and St.
Anthony which he had just been hearing, and from the voice
of neighbouring children that seemed to say, " Take up and
read." He, a North African, could not be sure whether
Italian children used such a phrase in their play, whether
it was a divine miracle, which he was with his contemporaries
quite ready to believe. Was it, as we should say, an
" audition," a subconscious impression interpreted as an
external voice, such as Bunyan, Sta. Teresa and others
have reported ? Augustine left this an open question,
while sure that somehow God had called to him. Here we
recall the story in St. John (xii. 28 ff.) of the voice from heaven
in honour of Jesus ; how some said that it thundered
(the naturalistic view) ; how others said that the angels
spoke to Him (the supernatural view) ; and how Jesus,
without explaining the natural event, enforced its religious
value in " drawing " men unto Himself.

Augustine's case also illustrates the close relation between
intellectual and moral difficulties in religion. Light, heat
and power interplay. While reason has a just right to
declare what is true for thought, it must be affected by
what is felt to be helpful for the more abundant life. The
moral attitude is in the long run decisive. Christianity
stands for a type and a power of spiritual life (VIII, v.–vii.).

4. The personality of the confessor is many-sided ; yet,
when he finds himself, the diverse elements compose a single
living whole. He is the man of feeling, the man of action,
the thinker, the mystic. His temperament is choleric, and
yet sanguine, and also melancholic with a " causeless sadness."

As a man of feeling, he was avid for life and the taste of all
things, with quivering sensibilities which made him subject

to the surge of diverse emotions and exposed him to sensuous temptations, subdued slowly by desperate efforts and Divine grace to moral reason and energetic Christian service. He craved love to the fullest measure, knew ambition, the pride of mastery, weariness, achievement, while " eager for the enjoyments which do not betray " (Bertrand, 6). His cries of penitence were as vehement as his passions had been. Like many highly-strung natures he could be tender and sympathetic and yet occasionally fierce in hard blows at opponents.

With æsthetic tastes as well as poetic imagination, he craved and loved beauty. " I used to say to my friends, ' Do we love anything except what is beautiful ? ' What, then, is beautiful, and what is beauty ? " (IV, xiii.). He took chief delight in music as the most fascinating of the arts—in liturgical chants such as swelled his soul at his baptism in the Milan Cathedral—and sometimes challenged this enjoyment as an unholy pleasure (X, xxxiii.).

Closely allied with the love of beauty was his passion for truth, for the real, the true and the good inseparable from one another. " How I sighed for truth. In Italy I often held converse with myself as to the method by which truth is to be discovered." Vast in the range of his horizons and inquiries, he was restlessly eager, not only for positive and assured knowledge, but for some comprehensive unity, an all-inclusive Whole of being. Philosophic doubt, with probability as the only guide to truth, as taught in the later Academy, proved to be a broken reed for him. It often seemed that absolute truth was unattainable. For this, cold reason did not suffice. Mystical insight also opened an avenue to the supernal realms. " I heard as the heart heareth "—a phrase instinct with the authority of the Spirit. As Canon Bigg says, " there can be no doubt that Augustine, like Pascal, reached his conclusion by throwing his heart into the scales." In the end he is fully assured of heavenly truth and grace as a Divine revelation guaranteed by the authority of the Church. Driven by the yearning to understand at the same time that he was impelled by the natural passion for life and love, he passed through swift alternations between intellectual interests

and emotional, even sensuous, impulses. In this respect
he has been compared by Harnack with Goethe's Faust.
But, among points of contrast between the two, it has been
well said, " the good which Augustine seeks is God : that
which Faust sets before himself is the knowledge of Nature,
the spirit of earth and its treasures." Faust is deficient
in the sense of sin and the peace of inward purity, though
in the second part he catches sight of Augustine's vision,
that " in a world of error and illusion, redemptive power
is to be sought in heavenly love and in the service of
man."

A heart for holiness governs his craving for beauty and
truth, and he is generally sound and always sincere. By
common admission his book sometimes shows false taste
and almost morbid overstrain. Some critics have declared
it " written up with an eye for effect " (M. Alfaric), or
accused him of being " theatrical " in making a stage-play
of his bleeding heart (McCabe). In this they are unjust or
victims of antipathies that spring from alien religious views.
We with our greater reserve could probably not indulge
in such display of our naked souls without a note of falsity.
But with his temperament and his rhetorical training he
was true to his own nature in writing as he did. If he seems
to pose himself for his own and others' observation, it is
only because he is frankly interested in self-study, as in all
human diagnosis, and because he is making an open penance
or sacrifice of himself to the praise of God and for the good
of others. In this self-analysis he usually displays a healthy
humanity, sometimes gaiety and humour, setting him above
mere pathological treatment.

His self-accusations are sometimes stated in extravagant
terms. He takes a curious interest in forecasting the sins
of his manhood by relating them to the faults of his earliest
years (I, xix.). Some of these early misdemeanours which
he brands as radically sinful were merely the thoughtless
pranks of boys—such as the theft of pears ; " sin sweetened
the pears," he remarks ; it was more probably the delight
of adventure in company with other lads that sweetened
them. He is projecting back upon his boyhood his later
theory of the natural depravity of the human heart and

original sin. When he comes to describe the wholesome innocency of his own son as a boy he forgets this theory.

Rousseau's "Confessions" have been compared with Augustine's. Both openly explore their own souls, though the former does so for self-vindication in a defiant spirit. Both lay stress on "the inalienable worth and interest of personality," and show the labyrinth of errors, half-truths and ideal efforts through which they labour to find an outlet, though the outlet for Augustine is a return to God, for Rousseau a "return to Nature." The contrast, however, is deeper than the likeness, because of the difference in moral tone. Rousseau betrays a nervous exasperation at people's watchful suspicions of him which is "a kind of cowardice before his own conscience." He is an Epicurean artist who finds curious unholy pleasure in drawing his own portrait with deliberate finish, complete complaisance and entire absence of all repugnance or recoil from his misdeeds. We are left with the feeling that it is rather charming to be salaciously wicked. He loves what "the degraded soul unworthily admires," so that portions of his book are almost unreadable.

In the other case, Augustine unveils the bitter truth with abhorrence and penitent thanksgivings for Divine grace. The account of his vagrant doings leaves no taint on the imagination. There is no false delicacy, and yet no lingering of fancy over unholy things that once delighted. In Archbishop Alexander's words, "here there is a coldness and a whiteness as of winter snow over the crater of an extinct volcano."

Cellini in his "Memoirs" makes jaunty avowal of vices and crimes because he must let the world hear the "trumpeting voices of praise and exultation" with which his own soul flattered itself. Byron sneers at—

> "St. Augustine in his fine Confessions,
> Which make the reader envy his transgressions."

Thus he reveals his flippancy, and needs no answer. But Cardinal Newman ("Historical Sketches," II, 144) made good use of the comparison of the poetry of Byron with the "Confessions." Byron, like Augustine, depicts himself "seeking for happiness in the creature, roaming unsatisfied from one object to another, breaking his soul upon itself, and bitterly confessing and imparting his wretchedness to all around. But, while each makes confessions, Augustine addresses them to the saints, Byron to the powers of evil."

Augustine's moral judgments in self-condemnation, sometimes over-scrupulous, bear the marks of the ascetic and monastic life to which he had been disposed (X, xliii.). The characteristic reaction of the sensuous temperament when awakened out of sensuality is to turn to asceticism, says Montgomery.

It is from the austere ascetic point of view that he undervalues and rejects marriage as inferior to the "religious" life of the celibate; that he speaks slightingly of the work of officials in the Roman Ministry of the Interior as "worldly service" to be abandoned when they are converted; that he abjures the profession of the rhetorician, and even apologizes for having retained his professorial chair in Milan for nearly twenty days; and again that he admits it may be viewed as a sin to have wept for his dead mother (IX, xii.). Of all the Christian Fathers he is most infected by the monastic or cloistral spirit. Yet, with all allowance for his ascetic ideal and his exaggerated account of his sins confessed for the glory of God, he was fundamentally right in his main charges against himself; he had been sensual, though not radically vicious and certainly never depraved; he had indulged the cravings of the flesh and the pride of wisdom and the vainglory of life (X, xxx., ff.).

It was not only the breach of moral law that he had reason to deplore, and the failure to observe the Christian ideal. Even before he became definitely Christian, he felt that he had been living below the level of his proper powers, that he was engrossed with the shows and sensational delights of life, such as the theatre and the gladiatorial fights, that he was mis-spending his personal forces on a "multiplicity of things," and had not found the Real, the True, the Beautiful, the Good. His own natural self-ideal condemned him. And from the Christian standpoint which he attained, all his careless hours as well as the self-indulgence which his pagan surroundings would have lightly excused were acutely felt to be wicked, especially owing to his Christian training in childhood.

His genius for friendship, which has often been remarked, illustrates the power of his personality. " He loved friendship as he loved love." He riveted men's hearts in loyal devotion ; and in turn he gave himself royally to others in the intimate fellowship of giving and receiving. Some of his comrades followed him over land and sea ; others followed him in his spiritual pilgrimage into error and then into the Christian fold ; among these were a brother, two cousins, and his companion Alypius—" brother of my heart, I had no secret which he did not share."

His chief enjoyment was in the camaraderie and solace of his friends. What delighted him was " to talk and laugh together, to do kind offices by turns ; to read together ; to jest or be earnest alternately, to dissent at times without ill-will, as a man might from his own self ; to long for one another when absent, and welcome the fresh comer with joy " (IV, viii., ix.). The anguish of bereavement is for him the greater because of the loss of love that answers love without asking personal gain. Is there in literature any finer description of and tribute to friendship than this ?

He writes also of the perils of friendship. " Men rarely laugh alone " ; and they are also apt to sin together. Bitter is his grief at the death of a friend whom he had corrupted (IV, iv.).

Most tender was the friendship between mother and son. The love with which she pursued him and her confidence that he would be given to her prayers for his salvation formed part of his conviction that God was ever seeking him and laying His hand upon him. When he gave her the slip and sailed away for Rome, he says, " I lied to my mother—and such a mother ! " (V. viii.). When in that city he nearly died in unbelief, " Thou didst not suffer me to die a double death. With which wound had my mother's heart been pierced, it could never have been healed." She " travailed of me in spirit more than in her child-bearing." In the retreat at Cassiciacum " she ruled us like a mother but served us like a daughter." Happy Monica, we say. For such were her kindly words and patience, " learned from Thee, her inward Instructor, in the school of the heart," that (he continues) " she gained unto Thee her own husband towards the very end of his earthly life ; nor had she to complain of those things in him now a Christian, which before he was a believer she had so meekly borne from him." For " she preached Thee unto him by her manner of living whereby Thou didst beautify her and make her reverent and amiable." She was " the servant of Thy servants." And she won her son Aurelius, and with him his son, as well as his brother Navigius.

His appreciation of his boy Adeodatus, who died a year or two after their return to Africa, fills out the picture of family friendships. Gifted and precocious, " Thou didst make him noble " who " was the offspring of my sin." And " we took him for our companion as of the same age in grace with ourselves, to be trained with ourselves in Thy schooling " (IX, vi.).

5. His singular gift of observation and his acute psychological insight impress all readers. With his strong sensibilities he responds swiftly to external impressions. He has sharp eyes, shrewd wit, and keen perception of sights and sounds and odours and of the characteristics of human life. He has watched the infant smile in sleep, and the boys who take their play like serious business, to be punished by elder folk whose follies they call business and who are enraged when worsted in such baser game or some petty dispute ! He has eyes for the hunted hare, the zest of sport, the bucking mule, and fighting cocks—imagery which he uses in his ecclesiastical controversies !

With his steady inward gaze, his faculty of psychological observation and peculiar genius for description of inner states, his penetration in self-study, his insight into the moods and motions of the heart, especially into the subtle back-windings and elusive tricks of the mind, win the wondering admiration of all readers. With skilful analysis he diagnoses the maladies of human souls, and shows powers of description which, it has been said, cannot be outdone by George Meredith or Henry James. Especially in matters of conscience and religion, " he knows every subterfuge and by-path by which man strives to escape from his God and his high destiny " (Harnack, 131).

There are many little touches of self-revealing human nature incidental to the story. " As one who has suffered under a bad physician is afraid to trust himself even to a good one, so was it with the health of my soul, which certainly could only be cured by belief, yet refused to be cured, lest it should believe what was false, resisting Thy hands " (VI, iv.).

We shall see the validity of his principle that if you love God enough you may do as you like, when we find it resumed and applied in Dante (*infra*, p. 121).

Among other examples of his faculty of mind-reading may be mentioned his description of the two wills in conflict in the same bosom, already quoted, and his critical examination of the love of praise (X, xxxvii.).

The psychology of the crowd has seldom been so acutely observed and so dramatically put as in Augustine's account of his friend Alypius when dragged by fellow-students against his will to the amphitheatre while he hated the cruel gladiatorial show. He told them that they might drag him bodily thither, but they could not force him to give his eyes and his mind to the bloody games. They bore him along to their seats. Observe his fight against what we call sympathetic mass-feeling. He closed his eyes. If only he could have sealed his ears likewise! But at the savage roar of the people in their mad delight, vanquished by curiosity and fancying himself steeled to despise the sight, he rashly opened his eyes, and was stricken inwardly with a wound deadlier than that of the gladiator, presuming upon his own strength. With his gaze fixed on the gore, he unawares became intoxicated with the fury of the bloody pastime, the din of battle and murderous delight. " He was no longer the man he came, but one of the crowd, a very mate of those that brought him. He shouted, applauded, blazed with excitement; he carried home with him the infatuation which might goad him to return with them who drew him hither, yea, even before them, and draw in others. Yet thence didst Thou with most strong and merciful hand pluck him, and didst teach him to put his trust not in himself, but in Thee, though not till long afterwards " (VI, viii.). This event clung to his memory and became an antidote to such hidden tastes in himself.

Happily the power of social suggestion operates for good as well as for evil, as he indicates in saying, " When many share a joy, each has a richer measure of joy, because they kindle themselves and are inflamed by one another " (VIII, iv.).

6. A higher range of insight lay in his powers as a mystic In the previous chapter the nature of mysticism has been indicated, and the mystical vision of supernal realms which he shared with his mother at Ostia has been quoted. He has by some writers been called the father of all Catholic mystics, while others have qualified the statement. The mystical element was not the constant characteristic of his works ; and where he gives it expression it is well restrained by common sense and free from visionary fancy and fantastical ecstasy. It was at the same time natural to one plane of his mind. He said that his mother could discern God's revelation to her by " a certain indescribable savour." Her son also sensed things Divine by that same savour. It was his psychological perception that made him sensitive to " the Beyond that is Within." He was absorbed, not so much with the scientific relation between the external world and the spiritual, as with signs and portents in the soul, theophanies in the innermost court where in " one moment of understanding " the beatific vision may be glimpsed.

He had been a mystic before he became a Christian. In his Neo-Platonist period he had entered the secret chamber within and beheld with the eye of the soul the Light Unchangeable, and with swift glance had the vision of " That Which Is," the " I Am that I Am." And " I heard as the heart heareth, and saw Thy invisible things, understood by those things which are made." From a height " I beheld the realm of peace. . . . But I saw not the way that leadeth to the beatific country, which is not for mere gazing on but to be an abode." The way thither was opened to him in Christ who is the way as well as the truth, while still he could not long retain the vision, which yet remained a gracious memory (as we shall see again in Dante's " Paradiso "). What had been bare vision to the Platonist eye became a " home " to Augustine as a Christian, because it became a moral and spiritual experience when " I had drawn from the wells of salvation " and known " the exaltation of Thy grace." " I was seeking Thee without, and lo, Thou wast within."

" God and the soul : this and this only," he exclaimed in his " Soliloquies." While signs descend through all things seen, it is up the stairway of the soul that we attain purgation, illumination, and union with God. In another book he says, " Our whole work in this life is to heal the eye of the heart by which we see God."

The same swift vision and a like conception of God as the " Self-Same " dwelling potentially within the human soul as native there are found in his prayers :—" O God, light of the minds that see Thee, life of the souls that love Thee, strength of the thoughts that seek Thee, enlarge our minds and raise the vision of our hearts, that with swift wings of thought our spirits may reach Thee the eternal wisdom, who art from everlasting to everlasting, through Jesus Christ our Lord." " Most merciful Father and Lord, although we sin we cannot cease to be Thy children ; because Thou hast made us, and re-made us, we humbly beseech Thee not to act toward us according to our transgressions, but according to that mercy of Thine which transcends the sins of the whole world. Our hearts are open to Thee. Scatter their darkness ; fill them with the brightness of Thy love ; and make us now and alway temples fit for Thee to dwell in, through Jesus Christ our Lord." " O Thou Good omnipotent, who so carest for every one of us as if Thou caredst for him alone ; and so for all as if all were one ; we behold how some things pass away that others may replace them ; but Thou dost never depart, O God, our Father supremely good, Beauty of all things beautiful. To Thee will we intrust whatsoever we have received from Thee, through Jesus Christ our Lord."

7. The place of Jesus Christ in Augustine's " Confessions " is implicitly vital, though not expressly predominant, and

is related to his mystical method of approach to God. Generally the mystic, just because his perception of God is direct and immediate, is apt in the highest reach of his experience to dispense with all mediation, whether of the Church, of the priest, or even of Jesus Christ, although Jesus Christ is antecedently honoured as the supreme agent in securing that immediate contact with God. He is conscious rather of the Christ who is in us than of the Jesus Christ who for us and our redemption lived and died. In this spirit Augustine wrote : " He (Christ) departed from our eyes that we might return into our hearts and there find Him," an ideal also fundamental in St. Paul's mind.

Seldom in his " Confessions " does he refer to the person of Jesus Christ and His redeeming work. The book is addressed directly to God the Father, not to Christ. He magnifies the glorious grace of God as a Divine gift. But he does not expressly connect the forgiveness of sins with the sacrifice of Christ on the cross ; and the healing medicine and the moral support for life in the Christian religion he relates to the general grace of God or to the ministrations of the Church with little recognition of the office of the historical Jesus.

Harnack (" History of Dogma," V, 86–7) has made use of this fact to assert that " he incurred the danger of neutralizing Christ's general significance," that his " doctrine of grace was relatively independent of the historical Christ," that he failed " to do justice to Christ's significance as the mirror of God's fatherly heart and as the eternal Mediator." But this charge is an over-statement of the facts as a whole, while true of most of the " Confessions." In the last chapter of the tenth book he dwells upon " the man Christ Jesus," the only true mediator between God and man, who shares mortality with men and perfect righteousness with God, and upon God's great love in giving Him to be our High Priest and sacrifice.

He dwells often on the great humility of Jesus Christ, which was so offensive to human pride and so corrective thereof ; on Christ as the way to the Father ; and on His indwelling presence as the law and living power of all godliness.

8. His intimate knowledge of the Bible is exhibited in his "Confessions," which is often woven of Scriptural language. Evidently the select pastures in which he grazed were the Psalms—" How did I cry unto Thee, O God, as I read the Psalms, those hymns of faith, whose pious accents leave no room for the spirit of pride " (IX, iv.) —the Pauline Epistles and the Johannine writings. The Bible was still in common use in the Christian Church (cf. Harnack's " Bible Reading in the Early Church "). It would be interesting to study the favourite reading of our Lord Jesus Christ in such books as Deuteronomy, the Psalms, and Isaiah—and the choice writings which fed the souls of the saints.

9. The literary qualities of the " Confessions," which have assisted its wide appeal, are manifest in the quotations already made. It abounds in graphic terms, trenchant and memorable phrases, which have passed into all European languages—" the biter bit," " life of my life "—and in shrewd sayings that describe a situation or give definition to character with all the suggestiveness of etching. It conveys the immediate perception of things and the feeling of life. It excels in vivid, imaginative touches and in picturesque imagery. " Thou didst free my soul from the deadly bird-lime, and now it cleaves to Thee." " The burden of the world lay softly on me as on a dreamer, and the thoughts in which my senses turned towards Thee, my God, were like the efforts of those who would rouse themselves from sleep, but, overcome by the depth of slumber, ever sink back again. And when Thou calledst to me, ' Awake, thou that sleepest,' I would give Thee no other answer than the words of delay and dream, ' Presently, but let me dream a little longer.' " It has expressions that pierce to the heart of life, aphorisms pregnant with significance. " Peace of mind is a sign of our secret unity." " Every forbidden longing, by an unchangeable law, is followed by delusion." " Every unordered spirit is its own punishment "—a moral principle to be reproduced by Dante.

There is nimble word-play, more than enough. Augustine

as a teacher of rhetoric or *belles lettres* and forensic oratory had acquired the art and the artifices which would make public speech popularly effective. Hence he indulges in clever conceits and acrobatic turns of phrasing, in antitheses that are forced and in assonances that are artificial, e.g. " I prated like one who knew, yet, unless I found Thy way in Christ our Saviour, what I deemed true was like to end in rue—*Non peritus sed periturus essem* " (VII, xx.). Sometimes his language is either heavy through over-elaboration, or is flamboyant and opulently Oriental in its exuberance ; but even his extravagances of diction are expressive of the passionate and imaginative nature of the man. The strained conceits in phraseology and the inflated rhetoric tantalize for a moment ; but always his language is vibrant ; his words are " alive and active " ; they strike fire ; and, as Luther's words were called, they are " half-battles."

His style of writing, without the finish and polish we find in Thomas à Kempis' " Imitatio Christi," has the same quality of imaginative emotion, and both books are lyrical, with musical cadence and rhythmic flow.

10. The influence of St. Augustine over subsequent generations is immeasurable and almost universal. While his personality became single and unitary, so complex were his life and his work that their impact is found operating in many diverse directions. It is not in place here to show how his theory of the Church in his " Civitas Dei " predetermined Mediæval Catholicism as an institution, how the system of theology which held sway for a millennium was entitled to be called Augustinian, how monasticism looked back to his leadership, how he originated problems in the philosophy of religion which still engage us.

It was as a religious genius that he was a pioneer and discoverer. Doubtless he derived renewing and refreshing grace from St. Paul ; but he was not merely digging the old wells. In his own separate experience there was dug the well of salvation from which streams of vital religion have flowed down through incoherent channels to bring life to many souls and turn desert places into green pastures. While he bowed before the authority of the Church, " he shows better than almost any other great religious teacher how impossible it is to separate 'religion of authority' and 'religion of the spirit' into two sharply divided groups; he is in both groups, and he is entirely unaware that they are inconsistent with each other."[1]   While the father of Roman theology, he was the only one among the Church Fathers from whom Luther drew instruction.   The Protestant and all other revivals of living and experimental religion own his influence.   " A new Christian piety dates from him, that which since attached to itself the name of ' evangelical.' "[2]

The sap or savour of the gospel of grace and life, at the heart of his doctrine, has infused mystical faculties of insight.   We shall have occasion to observe the profound spiritual impression he left on later classics of Christian experience, Dante, Thomas à Kempis, and their successors. In fact, he is " identified with the greater moments of life." By more than one writer he has been called " the first modern man."   For he touches our life on every side, as every side of his nature entered into his " Confessions."   It serves as the medium through which we make our own confessions.   We have found a voice, an interpreter, a priestly man.   And in him we see the grace that can overcome all things.   His message is one of rest; his dominant note is the JOY OF THE LORD.

A Prayer (based on St. Augustine) the author remembers as used daily in opening the Moral Philosophy class in Glasgow University by Professor Edward Caird, afterwards Master of Balliol :—

Almighty God, our heavenly Father, in whom we live and move and have our being, who hast created us for Thyself so that we can find rest only in Thee, grant unto us purity of heart and strength of purpose, so that no selfish passion may hinder us from knowing Thy will and no weakness from doing it, that in Thy light we may see light clearly and in Thy service find perfect freedom, through the Spirit of Him who taught us thus to pray, Our Father, which art in heaven, etc.   AMEN.

[1] Rufus M. Jones, " Studies in Mystical Religion," p. 87.
[2] " Encyclopædia of Religion and Ethics," II, 219 ff.

# III

# Dante's " Vision " : The · " Divine Comedy "

## (A) THE SEER, THE SITUATION, AND THE WORLD-VIEW

" THE VISION " was the name given in some early editions to Dante's supreme poem. In a dedicatory epistle to Can Grande of Verona as his benefactor during his exile Dante called it a " Comedy," explaining that a poem which ends happily, as his poem ends in Paradise, was designated a Comedy, in contrast with a Tragedy which ends sadly. Afterwards the attribute " divine " was given in token of admiration, first to the poet himself and then later to his work, which he called " The Sacred Song." " The Vision " as title is here deliberately preferred as indicating that the present study is mainly devoted to the vision of things spiritual and eternal within the massive structure of the " Divine Comedy." By " visione " Dante himself meant " something seen waking by the inner eye."

On two separate counts there may be some surprise that it should be included among the classics of Christian experience. On the main count, it is too vast, complex, and difficult, involving too much special knowledge, to be compassed within a chapter or two. In its scope it is a complete universe. In its rich erudition, comprehensive of numberless historical figures, mediæval science, philosophy, and theology, it demands, as it has created, an ample library for its exposition. As a literary composition of consummate art, whose original melody is lost in any translation, it is highly elaborated, every part carefully articulated into the whole structure, elusive owing to its symbolism, severely condensed, every sentence packed with meaning. An attempt to compress its contents must, to Dante scholars, appear impracticable if not preposterous.

The demur has reason in it. Yet experience makes one bold. Experience in lecturing on the subject has proved that, for those who already know little about Dante's " Vision," a broad survey of its general purport, of its structural scheme as a framework for its ruling ideas, however inadequate, may be made intelligibly interesting and stimulative to thought, and may as an introduction lead to a more thorough study of the subject. After all research the primary elements which constitute the universe known to physicists remain, they have told us, comparatively few and recognizable, while their combinations and operations are immeasurable. Such is true in the moral and spiritual sphere of which Dante is interpreter, and the vision is not " become unto us as the words of a book that is sealed " (Isa. xxix. 11).

On the second count, the inclusion of Dante in the classics of the soul is surprising ; the attempt to do so is unusual, perhaps unprecedented ; and his book lies outside the category of devotional writings. But the present volume, one must repeat, is not engrossed with devotional writings ; it seeks to cover a larger range in Christian experience. Dante's " Divine Comedy," while different in form from other Christian classics, is one of the great documents of religious experience. It is not commonly classed with " confessional literature " ; yet it is one of the most sublime and significant expositions of the human soul in all literature.

At first sight it deals with outward objective realms in Hell, Purgatory, and Paradise, and with a journey through the first and the second to the crowning heights of the last. But, while impersonal in literary treatment, it is fundamentally personal. It is the " Pilgrim's Progress " of Dante himself from sin and death through penitential discipline to newness of life, blessed and eternal. " It is

Dante's confession of his own salvation, and how it was brought about." Under an objective cover he is the centre and subject of the whole action of his own poem, which thus is self-revealing.

Yet it is not his own personal case alone. He is a representative man. What he saw in his own soul he saw to be the characteristic drama of the human soul in its deepest movements and progress—in his own words, " man in the exercise of his free will with the consequences of his action," and " the passage of the blessed soul from the slavery of the present corruption to the liberty of eternal glory." Within the external framework of the three realms of the Inferno, the Purgatorio, and the Paradiso, it is ultimately within the human heart as within his own that the realities are found. These inner personal experiences are projected on the screen of the eternal world.

The " Vision " of Dante was the first Christian poem (unless the compositions of Paulinus, friend of St. Augustine, and of Prudentius, be reckoned as ranking), as the " Confessions " of St. Augustine was the first autobiography. Carlyle speaks of him as the " voice of ten silent centuries, who sings us his mystic unfathomable song." More accurately, nine hundred years had passed since St. Augustine spoke as the voice of the human soul and as the exponent of his age. Dante derived from him both personal inspiration and structural ideas. In his " Banquet " (Convivio), which comprises a vindication of his life-course as well as an introduction to attainable learning motived to wisdom and mated to beauty, he appeals to the " Confessions " to justify his action in making known his own experience for the benefit of others : " for by the progress of his (Augustine's) life, which was from bad to good, from good to better, and from better to best, he gave us the example and teaching which could not have been received through any other such true testimony." Dante also entered into the inheritance of St. Augustine's ruling ideas, such as the relations between Church and State set forth in " The City of God," the relations between reason, revelation, and mystical vision, and the freedom of the human will.

## 1. THE SEER

The personal history of Dante (Durante) Alighieri (1265–1321) casts numerous projections on his apocalypse, besides explaining its origin and its inspiring motive. Only a brief outline of his life-course—enough to serve as introduction to his poem—can be given here, mainly because so much space is required for an explanatory survey of the " Vision " itself. Readers are referred to any considerable biography of the poet.[1]

Florence was the site of his life and action : not Florence with its great cathedral, its campanile, its Renaissance palaces and Uffizi Gallery—these were yet to come ; but Florence with its fortified castles, its " grandi " or old nobility, its merchant magnates, its guilds, and its feudal divisions within and defences against intrusion from without. Dante's father, a notary apparently, and his mother —both of whom he lost while still very young—he never directly mentions ; but evidently he was of ancient Florentine stock, though not of the nobility : of such family standing that he could enter into alliance with the powerful baronial house of Corso Donati, whose kinswoman Gemma Donati he married.

Pride, including pride of family, was one of the temptations and sins of which he was ever acutely aware, as we shall see later. In the " Paradiso " (xv. 134 ff.) with a thrill of pride he finds in the heaven of Mars his crusading ancestor Cacciaguida, who had been knighted for his heroic deeds by the Emperor, Conrad III. In reply to further questions he refuses to indulge the pride of blood. That hero's son, Dante's great-grandfather, he finds (" Par.," xv. 91 ff.) to have been circling for a hundred years in the Purgatorial terrace of the proud.

Of Dante's youth we know for certain little or nothing— beyond the capture of his heart by Beatrice. It is stated,

[1] E.g. by Paget Toynbee, by Federn, by Moore, or the concise sketch by E. G. Gardner in hi s " Primer " ; ultimately Villani's " Chronicle of Florence " (trans. by Selfe), Boccaccio (unreliable romancer), and Dante's " Vita Nuova " (poetic transfusion of biographical facts). See list of books at end of this volume.

but only conjecturally, that he completed his education at several universities and at Padua. As his own instructor he acquired considerable knowledge of Greek and Roman classics, as well as of Aristotle. An early sonnet of his won the favour of the most famous lyrical poet, Guido Cavalcanti, "the first of his friends," whom we find enshrined in his "sacred song." He says, "I had already (when but eighteen) learned of myself the art of setting words in rime."

Beatrice was the paramount factor in his early life, as he relates with rapturous glorification in his "New Life" (Vita Nuova). He first saw her when both were in their ninth year; she was "cinctured, and adorned in subdued crimson;" his spirit trembled, and love lorded it over him thenceforward. Other nine years passed, and, walking in the street between two ladies, she bent her eyes upon him, saluting him in spoken words for the first time. A fearful joy brought him bliss, and strange dreams haunted his mind with forebodings. He sang her sweet purity in sonnets, using other names as screens for herself. In that age of chivalry and Provençal poetry it was the custom to glorify woman. In worshipful homage he sang (in Dante Gabriel Rossetti's translation):

> "My lady is desired in the high heaven . . .
>                         As she goes by
> Into foul hearts a deathly chill is driven
> By love, that makes ill thought to perish there :
> While any one who endures to gaze on her
> Must either be ennobled or else die. . . .
> Also this virtue owns she, by God's will :
> Who speaks with her can never come to ill."

An authentic woman of flesh and blood she was, and no mere allegorical figure, though he idealizes her in his mystical imagination. She was, according to Boccaccio and Dante's own son, Beatrice, daughter of Folco Portinari, an honoured citizen of Florence. She married Simone de' Bardi, and died in 1290 in her twenty-fifth year. Dante was overwhelmed with grief. He broke out into the words of Jeremiah : "How doth the city sit solitary, that was full of people!" She was the "eternal womanly" with influence over man far above that of which Goethe sang in

"Faust." When "no comfort availed me, I set myself to read that book of Boethius ('The Consolation of Philosophy') whose contents are known to few, wherewith when a prisoner and in exile he had consoled himself"—a remarkable anticipation of his own self-consolation when in exile by composition of his veridical "Vision." Cicero on "Friendship" also solaced him.

He confesses that his eyes became "gladdened overmuch" with the sight and company of another young and beautiful lady whose compassion made him think too fondly of her. We cannot identify this lady with philosophy, which in his later book, "The Banquet," he says was the object of his second love. In his penitent confession in the "New Life"—foretaste of his confession before Beatrice in the "Purgatorio"—he calls the attachment "faithless" and "vile." There are other reasons for believing that he lapsed into ways of error, and this lapse, for which he came to reproach himself bitterly, would most probably occur in the few years between the death of Beatrice and his marriage with Gemma Donati. In the "Purgatorio" (xxiii.) Dante meets Forese Donati, his kinsman by marriage, and speaks of the grief they suffer at the remembrance of the life which they once lived together, and which Dante has been led to forsake.

A vision of the gracious Beatrice as he first saw her revived memories that caused his "heart painfully to repent of the desire by which it had so basely let itself be possessed, contrary to reason." With "whole humble and ashamed heart" his eyes could never "look again upon the beauty of any face that might again bring them to shame and evil." She, "the youngest of the angels," had come "from singing hallelujahs" to his rescue; as later, we shall see, she sent Virgil to show him in a Vision the piteous people of the dark pit for his conversion.

This Vision—doubtless the germ of the "Divina Commedia"—led him, he declares in the consummation of his "New Life," to a life's labour of love, if a few more years were allotted to him. "It is my hope that I shall yet write concerning her what hath not before been written of any woman. After the which, may it seem good unto Him who is the Master of Grace, that my spirit should go hence to behold the glory of its lady : to wit, of that blessed Beatrice who now gazeth continually on His countenance who is blessed throughout all ages. Laus Deo."[1]

He kept his word. In the " Divine Comedy " she is transfigured. She is made the personification of all holy beauty and holy love, the kinswoman of divinity, the symbol of Divine Wisdom and Revelation, his guide through celestial realms. It is a curious coincidence, in view of these selected classics of the soul, that, in the White Rose of beatified saints, Dante places Beatrice in a position on the fourth seat of the inmost row corresponding to that of St. Augustine.

Dante—to take another direction in his life-course—no " love-sick idler," was taking a part in public affairs. When twenty-four he fought as a soldier in the Florentine army, and was engaged in the fateful battle of Campaldino, in which the Guelphs, the Papal party, to whose side he belonged by family, defeated the Ghibellines, the Imperial party. It is impossible here to give more than the barest outline of his share in politics, " the forest dark " in which he lost his way, as told in the opening lines of the " Vision."

In the mid-year of his life, in 1300, he was sent on an embassy by the Florentine government, and became one of the priors of his city. France had displaced Germany in the control of the Holy Roman Empire, and in withstanding her the Papal Guelphs split into Whites and Blacks. Nobles, city magnates, and the people were rent by divisions in their allegiance to one party or the other. Dante publicly withstood the despotic claims of the Papacy, although his family had belonged to the Guelph or Papal party. He was driven to form a party by himself ; but he was disappointed—as later his high hopes of the coming of the new Emperor, Henry VII, were disappointed.

In the outcome of this civic and political tangle of party intrigues, while on a mission to Rome, he was subjected to false, trumped-up accusations ; his property was confiscated ; and he was sentenced to exile, to be burnt alive

[1] The above quotations from Dante's " Vita Nuova " are drawn from the translation by Dante Gabriel Rossetti, " Collected Works," Vol. II.

if found within the walls of Florence. Later decrees confirmed this sentence, the ban extending to his sons who
had accompanied him in his banishment. Time and again
he sought to reinstate himself, in vain. For the remaining
nineteen years of his life (1302–1321), as an exile he wandered from place to place, ever longing for the "sweet
bosom" of his native city, "almost a beggar," "a ship
without sail or helm carried to divers harbours and shores
by the parching wind of poverty," galled by the worthless
company he had to keep, often eating the bread of others,
the dependent's bread, which, with the humiliation it
brought him, tasted bitter in his mouth. In the "Paradiso" (xvii.) Cacciaguida predicts this as the first shaft
from the bow of exile:

> "Thou shalt make proof what salt and bitter fare
> Is bread of others, and what toils attend
> The going up and down another's stair."

In an amnesty offered by Florence to her exiles, before
he found his final refuge and his grave in Ravenna, he was
given the opportunity to return if he would confess himself
at fault, carrying a lighted taper through the streets and
paying a fine in penance. Conscious of innocence, he replied
in proud, scathing scorn of such ignominious terms that he
would never confound justice with money or treat his per-
secutors as though his benefactors. "This is not the way
to return to my country. If another shall be found that
does not derogate from the fame and honour of Dante, I
will take it with no lagging steps." But if not, "can I
not everywhere behold the face of the sun and stars, meditate on the sweetest truths under any sky, without
giving myself up inglorious, nay ignominious, to the popu-
lace and city of Florence? Nor shall I lack bread."

The proud, imperious spirit thus defiantly expressed,
badly fitting him for petty city politics anywhere, was
characteristic. Villani speaks of him, the great poet and
learned philosopher, as "somewhat haughty, reserved and
disdainful." Carlyle writes of his lonely, tragic face in
portraits (e.g. by Giotto) that have survived, filled with
silent pain and indignation, yet touched with a soft ethereal

soul, the face of a man who was not altogether unhappy in his great adventure.

In his banishment, the thinker rose above the statesman ; he had time to muse deeply upon the confusion between virtue and vice in the world ; and as he mused the fire burned. His life had been broken by ill-chance, sorrow, and worldly failure, while yet he kept his soul unconquerable. A devout Catholic, he suffered agony at the sight of the Church degraded and dishonoured by avarice, frauds, and political ambitions under the " new Pharisees." Like Milton (who knew his Dante), when displaced from public affairs as Secretary of State, saddened by his blindness, writing his visions of " Paradise Lost " and " Paradise Regained," Dante in his exile withdrew to the mountains of the prophets and in noble rage, disowned of men and thrown upon things eternal, with all his powers of intellect, imagination, and emotion, inspired by an ideal love, he reared his majestic " Vision " in ample symmetry. Therein, through all the chaos of the present complexities of the world, fundamental moral distinctions are made clear, and their natural ultimate issues are dramatically represented in three future realms. What he had learnt in suffering and in ideal love, he cast in immortal song.

Too late Florence repented of the ban she had laid on her greatest citizen. In 1350 she voted a gift in florins to be paid to Dante's daughter, Beatrice, a nun in Ravenna. In 1396 the republic voted a monument, and (in Russell Lowell's cutting words) " begged in vain for the metaphorical ashes of the man of whom she had threatened to make literal cinders if she could catch him alive." In 1429 she renewed her petition, but Ravenna refused to part with the body of the poet. Some five hundred years after his death Florence built in Santa Croce a cenotaph in his honour.

On the sixth centenary (1921) of his death his memory has been celebrated afresh. To the poem written in " eternal letters of fire " as " lightning writes its cipher on the rocks," to the " Sacred Poem " which " for many a year hath made me lean," as he said prophetically (" Paradiso," xxv.), " both heaven and earth have set their hand."

## 2. THE SITUATION

Dante, like St. Augustine, was the most significant man and the most representative mind in a transitional period of history. The earlier of the two embodied in himself through his mixed parentage the transition from ancient paganism to the Christian order of things. The later experienced and displayed the conflicts involved in the transitional movement from the feudal Catholicism of the Mediæval Church to the Revival of Learning and the Reform of the Church in head and members ; he was the epitome and the highest expression-point of the age now maturing for decay, and at the same time he transcended it, forecasting the new world waiting to be born. In his " Vision " the past came to a focus, yet from it radiate gleams of the future.

The very fact that, after attempting to conform to tradition by composing several cantos in Latin as the language of the learned, he abandoned it and wrote the " Comedy " in the Italian vernacular, was indicative of a new spirit. It was a bold innovation to clothe such lofty themes in the mother-tongue of the people, for the people as citizens enfranchised in the commonwealth of knowledge and the kingdom of the spirit. " The first noble piece of literature in a modern tongue," while working upon traditional material, comes out into the open air and the arena of humanity. It reveals a return to nature and human affections, in the spirit of St. Francis of Assisi. It has keen feeling for the meadows and green foliage, for running brooks and rivers, for the breeze, the sacrament of the dawn, the stars in their courses, for the colours and sounds of earth and sky. It glows with human passions, with chivalrous love as the fit human symbol of the Divine. " All's love, yet all's law," and nature's law is one aspect of love.

The theological doctrines in the platform on which his spiritual drama is staged are those of his master Thomas Aquinas. Yet he treats scholastic theology with considerable independence, with broader human sympathies and keener insight into the psychic founts of good and evil, truth and error ; he has caught wider horizons. This we shall see later in the sufferings of the impenitent in the Inferno. Aquinas viewed them as punishments inflicted from without as God willed according to men's deserts—a forensic conception; Dante with deeper psychological penetration traces them to the settled disposition of the will, and exhibits them as consequences inextricably bound up with the nature of the unrepented sins. In his treatment of the excommunicate who repented at the last moment he expands orthodox teaching to the utmost of Infinite Love.

'Midway upon the journey of our life "

is the first line of his poem. Midway in the allotted seventy years of the normal life, when he was thirty-five years old, that is in the year 1300, the action of the drama begins. It was the watershed between two epochs, the turning-point of history, midway between papal supremacy and decline. That year saw the vainglorious Jubilee celebrated by the corrupt Pope Boniface VIII, whom Dante daringly places in the Inferno as a usurper. In him the claim of the popes to absolute supremacy over both Church and State, heaven and earth, reached its climax. " They were the founders of the Empire, bestowed the imperial crown, carried the two swords, had authority to depose and set up kings." But now they overreached themselves. The tide of battle between the Church and the Empire turns in favour of the latter. France, being called to the rescue of the Papacy, transfers its seat to " Babylonish Captivity " in Avignon, and the Great Schism supervenes.

Dante here abandons the doctrine of Aquinas and his own early Guelph allegiance to Rome, and holds the Papacy chiefly responsible for the strife and for the degradation of both Church and Empire. The former has usurped the functions of the latter. " The sword is grafted on the crook."

" The Church of Rome,
Mixing two governments that ill assort,
Hath missed her footing, fallen into the mire,
And there herself and burden much defiled."

(" Purg.," xvi. 127.)

Let her restore herself to the original purity she had " before the fatal dower of Constantine " made her a central state and claimant to temporal power (" Inf.," xix. 115); let her rely only on her spiritual functions.[1]

Dante advocates the independent jurisdiction of " the two governments," Church and State. Each derives its authority within its own province from God, and neither from the other. They are meant to be complementary powers, as he had written in " De Monarchia ": " The sovereign Pontiff, to lead the human race to eternal life in accordance with things revealed; and the Emperor, to direct the human race to temporal felicity in accordance with philosophical teaching." At the same time the State (Cæsar) should pay reverence to the Church (Peter) for illuminating grace with which to " irradiate the whole circle of the world." Here Dante is prophetic, giving implicit sanction to the rising autonomous nationalism, though he falls far short of Marsilius of Padua with his assertion of " the original sovereignty of the people," involving representative government, and the purely voluntary nature of religious organization.

### 3. THE WORLD-VIEW

It is one world, a literal universe, which Dante sees and unveils in his flaming " Vision." This may seem superficially obvious; but it is one of the sweeping and most comprehensive conceptions of Dante, one of the most universally sanctifying principles revealed to man. It means, not that all things are alike as the workmanship of God, but that we find, in Tennyson's way of putting it,

> " One God, one law, one element,
> And one far-off divine event
> To which the whole creation moves."

---

[1] In the Terrestrial Paradise (" Purg.," xxxii.), after the Procession of the Spirit or Pageant of Revelation, the Chariot of the Church at its centre is described as perverted to the form of a Monster, corrupted by an Eagle (the Empire), with a " dishevelled harlot " seated in the Car in place of Beatrice on its way to ruinous misuse (in the Avignon captivity). In the " Paradiso " (xxvii. 22 ff.) Dante puts into the mouth of St. Peter a fierce invective against the Pope who has made of his place a " sewer of blood and stench," and against the avarice, simony, arrogance, and gross misconduct of the clergy.

According to Dante, in all worlds above and around and within, in all spheres of observation and experience, there is an all-embracing unity which lies in "order," one of his ruling concepts, and that alike a natural and a *moral order* ("Par.," i., 103–136).

Modern science, far beyond Dante's ken, has disclosed the physical order of the universe as coherent. In principle numbers of modern scientific discoveries were anticipated by earlier philosophic and religious insights. The principle of evolution had been announced by thinkers long before it was found true of the physical system. More relevant to our present purpose, the law of gravitation announced by Newton was observed and stated as a general principle by Dante and earlier observers of the moral and spiritual realms of experience. And this was so precisely because the world or system of spheres is one, and because the spiritual principle was observed in common experience before scientific physicists arose. The laws of nature are not all identical with moral and spiritual laws; their standards and methods are different. But in the long run the universe is found to be an exact system under a moral order.

A conflict had arisen, as we have seen, between the Church and the Empire. Dante shows that each, with its distinct function, is directly due to God, the one appointed to serve the eternal and the other the temporal felicity of men, the two being complementary manifestations of the one principle. They co-exist by Divine authority, though he does not show how, as two governments, they interpenetrate and how exactly they must sway each other. But at any rate Peter and Cæsar, Church and State, are working together for common ends.

An opposition had been set up, and still is upheld, between this world and the future life. "The times are very evil," ran a contemporary hymn still in use. The present world seemed not to be God's world, but to be an alien country in which God's laws did not obtain force. The devout man felt himself " a stranger here," and used this life simply as a preparation for the world to come, as his native country, where every injustice would be put right by supernatural act and all goodness gain its proper reward.

But Dante denies this dualism between this world and the next. The two are of one piece. The same moral and spiritual laws obtain in the two successive spheres. As we should say, goodness is always, like evil, rewarded "after its kind," with fruits in accordance with its nature. Dante translates the difference between the two realms into terms of eternal reality. The difference is not merely between two succeeding worlds, but between two planes of life, between qualitative distinctions, ever present in our experience. As the "Theologia Germanica" will indicate, and as Harnack has put in words, we can enjoy "eternal life in the midst of time." Long ere this, the Synoptic evangelists in their Apocalyptic contents thought of a spiritual body of powers in an upper realm ready to manifest themselves in the lower zone of life. According to Dante there is a vital continuity between this present life and the next, and the two are under the same moral law.

Likewise the spiritual and the natural had been set in antagonism to each other, because nature seemed alien to the spirit. But Dante shows that the two are kindred in meaning and value. Nature is a mirror of things unseen; its phases in stars, natural seasons, day and night, renewal and decay, are symbols of spiritual equivalents; the same spiritual presence pervades all. Here mysticism obtains its opportunity.

Dante observes a correspondence between natural and revealed religion (to speak in outworn terms). In his three spheres he gives a parallel place to pagan and Biblical representatives of virtue and vice. In the same scene ("Purg.," xv.) he exemplifies meekness from the Virgin Mary, from Pisistratus ("lord of the city" of Athens) declining to take vengeance for an insult, and from the young man St. Stephen, "whose eyes made gates to heaven," praying for God to forgive his murderers. Nimrod, Niobe, Jason, Arachne, pagan heroes from all quarters and ages are ranged alongside Christian rulers and teachers as characters typical of human civilizations. Cato, "the severest champion of true liberty," is set as guardian of the Purgatorial shore and mountain, and as example of moral as well as civic freedom. Men of action in the world of secular affairs, such as knights, are placed beside churchmen and martyrs. Many of the qualities for which historical and mythological figures suffer or are honoured are political or social vices or virtues—e.g. sedition, barratry (the jobbing sale of office and justice). " In his mind the heathen good stood for the Christian good,"[1] and the moral issues of the human conflict are akin in Christian and in pagan systems. The secular and the sacred, while distinguished as aspects of experience, are subject to the universal order under service of the Divine purpose.

In like manner, love Divine is continuous with pure human love. The ethereal love of the youthful Dante for Beatrice, romantically celebrated in the " New Life " (Vita Nuova), is germinal of the new life realized in his spiritual " Vision." It taught him, with her as a human image of the Divine beauty and goodness, to love the Supreme Good. Consecrated by her death, this idealizing love is the symbol and foretaste of the love of perfection in God. In his celestial world he takes her as the representative figure for Divine Wisdom. Devotion to her has acquired a religious value. Human emotions are not only thus recognized, but are purified by this spiritual association—an effective substitute for ascetic repudiation of natural affections in monastic celibacy. So it was that St. Paul's use (Ephes. v. 23 ff.) of the relation between husband and wife in expounding the mystical union between Christ and His Church had the effect of elevating wedlock. Love is one and sovereign in all spheres of the universal order.

It is this principle that enables Dante to gather all knowledge into a comprehensive unity and harmony, and to give a synoptic view of the world in all its planes and spheres. With his mastery of history, science (chiefly Græco-Arabian astronomy), surviving classical culture, Aristotelian philosophy, scholastic theology, the economy of Church and State, the Romantic poetry of chivalric love, mystical experience, he walks at liberty through them all. All are

---

[1] Cf., for ampler treatment of these principles in Dante, Taylor, " The Mediæval Mind," Vol. II, chap. xliv.; Edward Caird, " Essays on Literature," chap. i., ' Dante in relation to the Theology and Ethics of the Middle Ages.'

fused by his own creative mind in a concerted movement of Divine activity, visualized dramatically, subdued to the æsthetic purpose of his " miracle of song." By his prophetic insight they are transmuted into expressions of eternal reality and spiritual value. He makes abundant use of symbolism ; but things seen are not mere symbolic illustrations of things unseen ; they are modes and transparencies of the one all-embracing order. And they are presented as elements in a mutually related system because they were first combined in Dante's own experience and " conjunct view " of the manifold variety of life. Hence Ruskin could call him, " the central man of all the world, as representing in perfect balance the imaginative, moral, and intellectual faculties, all at their highest."

### 4. Various Meanings of the " Vision "

With the above multiform correspondence between spheres of life in view, we can see that the diversity of meanings in the scenes of the " Vision " is not an artificial device or a mechanical contrivance for the dramatic stage, but represents essential reality, a unity of order found in all planes of human experience, without and within, present and eternal. The poem has a fourfold sense, the literal, the allegorical, the moral and the anagogical (shadowing everlasting glory). Dante expressly says so in his Letter to Can Grande : " The first is called literal, the second allegorical. . . . Consider it in these lines : ' When Israel went out of Egypt, the house of Jacob from a barbarous people, Judah was His sanctuary, and Israel His dominion.' If we consider the letter alone, the departure of the children of Israel from Egypt in the time of Moses is signified ; if the allegory, our redemption accomplished in Christ is signified ; if the moral meaning, the conversion of the soul from the sorrow and misery of sin to a state of grace is signified ; if the anagogical, the departure of the sanctified soul from the bondage of this corruption to the liberty of eternal glory is signified."

As distinguished from the literal or historical, the other meanings may be classified together as moral and spiritual, though Dante calls them "allegorical." "The subject, then, of the work taken literally only is the state of souls after death. . . . But, if the work be taken allegorically, its subject is man as, by his freedom of choice deserving well or ill, he is subject to the justice which rewards and punishes." [1]

In Bunyan's "Pilgrim's Progress" the characters—Worldly Wiseman, Greatheart, and the rest—are ideas personified : the story is allegory throughout. In Dante's "Divine Comedy" they are real persons idealized, their distinctive qualities or acts being taken as representative. It is not mere allegory ; it is rooted in objective actuality, built up out of visible events and historical figures ; the narrative is not mere fiction fabricated to suit things unseen.

The temporal world-system is indeed a veil over our eyes, but that veil is translucent, and the real world of things unseen and eternal shows through the veil. It is the spiritual significance of the whole that supremely interests and inspires the mind of Dante as seer.

His ruling purpose in his "Vision" is self-confessed, both in the poem and in the *Convivio* (ii., 14, 15). Writing with the joy and power of poetic creation, he made his work of art independent of doctrinal teaching ; yet the poem is deliberately "the epic of man the pilgrim of salvation." In dramatized illustrative form, with occasional expositions, it is a "sum of saving knowledge." The high moral purpose in a deep spirit of faith with which it was written has been stated in peculiarly convincing and penetrative terms by Dean Church (83 f., 101 f., 115, 127 f.). To condense some of his paragraphs, "That which Dante held up before men's awakened and captivated minds was the verity of God's moral government. To rouse them to

---

[1] Toynbee, in his "Dante Dictionary," recognizes a five-fold interpretation of the poem, in these terms : "It represents in the literal sense the Florentine Dante Alighieri ; in the allegorical, Man on his earthly pilgrimage ; in the moral, Man turning from vice to virtue ; in the religious, the Sinner turning to God ; in the anagogical, the Soul passing from a state of sin to that of glory." Here Toynbee, representing the modern mind, introduces, in the first place, the life-experience of Dante himself as the historical original, and omits "the state of souls after death," which, however we may discount or question it, was integral to Dante's thought.

a sense of the mystery of their state ; to startle their common-place notions of sin into an imagination of its variety, its magnitude, and its infinite shapes and degrees ; to open their eyes to the beauty of the Christian temper, both as suffering and as consummated ; to teach them at once the faithfulness and awful freeness of God's grace ; to help the dull and lagging soul to conceive the possibility, in its own case, of rising step by step in joy without an end : this is the poet's end. . . . It is to stamp a deep impression on the mind of the issues of good and ill doing here, to do this forcibly by doing it in detail and in figure." The lot of all the numberless spirits who have ever lived here, spirits still living and sentient, is parallel with our present life in penalty, purification or the fullness of consolation. What Dante depicts through imagination enables us to see it, both there and here. It might be a scene now going on before a soul whose eyes were opened. " As he is led from woe to deeper woe, then through the tempered chastise-ments and resignation of the Purgatorio to the beatific vision, he is tracing the course of the soul on earth realizing sin and weaning itself from it, the course of its purification and preparation for its high lot by converse with the good and wise, by the remedies of grace, by efforts of will and love, perhaps by the dominant guidance of some single pure and holy influence, whether of person, or institutions, or thought."

It is no mere barren vision. The world to come we can know only in images, faint broken reflections. But he fills it in with the characteristic features of person and place here, and the events that determine humanity's great moments. Thus, and not by abstractions, he visualizes and vivifies what it is in this world that connects it with heaven and hell, and shows how this life and the life to come, however different, are parts of one whole. The history of men and states with which we are familiar, often apparently casual and fragmentary, is viewed in the light of God's final judgments. " The very men and women whom we see and speak to are now the real representatives of sin and goodness " in eternal issues. " He wrote, not for sport, nor for poetic pleasure ; he wrote to warn," and, one may add, to encourage with the assurance that every good effort has its eternal value.

The elaborate technical structure of the poem, which bores some students with its mechanism, should not be allowed by the average reader to divert his mind from the broad significance of its *tableaux vivants*. He will, no doubt, require as his companion a commentary, such as that which Dean Plumptre adds to his own translation. But while every scene has its peculiar reference and diverse meanings, and some of its imagery belongs to the " stiff and frozen forms " of the Middle Ages, he can find a truly catholic meaning in the successive scenes without slavish subjection to commentators upon details.

Dante's schema of numbers belongs to his system of symbolism consistently carried through his triptych. In keeping with the Trinity, three is the fundamental number, with multiples of three—nine and thirty-three. The poem is cast in three parts, the " Inferno," the " Purgatorio," the " Paradiso." Each of these contains cantos (allowing for the extra introductory canto of the " Inferno ") to the number of thirty-three, representing the thirty-three years of our Lord's earthly life. The number seven, probably derived from the seven planets, represents the six days of creation with the Sabbath as the seventh day, and again the seven deadly sins recognized in the Mediæval Church, exemplified in the seven terraces in the stages of purification in the " Purgatorio." The number nine, found in the nine circles of the Inferno, corresponds to the nine grades in the hierarchy of the Angelic Bodies—thrones, dominions, principalities, powers, etc.—as in the " Paradiso." Ten is the perfect number ; hence Dante's Ten Heavens, the above nine and the Empyrean. These numbers were adopted by Dante mainly as part of the symbolic tradition of the Church ; but according to ancient philosophy they belonged to the constitution of the universe, as when we assert that there is a natural three-ness of things. Thus in the seer's view they are part of the universal " order."

IV

# Dante's "Vision": The "Divine Comedy"

## (B) NIGHT—THE "INFERNO"

IT may be useful to have at the outset in outline a general synoptic conception of the cosmography and topography of the "Divine Comedy," even at the risk of some repetitions in subsequent pages.[1] The design given on an adjoining page is based mainly on the drawing in Zacchetti's "Manuale Dantesco" (Milan). The scale on which the Earth is drawn is deliberately made large, out of all proportion to the Purgatorio and especially the celestial universe, for practical illustrative purposes.

### 1. General Schema of the "Divine Comedy"

The Earth, according to the ancient Ptolemaic astronomy, was supposed to be the central point of the universe, with all the heavenly bodies circling round it—represented by Dante as globular in accord with Aristotle's conception.

Dante, for his dramatic purposes, imagines this world as comprising two hemispheres, to be traversed by him along with Virgil as guide. One hemisphere is the scene of Eden, with circles of heavens above it. Satan, Lucifer, in his fall

---

[1] See, for a fuller account, Dr. Moore, "Studies in Dante," Vol. III; Witte, "Essays on Dante," Chapter IV; and pictorial designs in frontispiece of Carroll's three volumes. For concise summary and small designs see Gardner's "Primer" on Dante. The design given herewith has been prepared by Mr. Morley C. Luke according to general directions and Zacchetti's plan.

from heaven, had torn his way through Eden down to the world's core. Ruined Eden, in its recoil, drew itself up into a lofty mountain, its flanks the terraces to be scaled in the penitential return to the lost Terrestrial Paradise (see II hereunder). The other hemisphere is the habitable Earth of men, crowned by Jerusalem, directly antipodean to the lost Eden.

(I) Underneath the surface of the Earth is the Inferno, the vast cavern formed under shock of Satan's fall, the abode of the finally impenitent, classified in circles according to the nature of their sins. It is an inverted cone, its vast base immediately under and co-extensive with the habitable Earth above, and its apex the centre of the globe where Satan sits. The interior of the conical pit is shaped like an immense amphitheatre in graduated sections, with an Ante-Hell and then nine successive circles or terraces, narrowing as they deepen to the bottom farthest from God, in which the impenitent endure sufferings, depicted in dramatic imagery, which express the natural outcome of their sins. Successive descending levels are divided by symbolic rivers—Acheron (with Charon as boatman), representing Death; Styx, meaning hateful; Phlegethon, flaming blood; and Cocytus, wailing: all borrowed symbolically from pagan mythology.

In the Ante-Hell are the Neutrals spurned of all. In the subsequent nine circles, graduated according to the gravity of the sins penalized, are (1) in the Limbo or border of Hell virtuous heathen and unbaptized infants; (2-6) those guilty of Incontinence, the Sensual, the Gluttonous, the Avaricious (Misers and Prodigals), the Wrathful and Sullen, and Heretics; those guilty of Malice, (7) the Violent (against neighbours, against themselves, against God, Nature, and Art); (8) the Fraudulent—Betrayers of Women, Flatterers, Simoniacs (buying Church functions like Simon Magus, Acts viii. 9 ff., or selling Church offices like Popes), Diviners, Barrators (trafficking in public office for personal gain), Hypocrites, Thieves, Evil Counsellors, Schismatics, Falsifiers; (9) Traitors, to kindred, to country, to friends and guests, and to benefactors. In the upper divisions the sins of incontinence, of hot blood, natural impulse, are punished less severely, as being in line with natural cravings though not under right moral restraint. In the lower divisions the sins of Malice are punished more severely, as being contrary to nature, committed in cold blood and inhumanity. So Satan, at the bottom of the pit, sits encased in ice, as representing the utmost of cold-blooded heartlessness. In an upper section Dante's Hell is fiery-hot ; in its depths it is icily cold, witheringly cold with a callous heart.

(II) On the other side of the hemisphere is the lost Eden elevated into a mountain of Purgatorial discipline. On its border, in Ante-Purgatory, are Excommunicates and other penitents of the last moment. Then comes the gateway with its significant *three steps of salvation* (among the most significant things in Dante). Then the seven successive terraces of the mount of cleansing which must be climbed. The first three terraces represent love distorted, pride, envy, anger, as fundamental sins of the spirit ; the fourth, love defective, as in sloth or accidie (depression of spirit) ; the last three, love excessive, for things permitted but liable to excess—avarice, gluttony, sensuality.

At the summit of the Mountain is the Earthly Paradise, the restored Eden, all green and fragrant. Virgil (as reason), returning to his own place in the borderland of the Inferno, yields up the guidance of the higher ascent to Beatrice as the representative of Revelation or Divine Wisdom. At her challenge of his defalcations, his memory or conscience is cleansed in the river Lethe (forgetfulness), and a bath in the river Eunoe (renewal of mind) brings him new vigour to pursue his upward pathway into the heavens.

(III) Above the Earthly Paradise are the successive heavens of the " Paradiso " in the circuit of celestial orbs and spheres.

First are the seven lower heavens located in the planets then known and the sun, presided over by angelic orders in gradations—Angels on the Moon, Archangels on Mercury, Principalities on Venus, Powers on the Sun, Virtues on Mars, Dominations on Jupiter, Thrones on Saturn. Each of these is temporarily tenanted by saints (visitants from their eternal abode round God) in classes whose special qualities correspond to the supposed virtues of the several

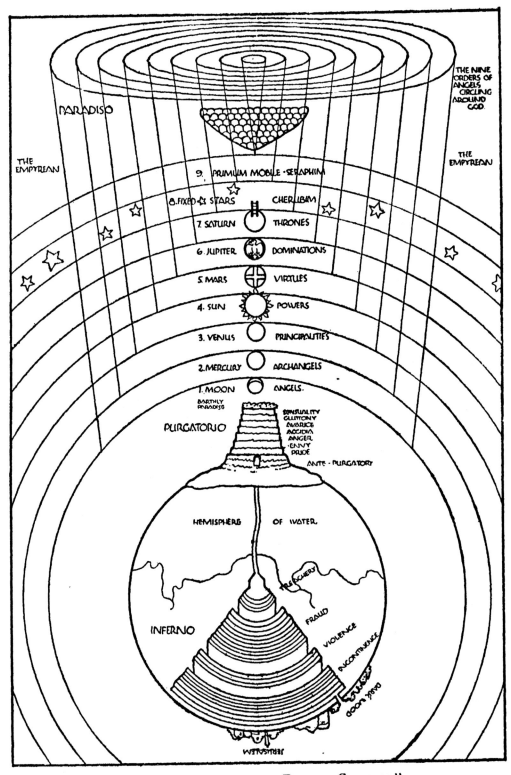

COSMOGRAPHY OF THE "DIVINE COMEDY."

orbs : the Moon by saints flawed by inconstancy, Mercury
by those whose greatness had suffered from mixed motives,
Venus by those under the lordship of love, the Sun by
teachers and doctors, Mars by representatives of manly
fortitude, Jupiter by just rulers, and Saturn by exemplars
of serene contemplation.

The eighth heaven in the Firmament of fixed stars, the
counterpart of Eden, is ruled by Cherubim representing
Divine Wisdom, with a vision of triumphant redemption
through Christ.   The ninth, the crystalline heaven ruled
by Seraphim of purest spiritual flame, is the " Primum
Mobile," from which all lower orbs take their motion.
Beatrice, as Dante's guide thus far, returns to her true place
in the White Rose round God, and St. Bernard, the great
mystic, representing immediate intuition, unveils to the
seer (his eyes specially illumined) the luminous Empyrean
of eternal truth and glory, the sempiternal White Rose,
composed of myriad saints and angels, all bent to the central
Light of God, and radiating the effulgence of the Divine
Essence and dazzling glory.   It is the Beatific Vision.

## 2. THE " INFERNO " :   REPRESENTATIVE SCENES

The introductory canto opens (in Longfellow's translation) :

> " Midway upon the journey of our life
> I found myself within a forest dark,
> For the straightforward pathway had been lost ! "

Deep in soul-slumber, " sleep-opprest," and wandering
astray, he has lost his way in a gloomy wood, the bemazing
thickets of worldly political affairs (as prior of Florence)
and in evil ways of life.

He has set out to climb the " delectable mount " that
caught the first rays of the morning sun, the mountain of
the ideal life.   But, as he begins to ascend, he is confronted
and driven back by three beasts, a lithe and spotted leopard
(panther), a ravenous lion, and a lean and greedy she-wolf.
These are apparently suggested to his mind by Jeremiah
v. 6 : " A lion out of the forest shall slay them, a wolf of
evenings (deserts) shall spoil them, a leopard shall watch

over their cities . . . because their transgressions are many and their backslidings are increased."

These beasts are symbolic—and let us recall that on his own authority his figures and scenes have various meanings, as already explained. They are variously taken as referring historically to political powers of the day, destructive and barring progress (e.g. Florence, France and Rome), but also and more especially representing in moral meaning three vices, such as the passion for sensuous beauty (leopard), pride (lion) and avarice (wolf), covering temptations and entanglements that beset him in those spring-time years of natural desire and ambitious spirit.

As he turns affrighted to descend again, the phantom figure faces him of one whose voice, from long-continued silence, seems hoarse. " Have pity on me, whether true man or shade," he cries in fear. " Man was I once "— and so Virgil declares himself. Then Dante: " O thou my master, my author, source of all honour, which I drew from that style I took from thee, save me from the beast that makes me tremble ! " (Here we are condensing in a free rendering of the substance.) Virgil: " Why dost thou return from climbing the mount ? To escape these dangers, then, thou must take another way to flee the ravenous beast (wolf) that must ruin mankind till the Greyhound come that will be her death."

Virgil bids Dante follow him as leader who will guide him through the infernal regions of the disconsolate and up the mount (of Purgatorial cleansing) where are those " content within the fire " in the hope of reaching the " blessed people," and under worthier guidance (Beatrice) see the best ones in the happy clime (Paradiso).

Shrinking from the fearsome adventure, mistrusting himself, confessing that Æneas (in Virgil's Æneid) had dared traverse the Underworld and St. Paul had been caught up into Paradise, he pleads to be excused, as if saying, " Who am I ? Why should I go ? "

Virgil warns him against cowardice, and tells him that he has come at the wish of the " gentle Lady " (the Blessed Virgin) and the bidding of Beatrice (with Sta. Lucia, Dante's patron saint) who, in pity and love, seeing what was befalling Dante, longed to save him from shame and death.

Beatrice, when he meets her in the Terrestrial Paradise, tells him that he had been given this fearful nightmare sight of hell in order to convert him from his downward course.

> " So low he fell, that arguments
>   For his salvation were already short,
>   Save shewing him the people of perdition."
>                    (" Purg.," xxx. 136 ff.)

While the animating human motive for the spiritual pilgrimage is the devoted memory of Beatrice, the ideal type of perfect purity, the originating cause is Divine Grace, employing Virgil as the first guide for the tremendous adventure of his soul.

Virgil is for several reasons chosen as his first guide in the eternal realms. He was Dante's favourite author, " my author," his most cherished poet, from whom by devoted study he had learnt his style (canto i.) ; in the " Æneid " Virgil had given a vision of Hades and described the realm of shades ; he had been the poet of Roman Empire (dear to Dante)—" born *sub Julio* and living under Augustus, he had sung the glories of Empire " ; he had written lines (Eclogue IV) which were long (mistakenly) viewed as a prophecy of the Messiah—really a fond forecast of the Augustan age—as reflected in the " Purgatorio " (canto xxii.). He had been the great seer-sage, and as such he is here introduced as the type of Human Wisdom or Science.

Human wisdom or insight can understand and describe the workings of sin and its consequences in human nature here and hereafter, in hell, and also in some measure the purgatorial discipline by which sin can be overcome through cleansing fires (in the " Purgatorio "). Thence Human Wisdom must fail, Virgil giving place to Beatrice as guide from the Terrestrial Paradise.

The spiritual pilgrimage opens in canto iii., the poem gliding into the eternal realm, to whose weird spell with its soul-subduing vision we must surrender our minds.

The total period of time supposed to be occupied by the journey in the " Divine Comedy " is one week of eight days. The journey from the descent into the Inferno to the reemergence into the upper light of the Purgatorio corresponds to the time between the death and the resurrection of Jesus Christ ; it starts on Good Friday, and on Easter morning the pilgrims rise with Christ out of the gloom of Hell into newness of life.

The gateway to the dark starless underworld has no keeper except the dread inscription : " All hope abandon, ye who enter here." The inscription goes on :

> " Through me the way is to the city dolent,
> Through me the way is to eternal dole ;
> Through me the way among the people lost.
> Justice incited my sublime Creator ;
> Created me Divine Omnipotence,
> The highest Wisdom and the Primal Love."

Within the gate there is Ante-Hell, a vestibule section not included in the circles. It is the region of the Neutrals. Listening, Dante hears laments and wailings :

> " Sighs, complaints, and ululations loud
> Resounded through the air without a star,
> Accents of anger, words of agony,
> And voices high and hoarse, with sound of hands."

They come from souls of men who had in their lifetime stood aloof from the conflicts of the world, taking no part with one side or the other, guarding themselves against hostile criticism, moral cowards and neutrals, living without praise or blame. Dante scorns such caitiffs more intensely than the worst of sinners. They are shirkers. " They never were alive." Now these men, who had been time-servers going with the wind of popular opinion whichever way it blew, under no banner of conviction, are carried in a restless swirl of sand and empty life. Neither heaven nor hell will have these men that never had enthusiasm. " The world admitteth no memory of them. Mercy and justice scorn them. Let us not speak of them. Look, and pass on."

Mr. J. Addington Symonds thought this contemptuous judgment unduly severe and inconsiderate. But these men were not mere weaklings ; they proved themselves cowards when great issues for human welfare were at stake. Those whom in the vision of judgment (St. Matt. xxv. 40) the Son of Man bids " Depart, ye accursed," are condemned for what they did *not* do to serve crying human needs.

We may compare Kipling's " Tomlinson " in " Barrack-Room Ballads," probably derived from Dante, and Browning's " Statue and the Bust," as to the merits of hesitating inaction.

Before the pilgrims pass, they see among the multitude " the shade of him who through cowardice made the great refusal "—probably Celestine V, whose weak withdrawal from the Papacy made way for the accursed Pope Boniface VIII, though others have identified him with Pilate, who washed his hands of responsibility in the case of Jesus. He is representative of many, who stand aloof.

The rivers already mentioned, delimiting the graduated sections of the Inferno, descend from the surface of the Earth (Crete as the pagan Eden) from a great image of Time in the form of an Old Man (as we say, Father Time), its head of gold (the Golden Age), its arms and breast of silver, its trunk of brass, its limbs of iron and feet of clay (cf. Dan. ii. 31–33). Between each of these is a fissure in the body, and from these clefts in the figure of Man-in-Time the tears of humanity, the " tears of things," of sin and sorrow, drip into the underworld, the source of the rivers that must be crossed by the wayfarer and that find their destined end in the abyss of the Inferno (xiv. 106 ff.).

Ferried across the river Acheron by Charon, the pilgrims of the realms of Night enter the first circle, the Limbo or Border of the Inferno, the abode of Unbaptized Infants and Virtuous Heathen. Dante here reflects the traditional idea that little ones could not enter the kingdom of heaven unless they had been baptized. The virtuous heathen, like Homer, Socrates, Plato, Aristotle, etc., who had never known Christ, are detained here on the outer hem of this region of shades. Incidentally Dante remarks upon the courtesy with which Homer, Horace, etc., received him as poet. " I was the sixth among five such men." He fore-knew his own rank.

Dante deals with them very gently. " Here there was no weeping, only sighs which made the eternal air to tremble." These noble, sweet unfortunates have sweet voices, and talk of wisdom whose castle stands close by. Rivulets flow through from Nature above, from the verdant hills and plains they loved, " making their channels cool and soft."

Topographically it is Hell, but climatically it is not. Yet, alas, the pathos of life lies not so much in what happens to a man as in what he misses. And these gracious shades miss the highest vision and the perfect day. Hither Virgil will have to return after serving Dante as guide up to the Terrestrial Paradise.

But, in the " Paradiso " (xix. 70–78, 103–109 ; xx. 67 ff.), the poet demands why should " a man born on the banks of the Indus, with none to tell or read to him of Christ, whose every wish or deed is good so far as human reason sees, be counted guilty in dying without baptism or faith. Where is the justice that condemns him ? "

> " Unto this kingdom never
> Ascended one who had not faith in Christ
> *Before* or since He to the tree was nailed.
> But look thou, many crying are, ' Christ, Christ ! '
> Who at the judgment shall be far less near
> Than some shall be who knew not Christ."

Technically Dante keeps within the traditional theory of the restricted destiny of the virtuous heathen—except in one case. He boldly places Rhipeus, whom Virgil in the " Æneid " called the justest of the Trojans, in Paradise, the heaven of Jupiter, on the supposed ground that, as " his heart was wholly set on righteousness," God gave him foresight of " our redemption yet to be," and that faith, hope and charity " were unto him for baptism more than a thousand years before baptizing." He thus extends to one—why not to many others on the same grounds ?— the principle on which faithful Jews from the patriarchs down to the prophets and national warriors were allotted their place in Paradise. Dante might have claimed Thomas Aquinas in support of his more generous hope. The master theologian taught that, while good heathen were excluded from the beatific vision, they were quite happy as we are happy without being kings. He went farther in saying : " God never suffers anyone to want what is necessary to his salvation, if he only desires it. No one loses his soul save through his own fault." According to his theory, " to many heathens a revelation of Christ was given, and if some were saved to whom the revelation had not been given, yet these were not saved without belief in the Divine Mediator, but by believing that God was the Saviour of men and would save them by ways which would best please Him and according to what the Spirit had revealed to some who could see the Truth." This principle could be held even if the terms stating it and the conditions presumed were differently conceived.

From the remaining eight Circles (given in a previous page) in which different classes of sins are punished, the limits of space will allow us only to select a few representative instances and scenes.

In the realm of the Incontinent, victims of unregulated natural impulse, those who had yielded to sensual passion (Circle ii.), are depicted as " darkened in their understanding " by self-indulgence and swept helplessly by a whirlwind of ceaseless unrest, the hurricane of passionate desire. We may rightly say that no amount of gratification, even if the life of the flesh survived death, would give full satisfaction ; that lust becomes a malady of the mind, especially of the emotional imagination, and not merely a demand of the body. Here are Paolo Malatesta and Francesca da Rimini—presented in a poignant picture of universal appeal (see G. F. Watts' painting, " Paolo and Francesca "). With gentle, piteous voice Francesca, saying, " There is no greater sorrow than in misery to remember the happy time," exclaims :

> " Love, that on gentle heart doth swiftly seize,
>     Seized this man for the person beautiful
>     That was ta'en from me, and still the mode offends me.
> Love, that exempts no one beloved from loving,
>     Seized me with pleasure of this man so strongly,
>     That, as thou seest, it doth not yet desert me ;
> Love has conducted us unto one death " (" Inf," v. 100–106).

It was, she tells, when innocently they were reading together of Lancelot's love, his enthralling passion kindled their " dubious desires." The momentary impulse that

once " united and undid " them swirls them ever here
together like doves flying through the air to their " sweet
nest." Dante's tender compassion for them reveals his
sympathetic understanding of such sins which, from no
wilful depravity, brought them to this " woeful pass."
Unlike Kipling, who says that people who sin two by two
suffer one by one, Dante shows them suffering together, as
does Tolstoy in his book, " Resurrection," in the process
of redemption.

There are few women, as compared with the number of
men, in Dante's Hell, though (significantly) five appear in
this circle where love easily lapses into passion. All but
one are drawn from pagan mythology or history. Francesca
is the only " Christian " woman in the Inferno. Here
Dante rises superior to the traditional idea—connected with
the story of Eve as the first sinner and tempter as well as
with priestly celibacy—that woman was dangerous.

In the next circle, gluttons, molested by the foul dog
Cerberus, wallow like hogs in the mire, under a cursed
rain of snow and hail, and bark like dogs.

Next are seen the Avaricious, both misers and prodigals,
treated together as guilty of essentially the same sin, greed
in hoarding and in reckless squandering, inability to use
money rightly as servant of good ends. They are here
rolling stones against each other. Ecclesiastics are prominent
among the Avaricious. Popes, Cardinals and other clergy
were, according to Dante, as to Chaucer, more than " a
little wee bit worldly," were indeed peculiarly liable to
greed and to profuse expenditure. Dr. Carroll [1] asks why
the very men who by their calling professed to have forsaken
the world were notoriously in bondage to it ; and he shrewdly
answers : " Perhaps the conjecture of an old commentator
is not far from the truth—' I own I cannot find a cause for
avarice in prelates, unless it be that perchance prohibition
engenders concupiscence.' " This is a piece of suggestive
psychological insight, instructive to parents, to churchmen,
and to many social reformers, who resort to an interdict
in advance of common enlightened persuasion for the

[1] " Exiles of Eternity," p. 117, quoting Vernon's ' Readings on the
Inferno," i. 217.

suppression by forced measure and bare majorities of all sorts of practices which most good men would strongly desire to have abolished by free predominant consent— " perchance prohibition engenders concupiscence."

Avarice is defeated in the long run ; for, as Virgil is made to say :

> " All the gold that is beneath the moon,
> Or ever has been, of these weary souls
> Could never make a single one repose."
> (vii. 64 ff.)

After the same manner, in Circle viii. (canto xix.), the higher ecclesiastics are severely challenged as Simoniacs, who sold rank and office in the Church to kinsfolk (nepotism) for material possessions. What price, the poet asks, did Christ demand of Peter for the keys ? Nothing but " Follow me." Church endowments, like those of Constantine (" Inf.," xix. 115 f.), had become perilous temptations.

The Wrathful and Sullen of temper (canto vii.), who had given way to morose melancholy, and who confess, " Dismal were we in the sweet air which by the sun is gladdened," are found bemired in the slimy swamp of the creek Styx. Having refused to see the sunshine (compare the Terrace of Accidie or Sloth in the " Purgatorio "), they are now blinded by the slime of the marsh, as angry resentment blinds the eye of reason, and are smiting each other, with gurgling sounds in their throats that raise bubbles on the surface of the marsh. It is a severe judgment on those who have been sulky in moods of depression. Who that has felt and thought deeply upon the world has not thus been sometimes depressed ? But the sulky mood is unfaithful to belief in the sovereign God.

Heresy, in the next region, is traced partly to lack of self-control and partly to wilfulness, coming between the sins of Incontinence and the sins of Malice. Dante had known by experience grave religious doubts. But the devout man must initially believe in order experimentally to understand (St. Anselm, as against Abelard who sought to understand in order that he might believe intelligently). As we shall see in a later chapter, faith according to Tolstoy is the vital force by which man lives and achieves happy results. Hence the tombs in which, in Dante, the heretics are buried, with fiery pains.

In the next realm are depicted Hypocrites, who are one thing to the eye, another in inner reality, all carrying the unbearable weight of a heavy mantle and hood, the mantle of pretence, golden outside, but leaden within, crushing them down, while with tears wrung from their eyes they are still compelled to go on.

In this nether Hell, governed by Malice, in Dis the city of Satan, fortified by castles and Furies, are (*a*) the malevolently Violent, against neighbours, against themselves (e.g. suicides), against God, against nature (e.g. sodomites, whose vice is unnatural and degrading, though shared by some men of intellect) ; (*b*) the Fraudulent in Malbolge (moats like pouches), betrayers of women, corrupt Church rulers (Simoniacs, already mentioned), corrupt civil magistrates, schismatics in the Church (e.g. Mohammed the false prophet), in the State and the Family ; and (*c*) in the bottomest Hell the Traitors to kindred, to country, to friends and to benefactors, and in the utmost depth to Christ. Here Judas, the arch-betrayer of Christ, is being chewed in the gnashing teeth of Satan. Within the lowest river of Cocytus which forms a lake of ice, Satan himself is depicted as huge, hideous, malignant, triple-mouthed, gruesome, with mighty bat-wings which issue wave-beats of freezing wind that with icy breath encrust the lowest infernal denizens in ice.

Dante's nethermost Hell, as already stated, is freezingly cold, not fierily hot. Which is a parable ! In its lowest depth sin is utterly cold to humanity, calculatingly callous, and petrifies the soul.

## 3. MORAL PRINCIPLES

Everywhere the moral order reigns inviolable, in the constitution of human life, in the fabric of the universe. Through all the topsy-turvy of mortal fortunes, through all the confusion between injustice, ambition, suffering, and honour, freedom and the common weal, through the blinding mists of disordered judgments, the seer looks

down on the world from the heights of calm vision and
proclaims that the eternal watersheds do ultimately dis-
criminate between good and evil among men and states,
that the rocks of righteousness and truth are unshaken.
Disrobed of artificial trappings, the accidents of time and
circumstance and all concealments, and exhibited openly
in their essential character and the moral issues inherent
therein, all are made manifest as in the day of judgment.
The final lines of distinction in destinies do not correspond
to but run athwart present classifications in society and
religious systems.  None, whether in Church or State,
in Christendom or heathendom, can escape this penetrating revealment for better or for worse.

The continuity of life and character is made clear.  Men
passing into other spheres carry their proper nature with
them, and are not changed by new conditions.  " He that
is unjust let him be unjust still. . . .  He that is righteous
let him be righteous still " (Rev. xxii. 11).

The inwardness of bane and bliss is a fundamental principle throughout the three realms of Dante's Vision.  His
Hell is a state of mind rather than a place, though a scenic
stage is needful for us to visualize it.  The real action
takes place in the subterranean chambers of the soul,
while interior states and disablements are projected on a
screen within a mediæval framework.  Underneath the
structural mechanism, a psychological exposition of sin
is given, neither spatial nor merely forensic.

Often we do not realize the enormity and obliquity of
our private individual sin until we see it with repugnance
exemplified in some one else, and perhaps see in his case
the mischief it brings about.  We need not suppose that
Dante dared to assume the role of arbiter of individual
destinies.  In placing historical persons in Hell, including
recent popes and politicians, he was not pronouncing the
final verdict of Omniscience on each individual.  He was
employing them and their characteristics as examples of
the sins condemned.  They were representative figures
through whom he could give dramatic embodiment to his
moral judgments and to the inherent nature of such sins.

The nature of the sin in each case is objectified, embodied

in form of punishment as well as in personal instance to express its character and its fruition. Sins are viewed here, not in their direct relation to God and their cost to God, but as they affect the man himself and society. And the penal sufferings depicted are a translation of the sin into concrete form, generally the fitting consequences of the sin. They are not imposed from without by another's hand like an inquisitor's lash ; the impenitent is punished by his sin, reaping the harvest of his own dispositions and habits, each after his kind. There are in some places tormenting demons at work, but they are only masks for the sins involved. The soul creates its own climate ; the nature of the sin creates the conditions that supervene. St. Augustine had already said, " Every unordered spirit (ill-regulated mind) is its own punishment." (" Confessions," I, 12).

These doleful people are here, not merely because they must receive what is justly due to them for sins done in the past (which was the forensic view of Thomas Aquinas, who did not show the inner moral relation between the sin and the suffering), but mainly because the same evil dispositions and tastes continue to rule their wills and hearts, which are still alien to God and goodness. They are here all for lack of " one sorry tear," for lack of a heart for holiness. Dante has no record of " unpardonable sin," no place in Hell's circles for those guilty of it : no sin whatever, no sinner, is potentially incapable of Divine pardon ; what is unpardonable is persistent impenitence. Some in these circles condemn what they had done, while others blame and blaspheme their ancestors or the whole human race as the criminal class usually do to-day ; but they manifest no softening contrition. We are accustomed to say that the pains of hell consist in anguish of conscience. Not so Dante, whatever imagery he may use, unless remorse be moral. Conscience, involving the sense of sin as sinful, is dead in the nether hell. If that moral nerve survived, it would be a token of a remaining element of good. Its place is taken by sullen, gnashing anger, despair, and the like. According to Eckhardt, the German mystic, Dante's contemporary, echoed in the " Theologia Germanica," there are two persons who have no sense of sin—Christ and Satan; and those nearest to each of these tend to lose it.

Those down in the Inferno don't seem to want to get out, it has been said; rather, they don't want to be good. They resent their agonies and would fain escape from them; but there is no escape from sin's effects without a change in moral attitude—for attitude is destiny. One of the direst effects of sin is that it brings loss of inward power, enfeebles the will, and so paralyses the wish to repent.

There is no closed door or shut gate at the entrance to the Inferno. Its denizens are not confined there by prison walls. What holds them is the " weight " of their desire or love, the action of gravitation. The idea, traceable in the apocryphal book, " The Wisdom of Solomon," was a favourite one with St. Augustine (" Confessions," xiii. 9), was taught by Thomas Aquinas, reigns in Dante's three realms, and reappears in Thomas à Kempis in diverse expression. All things come to rest in " order." As the body is moved by its weight, so the soul is moved by love, falling or ascending according to what it most desires, as we shall see again in the " Purgatorio " and the " Paradiso." The sin-weighted soul falls to its own natural level and stays there in virtue of moral and spiritual gravitation. None whose " own place " was in the circuit of the Inferno had ever, according to Dante, gone out from it—although One (not named, but manifestly Christ) had come once (to spirits in prison, 1 Peter iii. 19), and on Easter morning delivered Abraham, Moses, and others, that had foreseen Him and had believed. The old problem, when seen thus in its true light, is, not the eternity of punishment, but the perpetuity of moral gravitation and character.

Moral insight is shown in the graduation of penal sufferings which the inmates of the Inferno endure according to the degree of their depravity. It has been stated above that those who find themselves here through default or infirmity rather than vicious obliquity suffer mildly in loss rather than pain (Luke xii. 47), that those who yielded to natural passions of appetite unregulated suffer less bitterly than those whose sins sprang from deliberate design, malicious motive, and cold-hearted inhumanity—such as fraud and treachery—contrary to nature.

Here, and in the " Purgatorio " (as we shall see), Dante has given us a revised scale of sins and of virtues.[1] Whether his revaluation of all values, his principle of classification, be finally approved or no, it overturns the popular judgment which ostracises frail women of the Magdalene class and blindly honours Sir Gorgius Midas who has captured worldly success by crooked manipulation of men and markets regardless of others' well-being. He comes nearer Christ's standards of judgment—" many that are first shall be last, and the last shall be first " (St. Matt. xix. 30).

How, then, are we to view and how can we bear Dante's lurid pictures of Hell's tortures, which have become a byword for gruesome, ghastly, and sometimes loathsome horror ? They sear, and shock, and revolt our sensibilities, when we take them literally. Many of them are unthinkable, and no human constitution could stand them. True, they are no worse than the ingenious torments of the ancient Persian hell of Zoroastrianism (see G. F. Moore, " History of Religion," I, 401), and more charitable and discriminating than those of popular mediæval imagination, which consigned all the lost to a common torture-chamber in which they were tormented by fiendish and grotesque devils. They are to be taken as symbolical (whatever the poet's belief regarding a material hell may have been) ; but, even so, their inward moral equivalents are terrible enough. Rather we must take their moral impressionist value as the permanent gist of them.

They dramatize the measureless and unspeakable difference between right and wrong, the issues inextricable from man's choice between the two, and his penitence and impenitence. Mark Rutherford, Dr. Hale White (cf. his " Bunyan," 239), wrote : " Heaven, hell, and the atonement were the results of the conception that there is a generic, eternal and profoundly important distinction be-

---

[1] Much labour has been spent on a comparative study of the classification of sins and virtues in the " Inferno " and in the " Purgatorio." See Moore, " Studies in Dante," 2nd Series ; Witte, " Essays on Dante." cap. v.

tween right and wrong. It is because right is so right that there is a heaven, and because wrong is so wrong that there is a hell. God Himself became man to conquer sin."

So Dante showed the moral ground of hell, or has shown that such as remain impenitent in their sins depart into shame, loss and misery in the region of death.

" Oh the pity of it ! " we cry inwardly in echo of Dante's cry. Is there no gentle pity here ? One remembers Shorthouse's saying (in " John Inglesant "), " Only the Infinite Pity is adequate to the infinite pathos of human life." Yet is pity either proper or adequate here ? Virgil sees Dante weeping, and says, " Art thou, too, like other fools ? The death of pity is true pity." Yet pity leaps into their eyes unawares, in the case of Paolo and Francesca, as the judge who must condemn on moral grounds does so with tears in his eyes.

It is daring, even heroic, on Dante's part to declare, as it is written over the entrance to the Inferno, that it was erected, not only by the justice and omnipotence of the sublime Creator, but by " the highest Wisdom and the Primal Love."

It was in virtue of Divine love that the moral order of the universe should be maintained, that goodness, beauty, and truth should have their blessed garden protected against desecrating invasion by the " flaming sword which turned every way, to *keep* the way of the tree of life." It would not be love, it would be weakness ending in chaos, if good and evil fared alike. " God is love ; " " God is a consuming fire : " these two are really one. His holiness is one with His love.

Love, in diverse modes, is the keynote of Dante's three-fold Vision—he was the poet of love as well as the poet of righteousness, the two as one. In the Inferno love, the greatest gift to mankind, is, however, misdirected or per-verted by man. Love having been rejected, that under-world is characterized by its lovelessness, its darkened, motionless " dead air," with nothing green, no flower, no star.

Here it is NIGHT.

### 4. OUT OF THE DEPTHS

How were Dante and Virgil fittingly to emerge from the Inferno ? They could not be represented as returning on their path : there is no such return. The way taken is significant. They clamber over the haunch and head of Satan, turn completely round as if in a somersault (this inverted position taken by some to represent conversion), and, up the stairway passage cleft by Satan in his fall, the two pilgrims climb " with labour and with hard-drawn breath," " panting like a man forespent "—sin lowers the vitality. They hear " the sound of a small rivulet therein descending " to the abyss of oblivion and Satan, a pathetically " little rill " which is the wash of cleansing tears from the penitents on the Mount of Purification.

> " My Guide and I upon that hidden way
> Entered to return into the bright world ;
> And without care of having any rest,
> We mounted up, he first and I the second,
> So far that through a round opening I saw
> Some of the beauteous things which heaven bears ;
> And thence we issued forth to rebehold the stars."

Each of the three visions, the " Inferno," the " Purgatorio," and the " Paradiso," closes with the word " the stars."

# V

# Dante's " Vision " :   The " Divine Comedy "

## (C)  DAWN—THE  " PURGATORIO "

IT was on the evening of Good Friday that Dante with
Virgil " descended into hell ; " it was on Easter
morning that he rose into new life, having like Jesus Christ
been buried for the most part of three days, and reappearing
" in the end of the Sabbath when it began to *dawn* towards
the first day of the week."

Three realms of souls departed are set forth in the three
cantiche of Dante's " Vision." Most of us are accustomed
to think of only two. For that matter, his threefold classification of the dead resolves itself ultimately into a twofold
division, since those in Purgatory will in the long run,
when the process of purification is completed, enter into
the heavenly Paradise. But, apart from that remote
issue, those of us who disbelieve in Purgatory as a separate
realm take the " Purgatorio " in the second sense which
the poet deliberately gave to it, and find it profoundly true
in this present life of the poignant ordeal of moral discipline
promoting inward purification which we have reason to
know well.

The " Purgatorio " has not seized the popular imagination as the " Inferno " has done with its lurid pictures
which scare the eyes that look on them. But generally
it is more interesting to us than either the " Inferno " or
the " Paradiso " because it is in large part on the level of
our present experience, because we are not (pray God)
impenitently bad, whilst we are not celestially pure, but

mixed of good and evil in conflict, and enduring chastening on the way to be better. We are kin with these pilgrims of the Dawn ; " we understand their faith in the justice which appoints and measures their ' majestic pains,' the aim and purpose which sustains them, the high-hearted courage which endures," the steadfast hope that all will yet be well. Ours also is the Agony of Recovery, which one may offer as another name for the Mount of Purification.

We draw a sigh of unspeakable relief in sympathy with Dante as he emerges from the dungeon gloom and dead air of the " blind world " to " rebehold the stars " : his face stained with tears, his body forespent, but now in the open air and the glad morning light which fall healingly on his spirit, with the " sweet colour of the oriental sapphire up-gathering in the serene pure air," where the beauteous planet of Venus " makes all the Orient to laugh " and blends its light with the light of Dawn.

How different this—in keeping with the bold originality of his general setting of Purgatory on a mountain—from the conception of it current in the theology of his day—as an underground prison in close proximity to hell, with the same fire heating the two realms, and only a thin partition separating the penitent from the impenitent. The poet makes a new departure from tradition in giving an " open-air treatment " for the cleansing of contrite sinners. The long and arduous stairway of the towering Mountain must, indeed, be scaled through sore stress and fiery processes in the pilgrimage to final bliss ; but at any rate it will be under the canopy of God's heaven, with the light touching the mountain terraces at each dayspring. Hence the opening lines :

> " Of that second kingdom will I sing
> Wherein the human spirit doth purge itself,
> And to ascend to heaven becometh worthy."

Four stars—did he know of the Southern Cross ?—are seen in the southern sky which rejoices in their flames, representing the cardinal virtues, Prudence, Justice, Temperance and Fortitude, lost in the fall but to be re-covered in the ascent to the Earthly Paradise. The aged warder of these shores, Cato, " the champion of true liberty," challenges the two comers from the underworld, but is reassured, and sends them down to the shore to gird themselves about with the rush that grows in the ooze—the leafless rush that " in bending is not broken," and hardeneth not, symbol of humility of spirit which is the first requirement of those who, out of the miry clay, would climb the Mountain. Across the plain they come within the shadow of the Mountain where the dew withstands the sun, to have the grime and defilement of the infernal atmosphere washed away in the morning dew. Virgil's hands are outspread on the wet grass and then over Dante's tear-stained cheeks, until their hue that hell has hidden is uncovered and restored. The poet often makes use of the spiritual symbolism and sacramental values of Nature. This washing of soiled cheeks in the dew of Dawn, as a primary sacrament of nature's grace, is the first prophetic act in the long cleansing process of coming discipline.

At sunrise a birdlike boat—the ship of souls—glides in to shore from earth's borderland across the " trembling sea," wafted hither by the white wings of the Angelic Pilot (corresponding to Charon, ferryman over the river Acheron into the Inferno). It bears a freight of penitents arriving, all chanting Psalm cxiv., rendered (as in our hymnals) by Sir Walter Scott in his majestic version :

> " When Israel, of the Lord beloved,
>     Out of the land of bondage came,
>   Her fathers' God before her moved,
>     An awful Guide, in smoke and flame "—

which from the sixth century in the Western Church the priests had solemnly chanted as the bodies of the dead were borne into the church for the Burial Service.

### 1. The Mount of Purification

The mountain of Purification has three main divisions: first, the Ante-Purgatory—like the Ante-Hell—at the base of the mountain, from the shore to the gate of St. Peter ; second, within the gate, Purgatory proper, with seven terraces, each terrace narrower than the one below—the inverse of the cone of Inferno narrowing as it descended to the centre; third, the summit or tableland of the Earthly Paradise.

Virgil accompanies Dante in this second realm also, as the representative of Human Wisdom or Reason. But in this second realm of Christian half-lights, Virgil is unfamiliar with the way of the penitents, and has often to ask which direction to take, and has to depend on angels of light and grace. Natural Reason helps, but is inadequate.

The ascent is to take four days—symbolizing the four periods into which man's life is supposed to be divided. After the sleep of each night, when the pilgrim can make no advance without the light of grace, comes a vision that is to guide him for the day's climb, and then the sunlight, while once and again the sound of song and the beating of angelic wings are heard.

In Ante-Purgatory are those who had died while excommunicated by the Church, penitents of the last hour, but lingering like sheep without a shepherd; the indolent who delayed to repent until the eleventh hour, whose purification is now proportionately deferred, and who, with paralysis of will, say like lazy men " What's the use ? "; the over-active and energetic who, either coming to a sudden death without time for preparation, as soldiers did, or so busily engaged with crowding affairs of active life as to defer religious interests till the last, are therefore detained from purification by the same dilatoriness.

Dante denies that the Church has power to " bind or loose " apart from the moral and spiritual condition of the supplicant. So he was a prophet of the Reformation. But the persistent defiance of the Church on the part of the excommunicate deprives him of shepherd guidance and much of the grace of sacraments, and produces an infirmity of the will that paralyses action, so that, although penitent at last, he has to remain in the Ante-Purgatory for thirty times the period of his contumacy. It is bold of Dante to place on the doorstep of the Mount of Purification those who had been excommunicated by the Pope's curse but who had relented at the end. Man's judgment could cut them off from bliss for a time, but the ultimate judgment of God depended on the moral attitude of the excommunicate's soul. And if his soul turned towards God, Dante here says, in the spirit of the Evangel :

> " Infinite goodness hath such ample arms
> That it receives whatever turns back repentant to it."

The way through a cleft in the rock was so straight and narrow that only the swift wings of a vehement desire could carry one over it—so sore the struggle at the start of the new life, so precipitous the path to higher ground. Once on the next ledge, the law of ascent is explained to the wayfarer :

> " This Mount is such, that ever
> At the beginning down below 'tis toilsome,
> And the more a man goes up the less it pains.
> Therefore when it shall seem to thee so pleasant
> That the going up shall become to thee as easy
> As going down the current in a boat,
> Then at the pathway's ending thou shalt be ;
> There to repose thy panting breath expect."

It is the first step that counts : hard, but making the next step easier. With each advance the downward drag of natural disposition and habit diminishes, and the ascent becomes lighter in the increasing freedom of the soul.

The law of gravitation, not then known in the physical universe, holds good in the moral sphere. In St. Augustine, as indicated in the previous chapter, there is found the germ of Dante's " mystical doctrine of the law of spiritual gravitation, that the soul is moved by love as the body is by weight, the gravitation being to what it loves." He says in his " Confessions " (xiii. 9) that this principle holds good in the upward direction as in the downward. " Love lifts us thither (to Thee, our rest). In good will is our peace. Weight is not downward only, but to its own place. Fire tends upward, a stone downward. By their own weights are they urged, they seek their own place. . . . Out of order they are restless ; they are restored to order, they are at rest. My weight is my love ; by that am I borne, whithersoever I am borne . . . . We ascend by the ascents of our heart, and sing a song of degrees. By

Thy good fire we are kindled, and we go ; for we go upward
to the peace of Jerusalem." [1]

There are momentary reactions. In Miss Underhill's
words (" Mysticism," 215), " Each step towards the vision
of the Real brings with it a reaction. The nascent transcendental powers are easily fatigued, and the pendulum
of self takes a shorter swing." Therein is seen the victory
of grace, that at each upward step the pendulum takes a
shorter and shorter reactionary swing.

When evening darkness descends, they are assailed by
night-serpents, that is, by the evil dreams which are often
held as the last fastnesses of the devil in the heart of the
convert, those dreams of self-indulgence which (as we saw)
St. Augustine fought against. He wondered whether
vagrant memories in sleep were his true self as with devilish
art they essayed to reach the organs of his fancy and with
their polluting illusions drag him back to hell. They come
to Dante when the Compline hymn, " Te lucis ante," has been
sung (to give it in Newman's version) :

> " Now that the daylight dies away,
>    By all Thy grace and love,
> Thee, maker of the world, we pray
>    To watch our bed above.
>
> " Let dreams depart and phantoms fly,
>    The offspring of the night,
> Keep us, like shrines, beneath Thine eye,
>    Pure in our foe's despite."

---

[1] Cf. Dante in the " Convivio " : " Since God is the beginning of our souls
and the maker of them like unto Himself, this soul desires above all things
to return to Him. And even as a pilgrim who goes by a way he has never
travelled, who believes every house he sees afar to be his inn, and not
finding it to be so, directs his faith to the next, and so from house to house
till he comes to the inn ; so our soul, the moment that it enters on the new
and never-travelled path of this life, directs its eyes to the goal of its
Highest Good, and therefore whatever thing it sees which appears to have
in itself any good, believes that it is it. And because its first knowledge
is imperfect through want of experience and teaching, small goods appear
to it great ; and therefore it begins first to desire those. Whence we see
little children desire above all things an apple ; and then, proceeding
further on, desire a little bird, and then, further on, desire a beautiful
garment ; and then a horse, and then a wife ; and then riches, not great,
then great, then very great. And this happens because in none of these
things does it find that which it goes in search of, and it thinks to find it
further on." It continues unresting, disappointed with successive satisfactions, under a supreme attraction towards God who is its true home—the
thought of St. Augustine in a new expression.

These dream-serpents are only driven aside by two angels with flaming swords that guard the valley on the highway to the heights.

Up the mountain bastions they see a rift in the cliff—Dante calls it " the needle's eye ; " it proves to be the guarded gate to the Purgatorio proper, to the terraces of purification. Unlike the entrance to the Inferno which stood wide open, this portal has a warder and is narrow, the strait gate of life eternal.

We shall see how differently Bunyan conceives the gate of the pilgrim way, yet how fundamentally alike they are.

Outside and leading up to the gate there are three steps (" each stair mysteriously was meant," says Milton, who was influenced by Dante) :

> " There where we came, unto the first step,
>   White marble was so polished and so smooth,
>   I mirrored myself therein such as I appear.
>   The second, tinctured a deeper hue than perse (black purple),
>   Was of a rock rugged and fire-scorched,
>   Cracked asunder lengthwise and across its breadth.
>   The third, that uppermost rests massively,
>   Porphyry, seemed to me as flaming red
>   As blood which from a vein is gushing forth."
>
> (ix. 94 ff.)

Striking symbols, these three steps. (The idea of *steps* was often employed by mediæval mystics.) They have a first reference to the Roman Catholic sacrament of Penance, which consists of three parts—Contrition, Confession, Satisfaction; but, taken here in the order of Confession, Contrition, Satisfaction, the order in which they are brought to light, they have a wider and general symbolic meaning, not specially Roman.

The repenting sinner approaching the throne of grace must stand on this white, polished marble mirror in which, with awakened conscience, he can see his true self reflected as he is. The first step is " white," in Latin " candidus," signifying the absolute candour and sincerity of confession of sin ; and it is burnished clean, so that no sin may be unrevealed and unconfessed—else the confession is invalid and vain.

The second step is a rough stone, with no name, for it

is his hard and stony heart, and it is purple black (perse) and scorched with fire. But it is broken, split, with a crack across the breadth and another along the whole length, cleft with a cross. Hard and rough, this is the " broken and the contrite heart," scorched with sin-consuming fire ; but the cross cut in these transverse heart-breaks is the image also of the cross of Christ which is to take away sin and heal the broken in heart. It is when the love and cross of Christ powerfully impress the heart that it breaks in sincerest sorrow for sin, a repentance not like that animated by fear or self-interest.

The third step, of porphyry flaming red like blood spouting from an open vein, refers first to the " Satisfaction " demanded of the penitent by the Church of Rome as the temporal penalty for sin ; but it has the more general meaning of sacrificial love, heart's blood, spent in " works meet for repentance," in the self-denying service that attests redemption and establishes the heart in grace.

These three steps represent, as Miss Marie Rossetti puts it fervently in her " Shadow of Dante," " candid confession mirroring the whole man, mournful contrition breaking the hard heart of the gazer on the Cross, Love all aflame offering up in Satisfaction the life-blood of body, soul, and spirit."

The Angel-Warder of the gate stands first for the priestly confessor of the Roman Church—to others of us he is the Lord of all to whom we make confession. He has a sword in his hand : first the sword of authority, and then, in the second moral meaning, the " sword of the Spirit, which is the word of God . . . quick, powerful, and sharper than any two-edged sword, piercing even unto the dividing asunder of soul and spirit, a discerner of the thoughts and intents of the heart."

> " A naked sword
> Which so reflected back the sun's beams toward us
> That oft in vain I lifted up mine eyes."

He is seated on the threshold on a stone of adamant— the rock on which the Church was built—but his feet are rested on the uppermost step of blood-red porphyry, tender heart's blood combined with adamantine justice.

Up these three steps Dante goes with good will and begs for admission of the Angel-warder, " but first upon my breast three times I smote " for sins of thought, word, and deed. Then with the point of his sword the warder inscribes Dante's forehead with seven P's, *peccata*, the seven deadly or capital sins. They are no longer hid under cover, but openly shown to Him " who sets our secret sins in the light of His countenance." Compare the " Scarlet Letter " of Nathaniel Hawthorne.

> " ' Take heed that thou wash
> These wounds, when thou shalt be within,' he said."

One of these seven P's is to be purged off his brow on each of the seven Terraces he is about to scale.

The Angel-warder then takes two keys. " One was of gold, and the other was of silver," the silver key of knowledge, discernment of the fitness of the penitent, diagnosis requiring art and wisdom to unlock the soul and unloose the knot of the penitent's tangled case ; the key of gold, more precious than the other, because absolving from all sin. The Angel-warder says to Dante :

> " From Peter I hold them ; and he said to me to err
> Rather in opening than in keeping locked,
> If people but fall prostrate at my feet."

He is to lean well to the side of generosity—another softening touch of mercy from Dante's hand.

Then, with a warning that there must be no looking-back by any one fit for the kingdom,

> " He pushed the portals of the holy door,
> Exclaiming, ' Enter ! ' "

Entering, Dante hears a burst of sweetest song, the strains of the " first thunder-peal," as when at a cathedral door " we are wont to catch, when people singing with the organ stand, for now we hear, and now hear not, the words." It is the " Te Deum Laudamus " : " We praise Thee, O God, we acknowledge Thee to be the Lord "—the joy in the presence of the angels over one sinner's repentance.

The tradition as to the origin of the " Te Deum " was that it was composed by St. Ambrose on the occasion when

St. Augustine was converted from his wanderings astray and was admitted through the gate into the Church at Milan (as we saw in the previous chapter). We remember how St. Augustine, as he tells in his " Confessions," was deeply moved even unto tears by the music of the service when his black sins were blotted out and he was numbered among the children of God.

Tears and pain await Dante up the steep ascent, but happy will he be therein.

There are, as already indicated, three main divisions of the Mountain of Purification, each of them a stage in the return of the soul from the fallen state to Eden purity. First, Ante-Purgatory (outlined above), the low shores of the eternal sea, the base and foot-hill spurs of the Mountain. Next, the Purgatorio proper, with its seven Terraces representing the seven capital sins and the cleaning processes by which they are burnt out of the soul : Terrace I, of Pride ; II, of Envy ; III, of Anger ; IV, of Indolent Sloth, Accidia ; V, of Avarice ; VI, of Gluttony ; VII, of Sensual Indulgence. Third and last, the Terrestrial Paradise, the ideal of human existence, the restored Garden of Eden, in touch with Paradise, which forms the third and supreme vision of Dante.

In the literal sense, the Purgatorio is for the Roman Catholic the realm where penitent sinners pay the temporal punishment of the sins whose eternal guilt has been forgiven. In the more general sense, it is the purgatorial discipline whose cleansing fires of bitter-sweet experience purge the soul of the residue of evil habit and taste, of the deposit which sin has left, as a preparation for the ideal life of Eden purity and for the vision and ineffable bliss of heaven.

Man has a measureless capacity of loving ; but alas ! what to love, how to love wisely ? The root of both sin and virtue is love, which is also the final motive power of the universe. St. Augustine defined virtue as the ordering of love. " Every creature, since it is good, can be loved both well and badly : well, that is, when order is preserved ; badly, when order is disturbed." And " he liveth justly and holily who appraises things at their right worth ; it is he who hath ordered love, so that he neither loves what is not to be loved, nor fails to love what is to be loved, nor loves too much what is to be loved less, nor loves equally what is to be loved less or more." If the Creator is Himself loved, not aught else instead of Him, man cannot love badly.[1] "Set love in order in me," is the Vulgate version of the "Song of Solomon" (ii. 4) where the English Bible reads, "His banner over me is love." And so St. Francis preached, "Set Love in order, thou that lovest me." The native tendency of love is towards good, according to Dante; beauty and goodness are attractive; as one has said, "no one can hate God *as God*" in His goodness; and, as one of our own poets has said, "we needs must love the highest when we see it." Is not this the basis upon which the preacher must work, the ally in every bosom to which the Gospel must appeal? And may we not say that most of men's common sins are misdirected efforts after an imaged satisfaction which will fail to satisfy because of misapprehended estimates of abiding life-values? Hence Dante's lines ("Purg.," xvii. 91 ff.):

> " 'Neither Creator nor a creature ever,
>     Son,' he began, 'was destitute of love
>        Natural (i.e. instinctive) or spiritual (rational); and thou knowest it.
>  The natural was ever without error;
>     But err the other may by evil object,
>     Or by too much, or by too little vigour.

> " 'While in the first it well directed is,
>     And in the second moderates itself,
>     It cannot be the cause of sinful pleasure;
>  But when to ill it turns, and, with more care
>     Or lesser than it ought, runs after good,
>     'Gainst the Creator works His own creation.' "

All the sinful folly, the failure and the misery of men, is thus due to disorderd love. Hence in these seven penitential terraces we find Love Distorted in the first three—Pride ("love of one's own excellence"), Envy ("sadness at another's good"), Anger ("contrary to charity and justice"); Love Defective in despondent Sloth; and in the last three Love excessive—Avarice, Gluttony, Sensuality,

---

[1] Cf. Gardner, "Dante and the Mystics," 54 ff.; Wicksteed, "Dante and Thomas Aquinas," 162 ff.; Carroll, II, 225 ff.

the unrestrained craving for things not intrinsically wrong but wrong in immoderate measure.

In the " Inferno " were shown the demoralizing effects of unrepented sins ; in the " Purgatorio," on the other hand, we see the sources or inner springs of men's sins undergoing a process of purification ; the disposition is being cured, the habit of will reversed, through remedial and welcome pains, in order (as the poet says) to dissipate the last film of scum that dims the conscience. In the former the Wrathful were sunk in dismal marsh and given over to gurgling rage ; but on the third terrace of this mountain Anger is an acrid, pungent smoke that torments the eyes, blinding as anger does, while, however, the penitents are chanting the " Agnus Dei," calling upon the Lamb of God for cleansing mercy and the peace of purity. In the " Inferno," the glutton, his god his belly, was wallowing in mire ; but here on the sixth terrace Gluttony is portrayed in the leanness of the soul, wasted lean with intense hunger and thirst in sight of tempting food and drink which yet it must not taste and which Divine grace enables the penitent to refuse for love of true freedom.

Sins of the spirit, pride, envy and anger, are dealt with in the lower three terraces ; sins of the flesh, in the upper three terraces. Why this order ? Surely not, as one expositor thinks, because avarice, gluttonous appetite and sensual indulgence are the last sins to be conquered—such is not true in fact—but because sins of the spirit are more fundamental, if not also worse, than sins of the flesh, and because the spirit's victories over inner dispositions assist in the subjugation of physical desires. As St. Paul wrote, " Walk in the Spirit, and ye shall not fulfil the lusts of the flesh." First deal with the roots from which bodily tastes spring, and then the fruits in the sense-life will be found already withering.

This principle is significantly attested when, as Dante emerges from each terrace, one of the seven P's (*peccata*) graven on his brow disappears and all those that remain instantly become fainter. For our sins or vices, like our virtues, are intertwined, and the conquest of any one tends to weaken all the others.

At the entrance upon each of the seven terraces in succession there are sculptured on the wall or embankment examples of the virtue antipathetic to the sin under disciplinary treatment, as a " whip " to spur the aspirant to effort ; and at the exit leading up to the next terrace there are under foot repellent examples of the sin now purged away, as a " bridle " for the next stage. These typical figures are drawn both from sacred story and from pagan history and mythology.

At each ascent from terrace to terrace one of the Beatitudes is pronounced upon the aspiring soul.

To select a few illustrative instances : on the first terrace, Pride, regarded as the root or nerve of other sins, is purged from the hearts of penitents (canto x.). They are represented as, like corbels supporting a roof or floor, bent with breast down to knees, weighed down by a stony burden, and learning lowliness. They recite an expanded paraphrase of the Lord's Prayer. As Dante sees their pains, he bows his head humbly, recognizing that pride has been his own special sin. Pride that rises against God, pride of intellect, of art, of power, is exemplified by figures graven on the pavement, such as Lucifer (who fell through pride), Briareus, Nimrod, Niobe, Saul, Rehoboam, while on the marble wall are types of humility, chief among them being the lowly handmaiden Mary, and Christ who in the incarnation made Himself of no reputation. It is the law of things that the humble are exalted and the proud are cast down. The Angel of Humility with his wing smites the pilgrim's forehead so that the first " P " is expunged— although at first (such is the nature of humility) he is unaware that it has vanished. Voices chant the first Beatitude, " Blessed are the poor in spirit," as the step to the next stage is taken. The ascent is now found to be a little easier.

The Envious (xiii. ff.) on the second terrace, clad in irritating sackcloth, leaning feebly on others, have their eyes sewn with wire stitching. Envy, *invidia*, a sin of the eyes— envious eyes—as also of an ear open to evil rumours and of the tongue, is " sadness at another's good ; " and (said Jesus), " if thine eye be evil, thy whole body shall be full of darkness." Hence this terrace is flooded with the light of the sun, " for He maketh His sun to rise on the evil and the good." Here Dante's guide explains a most important principle, distinguishing between material and spiritual goods. To put it in our own terms, material goods are limited in quantity, and the more who claim a share in them the less remains for each individual, envy hence arising ; but of spiritual goods (such as love, knowledge, piety) there is no limiting stint ; the more they are distributed the more they multiply ; the more we have, the more we can give ; the more we give, the more we gain in ourselves. We are not impoverished by giving our best, nor selfish in self-culture. Is not this illustrated in the multiplication of the loaves and fishes ? Hence the Angel of Goodwill is here, like a mirror, not absorbing all the light of the sun, but multiplying its radiance.

The sin of Sloth, or rather of sluggish, gloomy Indisposition, which is purged away on the fourth terrace, is not commonly understood among us. It is not to be identified with indolence or habitual idleness. The term " accidia " in Dante, " accidie " in Chaucer (" The Parson's Tale "), derived from the Greek (ἀκηδία), means a state of not wanting or not caring, and signifies despondent torpor showing itself in listlessness and irritability. It is a distemper of the soul, akin to sickness, a heaviness and sadness which (as Thomas Aquinas put it) " so weighs down the heart that it has no mind to do anything, carrying with it a disgust of work and a torpor of mind—of mind neglecting to set about doing good." It was a malady which peculiarly afflicted residents in mediæval monasteries—doubtless through overmuch concentration upon religion—neglecting the other needs of wholesome human nature, harping always upon one of its various strings to the point of aversion, as further shown in the chapter on the " Imitatio Christi." It still visits earnest minds, in occasional and strange revulsion, felt by good people who are overwrought, from what they hold most dear, in weariness of well-doing, in an unnatural distaste even for the exercises of piety.[1] This is an indis-

[1] For a fine diagnosis and treatment of this state of mind in modern form, see an essay in " The Spirit of Discipline " by the late Bishop Paget. See also the chapter on " The Malady of Not Wanting " in the present author's book, " God's Gentlemen."

position of the human spirit of which account should be taken in the " cure of souls."

This gloomy antipathy to good, paralysing effort, is viewed by Dante as an evil from which the soul in this region has to be purged. Hence we hear the sound of running feet of penitents crying, " Haste, let not time be lost for little love."

In the terrace of Avarice souls lie pinioned face downward to the earth, crying sorrowfully, " My soul cleaveth unto the dust : quicken Thou me " ; and, when the pilgrims emerge from it, they enjoy a wonderful sense of lightness, so heavily does the love of money weigh men down.

At this point a mighty earthquake startles them, accompanied by a chorus of voices singing " Gloria in excelsis." All the terraces thrill and vibrate in sympathy, all the suffering penitents rejoice together, because one of their number has completed the process of purification and passed upwards to celestial bliss. Up and down the mountain runs the resounding rumour. There is thus a sense of company among the aspirants of the Dawn, as there is among the wayfarers in Bunyan's " Pilgrim's Progress."

Pains of fire burn the hearts of those, in the seventh terrace, who had formerly burned with sensual passion and who now eagerly run through purging flames singing the praises of chastity, echoing the Beatitude, " Blessed are the pure in heart." A ring of fire fringes the summit ; at the gate of Eden Lost were set " cherubim and a flaming sword which turned every way, to keep (i.e. defend) the way of the tree of life." After much shrinking, Dante, learning that only this wall stands between him and Beatrice, cleaves the fiery fence, and hears a voice greeting him, " Come, ye blessed of my Father," a foretaste of the welcome yet to come in Paradise.

These searching fires are not penal, nor are they searing as in the Inferno, but are cleansing like the discipline of affliction rightly borne. Here it is not (as there) the results of sin that are endured unwillingly, but the sifting process, endured gladly, which purifies the inward taste and desire. Many people, we know, would not mind their sins and would go on sinning if they were not afraid of the price they would have to pay. But the natural forces and the disorder of our nature with the warp that sinful habit left must be rectified, the stain on memory expunged, a pure passion aroused to consume all dross. The penitents, as Dante shows, do not merely acquiesce in the pains as just ; they love the cleansing fires, poignant sweet ; they are heard singing in the fiery ordeal, and do not want to escape from penitential anguish until the purgatorial work is done. As one of them says, " God pierces our souls with longings to see Him," but they do not wish to go into His immediate presence until in heart they are pure enough to see Him. This is the sign of their heart being changed, that they burn to be clean. When our cheeks are flamed at the memory of sin, we do not wish even to entertain the thought of its appeal again.

> " For who repents not cannot be absolved,
> Nor can one repent and will the sin at once,
> Because of the contradiction that assents not."

The changed attitude of the soul, the re-direction of the heart from evil towards God and towards goodness as yet unattained, makes all the difference in the universe, the difference ultimately between whatever heaven or hell there be.

St. John of the Cross wrote : " To comprehend it we must bear in mind that this fire of love, before it penetrates the inner parts of the soul, hurts her constantly while it is destroying and consuming away the weaknesses which come from habitual imperfections. By so doing the Holy Ghost disposes the soul to unite with God and to transform herself by love into Him. The fire that unites with the soul in the glory of love is the same that had beforehand encompassed her about in order to purify her " (" The Living Fire of Love," I).

The love of God, the recurring note in Dante, is a terrible love because it is so resolved by all means, " e'en though it be a cross " for Him and us, to secure our " saving health." Does Dante's demand upon human effort outrun that of the Gospel of Christ, or ignore redeeming grace ? He is far from suggesting that emancipation from sin is the victory won by our own sole efforts. " From on high comes down the power that aids me " (" Purg," i. 68). Divine grace is shewn at work at many points from start to finish. Saving grace is mediated through various agencies, through the sacraments of the dew and the stars, through angel visitants and songs, through guides sent to him by Beatrice and the drawing power of Beatrice herself; pains endured are operations of the same grace. Jesus Christ, indeed, is not introduced in person as a figure in the ascent of the mountain—He could not be so brought upon this stage, any more than in Bunyan's " Pilgrim's Progress," without incongruity. We shall see later the place of Christ in the whole of the " Vision." But He is represented in His ministrants throughout, and appears in the chariot of the Church on the mountain summit. By all revelations of light and love God is working together with the penitents, working within as well as without, to enable them to work out their own salvation.

At the same time the action of Divine grace is not seen in Dante so immediately triumphant as in the New Testament and in Bunyan. We should like to have more of the swift power of redemption. In many cases the " fire of love fulfilleth in one moment " of forgiveness more cleansing and renewal of life than our poet has set forth. But at any rate he exhibits firmly the moral order operative in salvation. He does not represent intercessory prayers for the dead as merely lifting them to a higher stage or even relieving their pains, but as quickening their heart and will for purification. Their entry into heaven is morally conditioned.

Everywhere on the Purgatorial mount there is Hope, the air of Hope, in contrast with all hope abandoned in the Inferno. Its pilgrim people are " prisoners of hope," hope singing " it is better farther on."

## 2. THE EARTHLY PARADISE

On the plateau that crowns the mountain, the Eden table-land lost in the fall but now recovered after the long ascent, is the Terrestrial Paradise (" Purg.," xxvii. ff.), the world and life attainable and blessed in the conquest of evil and in harmonious order restored. The pilgrims emerge upon it " slowly, slowly," forespent with the recent toilsome climb, scaling the heights of Recovery. In contrast with the entangling worldly thicket in which Dante had lost his way before starting upon his journey, here is a forest living-green which everywhere breathes fragrance. Here all is new, and " spring is evermore, elect to human nature for its nest." It is free from the mutations of storm and passion swayed below by " the prince of the power of the air," and enjoys the breeze that is the refreshing wind of the Spirit.

Limitations of space forbid explanations of the successive scenes and symbolic figures (Matelda as the active life, and some others) in this realm. In any case we must deal only with what is significant of experience.

Virgil is about to resign his function as Dante's guide, after catching a glimpse of the Car of Revelation, and return to his own place among virtuous pagans in the limbo of the Inferno ; one of the most pathetic things in literature is the parting between Dante and his beloved teacher. Human wisdom or Reason personified in Virgil cannot discern the things of revelation, and cannot guide the pilgrim farther. Before departing he says to Dante :

> " Take thine own pleasure for thy guide henceforth . . .
> Free, upright and healthy is thy will,
> And error were it not to do its bidding ;
> Thee o'er thyself I therefore crown and mitre."

In other words, a will which has been completely purified takes pleasure only in what is right and holy, and is its own law ; pleasure and duty are one. " Love God, and do as you like," said St. Augustine. This maxim might easily be misread and abused. It has been called antinomian, but is not so. Eckhardt wrote : " There are those who say, if I have God and His love, I may do what I like. That is a false idea of liberty. When thou wishest a thing contrary to God and His law thou hast not the love of God in thee." Precisely ; that is what St. Augustine, as Dante also, meant : if you only love God enough, you may safely follow all your inclinations. With love of God all-commanding, what you like is one with what God wills ; His law is your delight.   Goodness is now second nature, nay, your essential nature.   Gravitation is now towards holiness.

" Crowned and mitred," the expression used at a coronation in those days, is meant by the poet to refer to the muchdesired unity between the Empire (" *coronatus* ") and the Papacy (" *mitratus* ") in the interest of human harmony and happiness.   But in its moral reference it means that the one will is to rule over the two-fold nature of flesh and spirit ;  and in religion the redeemed are to be " kings and priests unto God " (Rev. i. 6 ;  1 Pet. ii. 9).

The pilgrims, beside an intervening stream, are filled with amazement by a vision of the triumphal Pageant of the Church, or the Procession of the Spirit, approaching through the forest (" Purg.," xxix. f.).   The figures composing it are marshalled in the form of a mighty cross, whose advance is accompanied by ineffable music and brilliant light.   At the front are seven golden candlesticks with candles flaming like pennons with rainbow splendour, seven yet one at base, representing the seven spirits or seven-fold power of the Spirit of God, and with them are the four and twenty elders, white-robed and lily-crowned, chanting praise, representing the Old Testament scriptures.   Then come animal-symbols of the four Evangelists (cf. Ezek. i. 10 f. ;  x. 14).   According to tradition Matthew is signified by the figure of a man, since he begins with the human origin of Christ ;  Mark by a lion, on account of the " voice of one crying " in the desert at the opening of his gospel ; Luke by the ox, the beast offered in sacrifice, since he sets out with the history of the priest Zacharias ;  John by the eagle, because he wings his flight at once beyond all created things to the contemplation of the eternal Word.   On the two sides in the transverse of the cross formation walk the Three Graces and the Four Cardinal Virtues, and, in the rear, figures symbolic of other New Testament writers, followed by one half-asleep " with face alert " (John), who from Mount Patmos wrote the Apocalypse.   At the central point of the cross comes the triumphal Chariot of the Church, drawn by the Gryphon (Griffin), at once lion and eagle, whose shining wings stretch upward to the heavens, symbolic of Christ in His natures, human (the lion) and Divine (the eagle).

While thus the Car of the ideal Church is drawn by Christ in typical figure, Beatrice, as personifying the spirit of Revelation, descends upon the seat therein out of heaven, robed in mystical colours. After a glimpse of her Virgil silently vanishes, returning to " his own place." Angels and heralds sing the " Benedictus."

Beatrice addresses Dante by name with a searching challenge. Although she is veiled, he knows it is she, for " not one drop of blood but trembles in his veins," as he feels " the traces of the ancient flame." She had remained his ideal of virgin grace, had inspired him with noble purposes, and her gaze becomes an impeachment of him for his delinquencies. He had looked forward to this meeting as the supreme joy that would crown his laborious climb. But, instead of rapture, he is smitten with shame at the very sight of her. Hanging his head, he sees himself reflected in the clear stream of water between him and her. When angels sing, " In Thee, O Lord, have I put my hope," her reproaches for his faithlessness which had frozen like winter snow in his heart begin to melt as under a south wind and break into tears and sobs. But self-pity is weakening, and must not, cannot, stay the searching sword of memory, made keener by his purification. Her accusing voice sounds as if it were his own, echoing his self-challenge. Why had he turned his steps astray, " following after false images of good," so that nothing would avail for his salvation " save showing him the people of perdition " ? Had he not deserted the high purpose which she had once inspired ? With a faltering " Yes " of confession and voice almost inaudible for tears, he pleads that the things of the present world with their false pleasure had turned his steps aside as soon as her face had been lost to him in death. But, she insists, should not her decease have weaned him from the world and made him renounce the things of dust for the beauty of eternal goodness ? As has been said, all the purgatorial fires of the mount are condensed in this culminating trial.

Relenting mercifully, Beatrice bids him lift his eyes and look on her, but the beauty of holiness is intolerable, his past folly is unbearably hateful, and he drops senseless in a

swoon beside the river.  He is plunged by Matelda in the
waters of Lethe, the river of forgetfulness, which washes
away the stains of remembered sin.  On nearing " the
blessed shore " on the other side, he hears the words softly
sung, " Purge me with hyssop, and I shall be clean ; wash
me, and I shall be whiter than snow."   On his landing, the
Blessed Damozel, taking off her veils, gives him " one
smile," as he is conducted to the Gryphon (Christ) in whose
breast he is hid.  St. Augustine taught that the memory
of our sin as an experience would be removed, but that it
would continue with us as a fact of knowledge, else our
praise of Divine grace would be impossible, being robbed of
an incentive.  Should we not rather say that the mercy
of God will transfigure the evil past so as to make the triumph
of grace an eternal theme of thanksgiving eclipsing the
painful memory ?

Two streams flow from the throne of the eternal grace,
according to Dante's Vision.   In Lethe memory is sweetened
when judgment has done its work.  But for perfect blessedness it is needful that the soul, devitalized by sin and
suffering, should be quickened with the memory of good
deeds and thoughts and the appetite for life.  So (after
scenic acts affecting the Car of the Church which do not
concern us here) Dante is bathed in the stream Eunoe
(εὔνοὅς, well-minded) or " kindly thoughts," to " revive
his fainting memory."   It is noon on Easter day when with
this infusion of grace he rises into newness of life in a world
where all is ever new.

> " I returned from the most holy wave
> Re-made even in fashion of new plants
> That are renewed with a new foliage,
> Pure and disposed to mount up to the stars."

The " Purgatorio " thus, like the " Inferno " and the
" Paradiso," concludes with " the stars."

## VI

# Dante's "Vision": The "Divine Comedy"

### (D) NOON—THE "PARADISO"

AS it was Night when Dante explored the Inferno, and Dawn when he adventured upon the "second kingdom" to climb the Mount of purgatorial discipline, so it is Noon, the noblest hour of the day, the hour of Christ's crucifixion and of His ascension, when the poet is exalted to the successive heavens of eternal Bliss. The splendour of the noonday glory sorely taxes his powers of vision, and, he confesses, no words of men can adequately describe what he sees—it is ineffable. Not only does language fail him, but even his memory fails to retain the full apocalypse—"memory faileth to renew the spell."

The seer must in these supernal spheres resort to poetic symbols which suggest to the visualizing mind much more than can be cast in exact terms. The mythopoetic faculty of instructed imagination must be free to expand our inadequate knowledge of these transcendent regions. Any definite forecast of the future world, above or below, must in the nature of the case be mythological, casting ideas (presumably true) in pictorial dress or dramatic scenes. Divine revelation itself is built out of and interprets experience, and is not supernatural information. Of the life to come, of which man has had no experience, we really can be sure of nothing formal beyond the moral and spiritual implicates of the present life. Moral certitude is valid when we follow the extended line or curve of human experience in its highest magnitudes. Dante's genius here as a spiritual geographer lies in his perception and delineation of symbolic scenes in which these infinite magnitudes of the soul can be translated into forms of imagination which shall adequately convey impressions true to the finest Christian experience.[1]

To give an apocalypse from his own Patmos standpoint of the Paradise of God was the supreme effort of Dante's prophetic mind ; no wonder that this labour of years left him " lean." The " Paradiso " is the most sublime, coherent flight of sanctified imagination in the world's literature, imagination marvellously sustained to the crowning height in the Beatific Vision. It is the favourite field for expert Dante scholars ; but it is the least popular of the three movements of his " Vision." Why ? Because it contains much technical mediæval theology and the discussion of abstract problems, requiring special knowledge. It also outruns the scope of most human life and the powers of common imagination in its resplendent conceptions of the infinite power and goodness of God throughout the universe. And further, as Ruskin said, " it requires far greater attention, and perhaps for its full enjoyment a holier heart." It is partly due to this lack of the " holier heart " and of spiritual interest, as well as to imperfect experience, that Milton's " Paradise Regained " could not obtain the appeal of the tragedy of " Paradise Lost."

The cosmographic structure of the Paradiso has in a previous chapter been partially outlined (see also the Diagram of Dante's universe). Nine heavens encircle and revolve round the Earth. Seven of them have their visible centre in the known planets and the sun ; the eighth, the highest heaven visible to human eyes, is identified with the fixed stars of the firmament. Above them, and introduced to meet the requirements of the poet's Vision, are the ninth or crystalline heaven, entitled " Primum Mobile " as being the source of all motion in the other orbs, and subtending all worlds the Empyrean or Luminous Heaven, the

---

[1] For timid godly souls, Mrs. Oliphant's book, " A Little Pilgrim in the Unseen," not referring to a child but to the simple-hearted, has, in its tender imagination of the soul's awaking and possible adventures in the heavenly world, been found very comforting.

tranquil, transcendent and eternal abode of Supreme Deity and of spirits perfected in unison with Him.

According to the " Celestial Hierarchy " of the Neo-Platonist Dionysius, long held to be valid, there are nine Orders in the Angelic Hierarchy which in their mediating function reflect and transmit the Divine activity and grace, the function of the lower three being to purify, of the next three to illumine, and of the highest group to perfect the soul. These nine Angelic Orders are supposed to be identified with the nine moving spheres or graduated heavens, the nine successive celestial orbs : Angels with the Moon, Archangels with Mercury, Principalities with Venus, Powers with the Sun, Virtues with Mars, Dominations with Jupiter, Thrones with Saturn, Cherubim with the Fixed Stars, and Seraphim with the Primum Mobile.

Each of these orbs, in line with ancient astral religion, is supposed to be possessed of distinctive virtues, and the denizens assembled in each possess qualities of character to match its peculiar virtues. The true and abiding home of all beatified saints is the Empyrean Paradise beyond the stars, where they compose the White Rose with its focal heart in God. But, for the symbolic purposes of his Vision, the seer in his Patmos panoramic outlook represents them as for the nonce stationed on the several planets, having descended thither to receive him. As " fellow-citizens come forth to meet him who returns from a long journey, even before he enters the gates of his city, so to the noble soul come forth the citizens of the eternal life."

The allocation of the saints to the several astral spheres to whose virtues their qualities of character correspond is intended to exhibit the graduated scale of spiritual attainments, as in the " Inferno " and the " Purgatorio " sinners are classified according to the nature and the measure of their sins. Dante has too keen psychological insight and sense of reality to place all saints on an undifferentiated level, to represent Paradise as a flat plane of democratic equality. All are clad in glowing light, but they shine in brilliance according as they burn inwardly with divinest fire. Higher than those who excelled in action, and again than those completed in knowledge, are those who are

perfected in love. "One star differeth from another star
in glory." According to Dante, "The house is one, but
there is a diversity of mansions here." "Everywhere in
heaven is Paradise, although the grace of Good Supreme
there rain not in one measure." Degrees of beatitude are
determined by capacity, and every spirit is perfect in bliss-
fulness according to the compass of his faculty for wisdom
and love. Thus Divine grace does not, there or here, tend
(as does monastic rule) to reduce all to a uniform type, but
maintains the force and distinctions of personality.

Hence no one envies the rank enjoyed by others ; all are
content, wishing for nothing but what they have as the
utmost they are capable of having—as St. Augustine had
taught in almost the same words in the "City of God"
(xxii. 30). If they should wish to be up higher than they
are, their wills would be in discord with Him who put them
there.

> "Rather it is the law of this life beatific
>     To keep ourselves within the Will Divine,
>     So that our several wills shall make but one . . .
> And His will is our peace."

In the music of the spheres, while each of them in its orbit
has its distinctive note, all blend together in a rich ethereal
harmony, and, "as diverse voices make sweet melody, so
do the ranks of life render sweet harmony amidst these
spheres" (vi. 125). In this unison of tones between the
natural and the spiritual planes we may surely find the
eternal symphony.

Does Dante come short in not representing a progressive
movement of saintly spirits in heaven "from glory to
glory"? In Tennyson we read :

> "Eternal process moving on,
>     From state to state the spirit walks."

Dante moves on "from state to state," but it is as an
observer. There are signs of a progressive movement in the
"Purgatorio"—naturally as it is an intermediate and
temporary state. In the "Inferno" the spirits are not
depicted as descending from bad to worse, in the "Paradiso"
rising from good to better. Bunyan's "Pilgrim's Progress" by

the nature of the imagery provides for advance, for its scene is the present life. But Dante's structural schema of Hell and Heaven stages an eternal order of reality and dramatizes existing personal character as determinate. Moreover, as he shows every saintly soul perfect in bliss according to the measure of his capacity, it would be difficult to represent advance, unless it were in the growth of capacity.

In these spacious skies the law of " weight," already noticed, obtains completely; if no personal progress is worked out, the natural inclination or appetence is upward; Dante soars without effort. All are drawn, like streams, to " the sea whereto all beings move," as in Keble's hymn—

> " Till in the ocean of Thy love
> We lose ourselves in heaven above."

Beatrice, expressive of Revelation or Divine Wisdom, is Dante's guide from sphere to sphere, instructing him upon the ever-waxing wonders of heaven, the various manifestations of love in nature, beauty and God's will, the mystery of man's redemption, and the agency of the spheres in human lives and destinies. Her eyes, symbolizing the demonstrations of the truth, look upward and receive the rays of the Eternal Light, which he sees reflected in gazing on her face (i. 47). We recall Browning's line, " The vulgar saw thy tower, thou sawest the sun." It is by the growing radiance in her countenance that Dante is made aware he is ascending. Yet in the upper heavens he cannot see her face for the effulgence shining in St. John the Divine as he talks of celestial mysteries. According to Thomas Aquinas, followed by Dante, man has a threefold knowledge of things divine. The first is an ascent through things created by the light of natural reason. The second is a descent of divine truth by revelation exceeding human understanding. The third is a rapt supernatural elevation of the spirit giving direct and perfect insight transcending both reason and objective revelation. Hence in the crowning trance Beatrice as Revelation has to yield place as guide to St. Bernard, who, as mystic, represents *visio intuitiva,* or immediate apprehension of the Eternal.

Only swift glimpses of successive heavens can here be given.

Over the three lower heavens—the Moon, Mercury, Venus —the shadow of earth falls; the denizens owing to their human frailties lack the fullest beatitude in loss of power or faculty for the finest vision. On the Moon, with its changing phases, are spirits who waxed and waned in their devotion through inconstancy to sacred vows. On Mercury are those who were animated by mixed motives, by personal ambition or love of fame, " so that the rays of true love mount upwards less vividly " (vi. 117). Venus, with its twofold movement round the sun and round the earth in cycle and epicycle, now the morning and now the evening star, comprises spirits who had suffered from a divided heart, dissipated love, impure love circling round an earthly object, with love for God as the conquering counterpoise. Rahab, though she had been a harlot, is placed in this heaven because quoted in a genealogy of Jesus and among exemplars of faith, and because her scarlet thread signalling to the Israelites at Jericho became a prophetic symbol of Christ's redeeming blood and a type of the Church

Beyond the shadow of earth, the Sun is the sphere of the great teachers and theologians like the seraphic St. Francis, lover of Poverty, and St. Thomas Aquinas, expounding the doctrine of the Trinity. Feuds between Franciscan and Dominican monks as rival orders who should co-operate in their twofold work are rebuked when Dante represents a Dominican as singing the praises of St. Francis's splendid work like " a sun in the world," and a Franciscan glorifying the wisdom of St. Dominic; each is made to delight in the best that the other did. In Mars, signifying manly valour, Dante sees in the form of a Cross a constellation of stars that are the Christian knights and saintly martyrs who as warriors for truth and liberty had been soldiers of the cross, whose slogan song was " Arise and Conquer ! " Of the cardinal virtues embodied on these orbs, justice follows fortitude. On Jupiter, accordingly, white with pure justice, ruled by the order of Dominations, is presented the ideal government of men, the eagle (Roman) whose features are composed of righteous rulers such as David, Hezekiah, Trajan (by special grace), and Constantine the Great. On Saturn, the stead-fast seat of calm serenity in reflection, the poet sees the contemplative saints, who deep in restful meditation receive the promise, "Be still and know that I am God." They are going up the Ladder (like Jacob's) or Stairway of Contemplation to catch the golden splendours of realms supernal which "eye hath not seen." [1]

Having accepted the "upward calling" of that "scala santa," "his eyes made clear and keen," he is bidden look down retracing his past way through the seven spheres, and gains a momentary glimpse of the earth far below :

> "I saw this globe
> So pitiful of semblance, that perforce
> It moved my smiles, and him in truth I hold
> For wisest who esteems it least."
>
> (xxii. 128 ff.)

Having had his estimate of relative values adjusted *sub specie æternitatis*, the seer is able to enter the eighth heaven, the Firmament of fixed stars, the sphere of the Cherubim, the celestial counterpart of the Terrestrial Paradise. There the fall of man was seen; here are shown the harvest of

---

[1] "Fiery brooding" is the pregnant phrase used for "Meditation," by A. E. (George Russell) in "The Candle of Vision." The experience has its present-day equivalent in a modern mode in his pages. "On that path of fiery brooding I entered. At first all was stupor. . . . At first we struggle blind and baffled, our meditation barren. . . . But let us persist, and that stupor disappears. Our faculties readjust themselves, and do the work we will them to do. The dark caverns of the brain begin to grow luminous. We are creating our own light. By heat of will and aspiration we are transmuting what is gross in the subtle æthers through which the mind works. . . . How quick the mind is now, how vivid the imagination ! We are lifted above the tumult of the body. The heat of the blood disappears below us. We draw nigher to ourselves. The heart longs for the hour of meditation and hurries to it ; and, when it comes, we rise within ourselves as a diver too long under seas rises to breathe the air, to see the light. We have invoked the God and we are answered according to old promise. As our aspiration so is our inspiration. We imagine It as Love, and what a love enfolds us. We conceive of It as Might, and we take power from that Majesty. We dream of It as Beauty, and the Magician of the Beautiful appears everywhere at Its miraculous art. . . . This vision brings its own proof to the spirit, but words cannot declare or explain it. We must go back to lower levels and turn to that which has form from that which is bodiless." (Compare St. Augustine's vision on the balcony at Ostia, and the closing lines of the "Paradiso"). "Our highest moments in life are often those of which we hold thereafter the vaguest memories."

redemption, the spoils of Christ's triumph, the myriad souls redeemed shining with the light they derive from Him.

> " O happy band, elect to fullest joy,
>     At the blest Lamb's great supper duly placed,
>     Who feeds you still with bliss that cannot cloy."

Here St. Peter examines Dante on Faith, St. James on Hope, St. John on Love. In the suggestive study of these three theological virtues Dante's Creed begins :

> " I believe in one God,
> Sole and everlasting, who, Himself unmoved,
> Moveth all the heavens by love and longing."
> (xxiv. 130.)

After the Creed and expositions of belief, the *Gloria*, " To Father, Son, and Holy Ghost," is chanted by all Paradise. It comes like the exuberant smile, the victorious laugh of the universe, at the glory of redemption, all creation blushing in eclipse. Note how it consummates the devout " hilarity " of Christian saints which had deeply impressed St. Augustine before his conversion in hearing anthems sung in Milan Cathedral. If this Christian " hilarity " is lacking to-day, we lose much of the supernormal, healing power of faith experienced of old. And why ?

Above the sidereal heavens, the ninth is the crystalline heaven, from which all the universe draws its various motion, therefore called the " Primum Mobile." Here the nine circles (see diagram) of the angelic hierarchy revolve round the central Point of Light, which signifies the unity of God, and which is broken (we think of prism and spectrum) into diverse angelic orders. These are " so many mirrors " manifesting and mediating the Eternal Goodness by sharing its height of power and breadth of love. Here in the inner circle are the Seraphim who " love most and know most." Motion, everywhere observed in these celestial spheres, is Dante's symbol of vitality. The nearer these angelic circles are to the Central Point, the swifter they revolve (contrary to the law of physical nature in lower realms). In the life of the spirit velocity of motion signifies and is proportionate to the intensity of yearning for union with God, and the brighter is their sacred flame, the penetration of truth in their " spark " from the Eternal Light.

As the seer emerges in the luminous empyrean, the true Paradise of God, all stars and other lights pale and vanish before the Uncreated Light, in the heaven that is pure light :

> " Light intellectual replete with love,
>   Love of true good replete with joy,
>   Joy that transcendeth every sweetness."
>
> (xxx. 40 ff.)

Here the " shadowy prefaces of truth " in sense and symbol are transcended in the vision of ultimate realities. Dante's natural sight is blinded, but his inner eyes are specially illuminated by drinking of the " river of light," so, by such a river of grace, made capable of celestial insight. " In Thy light shall we see light " (Psa. xxxvi). How can we summarize what the poet sees but can scarcely compass in a " flying plentitude " of imagery ?

Beatrice has vanished from Dante's side and, seeing her throned in the Mystic Rose, he addresses her with blessings for her gracious help that drew him out of slavery into liberty. She looked back on him and " smiled, then turned her to the Eternal Fountain." Beatrice had three smiles for Dante : " one smile " she gave him when he emerged from the river Lethe with memory cleansed through forgiveness ; another in the eighth heaven in rapture at the Triumph of Christ (xxiii. 48, 59) ; another she gives him when their pilgrimage through the heavens is finished. Then he finds St. Bernard of Clairvaux by his side. Strangely he is spoken of as an " old man," although Thomas Aquinas, like St. Augustine, taught that the saints will rise, like Christ, at the prime of life, say about thirty, whatever the age at which they died. Under that contemplative mystic as interpreter the poet gains direct intuition of things transcendent and ineffable.

The White Rose, which is the consummation of his " Vision," is composed of petals rank upon rank, representing the innumerable company of prophets, apostles, and saints of all ages, with little children, all pulsating with vibrant life. Their devout gaze is directed to the central Sea of Light, the Ocean Circle of the Eternal, appearing as " three circles of three colours yet of one dimension," GOD Himself in Unity and Trinity. Looking into that " great deep " of the inscrutable mystery of the Divine Essence, the piercing glory of the Beatific Vision in that " one moment of understanding " exhausts his powers of expression ; and the " Divina Commedia " ends, with Love all-moving : [1]

> " Here vigour failed the lofty fantasy :
>     But now was turning my desire and will,
>     Even as a wheel that equally is moved,
> The Love which moves the sun and the other stars."

When Dante awakes from his " mighty trance," he hears the sound " of this importunate earth." The dream fades into the light of common day ; yet the dream remains the Reality—much of it erased from memory, " yet " (he says) " does the sweetness that was born of it still drop within my heart." We pant for breath in these celestial flights. In the closing words of an old Italian commentary, " To that Beatific Vision may He bring us all *in patria* Who deigned to bring this most fortunate author thereto *in via* : *Deo Gratias.*" So, we shall find, Bunyan, having brought his pilgrims to the gates of the Celestial City and caught a glimpse within as the gates shut upon them, exclaims, " Which, when I had seen, I wished myself among them."

The Apocalypse of Dante, like the Apocalypse of St. John the Divine, sets forth a City, is cast in terms of a community-life rather than of individual happiness, and takes its place among other conceptions of the City of God (mentioned in our closing chapter) which are recapturing the social interest of the new generation.

Science somewhat shocks our imagination when it assures us that the vast vacant space of the universe is deep darkness, black as night, in which we should see nothing but points or discs of light in stars or suns, since an atmosphere round a globe is the necessary medium in which light waves are scattered and produce light diffused in the sky. Dante's universe, conceived spiritually, is luminous ; in the words of Dean Church, " light everywhere, in the sky and earth and sea, in the star, the flame, the lamp, the gem, broken in the water, reflected from the mirror, transmitted through the

---

[1] Dante adapts Aristotle's saying, " He moves all things as the object of their love."

glass . . . quivering in the lightning, mellowed in the pearl, copying itself in the double rainbow." So it is in the personal centres and atmosphere of life and experience that the true light becomes visible and transmits itself, light in the eye and the smile of joy, luminous souls (estimated by Ruskin at ten thousand) passing on light from life to life. With light Dante sees life, throbbing, abundant life and not sleepy stagnation, and, supremely, love as the essence and moving law of all creation.

Jesus Christ radiates light and grace wherever there is an atmosphere in which His rays can become part of the Vision. He is not once personally mentioned in the alien realm of the Inferno proper, although in the Ante-Hell, the Limbo of good heathen, He is alluded to as " a Mighty One, with victorious trophy crowned." In the Purgatorial ascent He is five times referred to as lending succour to the pilgrim, e.g. " on the tree when with His blood Christ made our spirits free " (xxiii. 74) ; but, as stated in the previous chapter, His grace is also experienced through the ministries of nature and angels. In the Earthly Paradise of the Purgatorio He is represented by the Gryphon drawing the Chariot of Revelation in the Procession of the Spirit in the form of the Cross. In the Paradiso the name of Christ occurs thirty-four times. On Mars the soldier-saints are arrayed like a Cross ; the quadrant " so flashed forth Christ that I may not find example worthy."

> " But whoso takes His Cross and follows Christ
> Will pardon me for that I leave untold,
> When in the fleckered dawning he shall ' spy
> The glitterance of Christ.' "
>
> (xiv. 106 ff.)

Another vision of Him is given in the Heaven of the Fixed Stars, where in His triumph over death and hell He appears as " above ten thousand lamps, the bright Sun that kindled every one " (xxiii. 28 f.). A final vision of Him is presented in the White Rose of glorified saints, " whom with His blood Christ won to be His bride " (xxxi. 1 ff.).

The Incarnation is integral to Dante's ruling conception of God's relation to His creatures ; and, as " the Son of God willed to load Himself with our pain," the ruling purpose of

the Incarnation was the work of Christ as Redeemer and as
Conqueror.  He is the central glory of the redeemed, and
in the Mystic Sempiternal Rose, to use the words of Sir
Wyke Bayliss, " the wide circles of the saintly host as they
approach the centre become incarnadine with the very life-
blood of Christ."  Thus, while Dante reflects generic human
experience, it is distinctively Christian experience that
becomes dominant in his stupendous and piercing Vision.

# VII

## Tauler's "Sermons"

THE so-called "Sermons" of Tauler are not strictly sermonic in ordinary form, but close analytical studies of Christian experience in expository manner.

Tauler's "Sermons" and the "Theologia Germanica" call for short notice, first for their own worth, and again for the illumination they cast on the spiritual antecedents and background of Thomas à Kempis' "Imitatio Christi," which is the subject to follow.

For our present purpose little need be said of Eckhardt, who set the standard of speculative mysticism transmitted from Plotinus, pseudo-Dionysius, and Erigena, and quickened the passion for direct perception of "Infinite Being." The type of mystical piety of which Gerard Groote and Thomas à Kempis were born was less transcendental and more experimental than his, and was found among the "Friends of God." Our Lord had called His disciples "friends." "Henceforth I call you not servants . . . but I have called you friends; for all things that I have heard of My Father I have made known unto you" (St. John xv. 15). Chief among these were John Tauler, Henry Suso, Ruysbroek, and the unknown author of the "Theologia Germanica." Contemporaries in England of kindred spirit —of the same period also as Wycliffe and Chaucer—were Richard Rolle, whose writings the "Imitatio" resembles in essential ideas, and Walter Hilton, who is one of those for whom the authorship of the "Imitatio" has been claimed.

Tauler's "Sermons" might well be included among the classics of the soul, with his own spiritual record as illustration, and Whittier's poem on Tauler to help. The story is well known how he, the Dominican monk, of Cologne and then of Strassburg, when about fifty years of age, became a " new creature in Christ Jesus " under challenge from a stranger-layman, who heard him preach five times and told him that, however gifted and gentle, he was still in the dark as to the spiritual life of grace (" Life," chap. i., p. 13). Whether the story is sufficiently authenticated or not, Tauler kept a two years' disciplinary silence in which his soul was " unmade and remade," and after which his message was a " Sursum Corda " to many.   During the Black Death, when priests were fleeing, and during a Papal interdict, he ministered among the sick and dying, and, it is told, " produced such effect that the people died content or were no longer much afraid of excommunication."

We have room for only a few samples of his teaching. " As a sculptor is said to have exclaimed on seeing a rude block of marble, ' What a godlike beauty thou hidest!' so God looks upon man in whom His image is hidden."   Yet this " Divine soul-centre " is not operative but only potential until " the outward man is converted into the inward, reasonable man, and the two are gathered up into the very centre of the man's being, the unseen depths of his spirit, where the image of God dwelleth " (Sermon xxiv).   " There is nothing so near the inmost heart of man as God."   " God illumines His true Friends (i.e. not mere servants, cf. John xv. 15) and shines within them with power, purity, and truth, so that they become supernatural persons,"—or, as we to-day would put it, the truly spiritual is the real super-natural.   He traces three stages in the upward journey from negative to positive goodness.   The first lies in self-denial from fear of hell and hope of heaven—a self-centred stage.   In the second a man bears " undeserved injury with quickened activity," and, when " our Lord shows him some kindness, he feels as if all were well between his soul and God, and feels himself so rich as if he could never more be poor . . . ready to believe, so to speak, that our Lord is at his disposal."   But, seeing how he is apt to rely on his imagined powers and lose the ripest fruit of faith, our Lord withdraws Himself, " stays His hand from bestowing sensible tokens of His mercy, because the man fancied that he was really as he stood in man's opinion, fancied that he was something : now he sees clearly that he is nothing." Our kind Lord, " like a tender mother or a wise physician, suffers him to fall into temptations he never knew when he fancied himself, overclouds the light, and hedges him in with the thorns of an anguished conscience." He is made miserable about himself from reading passages of Scripture, sheds tears sometimes when weighed down to earth, at other times he is not even able thus to lament with weeping, yet is exasperated at himself. If he would be healed, he must not yield to such mortification. Let him gather courage from remembering how he has striven to endure cheerfully rebuke and shame for the sake of goodness, how he has often glorified God and shown kindness to his fellows—what we would call signs of grace ; while yet he must examine himself whether he has really and prayerfully cared for those who opposed him, " until the workings of self-sufficiency are driven out from all the secret corners of his spirit." Much of the above description of the alternations of the soul might have come from Bunyan, his gleams of cheer alternating with despairing gloom, though Tauler's terms are less imaginatively vivid than Bunyan's. One wishes Bunyan had known this passage in Tauler, for his comfort in such " barren seasons."

The third stage is one of " clear intuition and perfect fruition," to which the faithful are raised in Christ by the power of the Holy Spirit, in joyous triumph through the complete union of the human with the Divine will.

" Evangelical poverty," he taught, was necessary to this end. He did not mean simply that they should practise poverty in respect of worldly goods, but that they should bring about " inward disconnection and distance of the soul from all things, and be ' poor ' in spirit, poor in all that belongs to self, in the works and virtues which are of creature-growth, empty of all that feeds self, and possessed of God in self-oblivion " (Sermon xxv. for St. Stephen's Day). The temple within man must be a " clean, pure house of prayer," and all the " traders," human fancies and self-gratification, must be driven out, that God may abide in His own house.

Yet he is not a Quietist ; he enjoins activity, works of

love. " Spiritual enjoyments are to be taken, as food, for nourishment and support to help us in our active work." It may be sloth that makes a man seek the life of contemplation : " no virtue is to be trusted until it has been put into practice"—which reminds us of William James's principle that any moral purpose must be acted upon if it is to be securely established. Tauler does not oppose the spiritual to the secular. " One man can spin, another can make shoes, and all these are gifts of the Holy Ghost. I tell you, if I were not a priest, I should esteem it a great gift that I was able to make shoes, and I would try to make them so well as to be a pattern to all."

Another of the " Friends of God," Henry Suso (died 1365), who wrote his realistic Autobiography in the third person, with keen psychological self-analysis, tells how at eighteen he experienced his " commencement " in a spiritual awakening, what cutting austerities he practised on his " refractory body," how as a " love-token " he cut the name of Jesus in his breast, what visions he received, what ecstasies he enjoyed. In all this he is more akin to the Spanish mystics like Sta. Teresa. But in a vision God calls on him now to " Be a knight, and thou shalt have fighting enough." For years thereafter he took long journeys on errands of love, encountered robbers, and in his pastoral work strove to reclaim fallen women. One of these under guise of a penitent treacherously slandered him. The heads of his own Order in due time vindicated his character. Yet meanwhile, though aware it would foster suspicion, he took the child left with him by its mother, the false-accuser, into his arms as it smiled into his face, and provided for its maintenance, rather than leave it to die from neglect (Inge, " Christian Mysticism," p. 178).

# VIII

# " Theologia Germanica "

THE anonymous little book to which Luther gave the name " German Theology " would not be recognized as peculiarly German to-day ; neither is it formal Theology, although theological principles are implicit in it. It is essentially a document of the spiritual life of rare quality. If it had not had to carry the burden of such a title, it would have been more widely known and read. It should be classed with Tauler's " Sermons."

It gives the most intensified expression to the purest principles of which the " Friends of God " were spokesmen and exemplars. It quotes Tauler's "Sermons," and 1350 has been given as its approximate date. It thus preceded Thomas à Kempis' " Imitatio Christi," with which it has been favourably compared in its essential quality though not in its range of subject-matter. Luther translated and published it in 1516, a year before his " hammer " nailed his ninety-five Theses to the Wittenberg church door and struck the keynote of the Reformation. What it had done for his own spiritual life is told in his preface to it. While criticizing its " bad German and crabbed words," he avows, " next to the Bible and St. Augustine, no book hath ever come into my hands whence I have learnt or would wish to learn more of what God, and Christ, and man and all things are " ; and during his lifetime it passed through sixteen editions.

No author's name is attached to it. The only external indication of its source is found in the introductory note, possibly written by a disciple of the " Friends of God," given in the earliest Manuscript extant (dated 1497), which states : " This little book hath the Almighty and Eternal

141

God spoken by the mouth of a wise, understanding, faithful, righteous man, *His Friend*, who aforetime was of the Teutonic Order, a priest and warden in the house of the Teutonic Order in Frankfort ; and it giveth much precious insight into Divine truth, and especially teacheth how and whereby we may discern the true and upright *Friends of God* from those unrighteous and false free-thinkers, who are most hurtful to the holy Church." Clearly, while primarily intended for instruction in positive truth among the faithful, it was also meant to counteract the false notions and lax morals of sectaries, who made claim to live by the " Free Spirit " without other light or restraint.

Why was the book issued anonymously ? For one thing, voluntary Associations like the " Friends of God " were in those times exposed to suspicion by official ecclesiastics as possible hotbeds of heresy, and, while not secret societies, they avoided acts liable to call the public attention of inquisitors.

The main reason for its anonymity, however, was the vital principle which it taught—that one must screen everything calling attention to Self. The author hides his personal identity because in the true Friend of God there must be no I, no Mine, no " creature " glory. Of this we shall see more later ; " ama nesciri," " love to be unknown," will reappear in Thomas à Kempis. The unknown author's saying, " I would fain be to the Eternal Goodness what his own hand is to a man," illustrates both the heroic self-oblivion put into practice and the danger of overstraining the Divine requirement.

He shares the common stock of Christian principles current in the circle of Tauler and other Friends ; there is no need to repeat those previously stated. But there is an individual distinction in much that he writes, in the searching, sure, and pithy way in which he puts it, in his concentration of mind upon a few master-truths. From Eckhardt he derives the mould of formal concepts, but he subjects them to devotional and practical uses.

His fundamental theorem is that God is the Substance of all that has true being—by which he means, not the " stuff," but the underlying Reality of which all holds its life. " All things have their being more truly in God than in themselves ; He is the Being of all that are, the life of all that live " (chapters 1 and 36). This immanence of God in all that is real escapes the deification of man somewhat narrowly in places. Generally he affirms that man partakes of the Divine nature, not through identity of essence, but on moral terms, by unity of will and love.

According to his ruling principle, Self, everything of " creature " nature, must be surrendered as of God and for God. There must be no " I, I, Mine," nothing in or done by me accounted to me and my credit. If a man values anything *as his*, " so long as a man seeketh his own will and his own highest Good *because it is his*, for his own sake, he will never find it ; for, so long as he doeth this, he seeketh himself," and " he cometh not unto the life of Christ " (44) Again, in true obedience a man " should be so quit of himself that in all things he should no more seek or regard himself than if he did not exist, and should as little account of himself as if another had done all his works."

It is a hard saying—an instance of " the hardness of the saints." It looks like a Buddhistic attempt to abandon one's individuality as an independent centre of moral action. The author is not content to require unselfishness in the Gospel sense. He falls short of the pure Christian conception of fullness of personality as the goal of Divine tuition by rectifying the spirit of our mind. Yet it is not a vacuum he has in view ; the gist of it is sound, as when he proceeds to say that " there is nothing without God except to will otherwise than is willed by the Eternal Will " (44), and that " if there were no self-will, there would be no devil and no hell. . . . Nothing burneth in hell but self-will." Sin is self-will.

" It is said, it was because Adam ate the apple that he was lost, or fell. I say it was because of his claiming something for his own, because of his I, Mine, Me, and the like. Had he eaten seven apples, and yet never claimed anything for his own, he would not have fallen ; but, as soon as he called something his own, he fell, and would have fallen if he had never touched an apple " (3).

The same principle, acting conversely, opens the way of

salvation, namely, by the union of the human and the Divine as sin came from disunion between them.   How was the healing of the breach brought about ?   " Man could not without God, and God could not without man.   Wherefore God took human nature or manhood upon Himself and was made man, and man was made Divine.   So must my fall be healed.   I cannot do the work without God, and God may not or will not without me. . . .   God must be made man, in such sort that He must take to Himself all that is in me, within and without, so that there may be nothing in me which striveth against God or hindereth His work. . . .   I can do nothing of myself, but simply yield to God, so that He alone may do all things in me " (3).   Here it is, not Christ's sacrificial Cross, but His Incarnation and its equivalent in man's inner experience that is the means of redemption.

Yet again, with deep insight and in modern fashion, he shows the function of Divine and human suffering in redemption.   We shall meet it later in a different setting in Tolstoy, in his novel of " Resurrection."   According to the unknown author of this monograph, wherever God as personal reveals Himself, He reveals His suffering sorrow over sin.   There are only two persons who have no sense of sin, Jesus Christ and Satan, as Eckhardt taught (see Dante's " Inferno "). " It grieveth Him so sore that He would willingly suffer agony and death if one man's sins might be thereby washed out."   In Jesus Christ this suffering sorrow over sin is supreme—in Him who unites God and man.   " From this cause arose the hidden anguish of Christ, of which none can tell save Himself, and therefore it is called a mystery." But likewise a truly godly man sorrows over sin, and must mourn over it until death (37).   The more holy he grows, the greater is his sensitiveness to sin, the deeper is his suffering sorrow over it.   The implication is that God's sorrow over it finds an echo in man, who is esteemed the more on that account, and that the common sentiment is healing and reconciling.   Whether this is an adequate account of Christ's atonement for sin may be debated.   But at any rate it enforces from a psychological standpoint facts of Christian experience.

Sympathy with God in His purpose of love is involved herewith. Love must be disinterested, like His. The Good desired must be sought, not for personal ends, but for its own sake, simply because it is good. Neither fear of hell, desire of heaven, nor any other adventitious benefit must affect us. Those who are swayed by these considerations are hirelings, thinking of their private gains and their present hardships. " It is a sure token of an hireling that he wisheth his work were at an end. But he who loveth it is not offended at his toil nor the length of time it lasteth " (32, 38). To know what is true we must love what is good. And true knowledge comes, not by questioning, but by practical action (19). The Christian life is the best and noblest life—and we ought to love what is best—though it may be bitter to human nature (6, 18, 45). A man, while yet in the body, may now and here enter into the eternal life, which is a present experience, a foretaste of eternal blessedness in Paradise (8, 50).

Clearly this little book, bearing the ripe fruit of Christian experience and reflection, however incomplete, was germinal of future experience and reasoned thought.

# IX

## Thomas à Kempis' " Imitatio Christi "

THOMAS À KEMPIS appears in the course of history about one thousand years after St. Augustine, one hundred years after Dante, and one hundred years before Luther, and forms a link in the golden chain of spiritual succession.

The " Imitatio Christi " presents a third type of classics of the soul, in singular contrast with the " Confessions " of the first and the " Vision " of the second. It has nothing of the romantic interest and tragic passion of St. Augustine's personal record. Much spiritual combat went to the making of it, and, like the petals in the White Rose of saints in Dante, it vibrates with refined emotional life ; but the storm of battle has overpassed the soul and left " a season of clear shining." It has no objective world-outlook like Dante, no dramatic framework or picturesque stage on which men, bad, bettering, and best, are shown in action. It has no story or imaginative dressing, like the allegorical tale of " The Pilgrim's Progress," to lend it popularity. Its steady, piercing gaze is entirely inward ; its method is analytic as well as introspective ; its action is an antiphony between God and the soul, the soul and God. It is a finely wrought scroll of self-utterance in purest terms and simplest form. It is a transcript from experience of that regimen which disciplines the soul for the perfect service of God in worship and holiness. All the more wonderful on this account is the immense circulation it has obtained.

Next to the Bible the " Imitatio Christi " is the most popular book in the literature of the world ; more copies of it have been printed than of any other book. The Bible or portions of it have been translated into some seven hundred and fifty versions—over five hundred by the British and Foreign Bible Society. So often has it been reprinted in the various tongues into which it has been translated that it is not possible for us now to tell the stupendous number.

Of the " Imitatio Christi " Dr. Samuel Johnson said, " The world has opened its arms to receive it," and he quoted a statement that it " had been printed in one language or other as many times as there have been months since it first came out." This statement was decried as extravagant, but it is borne out by the facts. Years ago it had appeared in some 6,000 editions or reprints—in more since then.

Bunyan's " Pilgrim's Progress " is said to have been issued in one hundred and twenty tongues—in how many editions or reprints we know not ; the " Imitatio Christi " is in some forty translations, Shakespeare in some twenty-seven. Although Bunyan's " Pilgrim's Progress " has passed into more versions or languages, the " Imitatio " is believed to have had a wider circulation.

The " Pilgrim's Progress " has lost much vogue among Roman Catholics and cut itself off from their sympathy by its severe picture of " Giant Pope " and by its other Protestant contents—though an expurgated edition, omitting " Giant Pope," has been issued.[1]

On the other hand, the private use of the Bible being commonly withheld from the laity, the general use of the " Imitatio " with so much of the Bible in it was not efficiently encouraged by Roman churchmen. Hence De Quincey's shrewd remark (in the preface to Vol. 1 of his Works) that the wide currency of this little book throughout Christendom " is virtually to be interpreted as a vicarious popularity of the Bible. At that time the Bible was a fountain of inspired truth everywhere sealed up, but a whisper ran through the western nations of Europe that the work of Thomas à Kempis contained some slender rivulets of truth

[1] Gladstone could say, with truth yet curious innuendo : " I have given Thomas à Kempis to men of uncultivated minds, who were also Presbyterians, but all relish it. I do not believe it is possible for any one to read that book earnestly from its beginning and think of Popish or non-Popish, or of anything but the man whom it presents and brings to us."

silently stealing away into light from that interdicted fountain. . . . The book came forward as an answer to the sighing of Christian Europe for light from heaven."

1. We must assume that Thomas à Kempis was the author of the " Imitatio Christi," although the authorship has been and still is the subject of controversy whose bitterness has been in sad contrast with the sweet spirit of the book.  It has been ascribed to St. Bernard of Clairvaux, the great mystic of the mediæval Church, who is represented by Dante at the crowning vision of the Paradiso as unveiling the White Rose.  It reflects the mystic spirit and influence of St. Bernard, but could not have been written by him, · and that idea is now abandoned.

The claim of Gerson of Paris to be its author is based largely on the fact that an early edition in the fifteenth century bears his name as author on the title-page, but is upheld to-day by few scholars outside of France.  The book is out of keeping with Gerson's type of mind and his antagonism to the mystics and the monastic order.  He, the great chancellor of the University of Paris, was a notable doctor of scholastic learning, deeply dyed with Scholasticism in its philosophical subtlety, and he could not have made the attacks on all theological science with its " genera et species " which are repeated in the " Imitatio."

It is significant that the author did not obtrude but rather veiled his personality.  It is a fine illustration of the spirit of the book, of the utter self-abnegation and repudiation of all pride in personal achievements, that there should have been any possible doubt as to his identity, that he should leave the book to speak for itself—although in early editions his name is given.  He writes in it, " Search not who said this or that, but attend to what is spoken."  And again, " If you wish to be divine, remain hidden as God."

The lack of final evidence as to the authorship of the book might explain how it is that the Roman Church has never canonized Thomas à Kempis as one of its saints.  But, indeed, he was not in great favour among certain classes of Roman Catholics.

A book of the same lofty order from the same age, the

" Theologia Germanica," is anonymous to this day—the writer wished to deny self to the extent of his personal identity being unknown. How far away and foreign that spirit seems to our modern self-advertising minds ! " Ama nesciri," says this book ; " love to be unknown "—a phrase which was in common use among the Brethren of the Common Life, to whom Thomas à Kempis belonged. This is a slight confirmation of the belief now general that he was the author, although both writers were anticipated by St. Bernard in the use of the phrase.

The interest of the book, then, lies, not in its authorship, but in its contents and spiritual vision.

2. The man and his life-work (1380–1471) have comparatively little to be told about them that would add to the significance of his immortal book.

His own name was Thomas Hamaercken (or Haemerlein), in Latin Malleolus, mallet or little hammer, the family name supposed to indicate (like Smith) that the ancestral trade had been that of a worker in metal. He was born at Kempen, a small town near the lower Rhine, forty miles north of Cologne, and according to a custom of the time he came to bear the name of his birthplace, Thomas à Kempis (more accurately Kempen, as Kempis is a contraction of the Latin adjective Kempensis). His parents were plain folk, his father John an industrious artisan, his mother Gertrude a devout *Frau* who imparted to her sons her own religious spirit.

An elder son, John, they had already given to the Church, to the religious House established at Deventer in Holland, and at the age of thirteen Thomas was sent to join him there, though on arrival he found that John had removed to another hostel of the Brethren of the Common Life at Windesheim, of which he became prior. Making the twenty miles' journey thither, he was sent back by his brother to Deventer for the benefit of the invaluable education to be had there under the tuition of that man of God, Florentius, whose " Life " Thomas wrote in later years, calling him " my father and sweet master." The good Florentius took kindly to the lad, received him into his own house and personal care, lending him books, treating him as a son and receiving more than a son's loyal and ingenuous devotion. "I would sing of the kindnesses of Florentius for ever, for in fact for seven whole years I experienced the greatness of his kindness in my own knowledge and feelings." Both master and pupil were avid for Church Music (note this link with the title of his book, " Church Music "). Thomas was one of the choristers, and in his memorials of Florentius exclaims, " As often as I saw my superior standing in the choir, the mere presence of so holy a man inspired me with such awe that I dared not speak when he looked up from the book. On one occasion it happened that I was standing near him in the choir, and he turned to the book we had and sang with us. And standing close behind me, he supported himself by placing both his hands on my shoulder ; and I stood quite still, scarcely daring to move, so astonished was I at the honour he had done me."

This " laying on of hands " is the most natural and surely the most quickening symbolic act in " blessing " those called on to take up the spiritual succession. Here comes to the present writer's mind the significant note of Dean Plumptre on " the firm clasp of hand " which, at their first meeting, Virgil gave to Dante (canto iii.) : " The ' clasped hand ' tells of an experience which had felt the power of that sacrament of human help. One wonders that no master of spiritual therapeutics has written at least an essay on the evangelizing power of the hand as distinguished from the voice. In this case it brought, as by a mesmeric influence, to the perplexed mind of the pilgrim something of the serener joy with which his more experienced guide had learnt to look even on the most terrible manifestations of the Divine righteousness." Thomas never lost the impress and " evangelizing power " of his spiritual father's hand.

Of the Community called " The Brethren of the Common Life " one might say what the Psalmist (lxxxvii. 5, 6) foretold would be said of Zion : " She shall be called Mother." Jehovah shall count, when enrolling the peoples, " This one was born there, and that one was born there." " All my springs are in thee." " Born there "—that is what we like to know concerning any great book or man : the fertilizing soil, the endearing background, the heritage, the mental and spiritual climate. The "Imitatio Christi" could scarcely have been born anywhere else or at any other period of time; yet it is at home in every country and in every age.

The father of the "Brethren of the Common Life"—who was called "the first father of our Reformation"—was Gerard Groote, Gerardus Magnus, born in Deventer forty years before Thomas à Kempis. Enjoying wealth, social distinction, and a place among the learned in Cologne University, he had the brightest of worldly prospects, and received various benefices. His fond biographer, Thomas à Kempis, observes: "He was not yet seeking the glory of Christ, but in the broad ways of the world was following the shadow of a great name." But the outward touch of the invisible Divine hand was working together with inward reactions. A plainly clad stranger, one of the "Friends of God" to whom Tauler belonged, bringing a challenge of God such as another stranger had brought to Tauler, found him one day a spectator at a public game in Cologne, and said to him, "Why standest thou here? Thou oughtest to become *another man*." The word thus spoken by the wayside lodged and wrought in his heart. Grave sickness, and the influence of a former teacher in Paris University, who bade him follow Christ, reinforced the summons. His "great possessions" did not induce another "great refusal."

Gerard went into retirement and spiritual training for a while, learning what Tauler had taught as "evangelical poverty," to make nothing of his own acquirements and everything of a simple message and the obedience of Christ. He was influenced by fellowship with Ruysbroek and the study of St. Augustine. Surrendering his benefices and accepting deacon's orders (not the office of a priest), he went out in simple guise, like George Fox and later John Wesley, to preach to the common people the "common salvation" in terms of human and Divine love, free from professionalism and without pay. The itinerant preacher, who has been compared to the friars of his contemporary Wycliffe, preaching in markets and fields, drew crowds to "the New Devotion," shamed the regular clergy whose jealousy and protests caused the withdrawal of the episcopal licence and an inhibition. Good came out of this misfortune.

The education of the people had already been a ruling interest in his life, as it was with other Friends of God who were friends of man. On the advice of Ruysbroek, and on seeing the happy community at Grünthal of which Ruysbroek was a member, he resolved to establish a community of brothers for the education and spiritual instruction of the young.

Florentius Radewyn, formerly a wealthy canon of Utrecht Cathedral, the earliest disciple of Gerard Groote, whom he gave up all to follow, led with him in setting up a hostel in Deventer for a Brotherhood of Goodwill devoted to the above objects, and was put at the head of the Brother House there. "Live together" was his counsel to his spiritual benefactor. They would gather young men together, to gain "not more learning but a better learning," to multiply good books by making copies and pooling the revenue therefrom for their common maintenance.

Thus originated the "New Devotion" of the "Brethren of the Common Life," of which Thomas à Kempis was the pupil and the most memorable product, which reformed vital religion, and to which Luther paid high tribute. The movement, meeting a felt want, spread over the Low Countries and northern Germany. Its head-quarters was established at Windesheim, with John the elder brother of Thomas à Kempis as its prior. Mount St. Agnes, near Zwolle, to-day Berg Cloister, to which Thomas went for most of his lifetime, was one of its chief seats. Within thirty years, we are told, it had given rise to thirty-seven brother-houses for men and eight similar institutions for women.

These Brethren undertook only voluntary vows; they could quit when they chose. They lived and laboured in close touch with the community of common people. They earned their livelihood, not by begging or endowments as many monks did, but by the fruits of their own labours, some brethren tilling the soil. Their main undertaking was educational. This included the multiplication of holy books in manuscript copies, including the Holy Bible. They were encouraged to draw up collections of spiritual sayings from New Testament sources, and from the writings of St. Augustine, St. Anselm and St. Bernard. These selections were the precursors of the " Imitatio Christi."

To resume the story of Thomas à Kempis, he spent seven years in the Deventer school under the Brethren of the Common Life. Then Florentius charged him to choose between the dangers of the world and the safety of the " religious " life. Making his choice of the latter and the better, he was duly passed on to the Brother-House at Mount St. Agnes, set away from all earthly ambitions and controversies. Here he remained for about seventy years of his life, instructing novitiates and copying Holy Books, with only a slight break, and with few events in his life, until he died at 91 years of age. He was exiled, like his brethren, for over a year under a Papal interdict laid upon the diocese. He went to nurse his elder brother John in his last sickness. He was once, and then again, chosen as sub-prior of the Brotherhood. But he was not a man of affairs, was what we call " absent-minded," and was displaced. He has been described as " a little fresh-coloured man with soft brown eyes, short-sighted, somewhat bent in the shoulders, whose body stood upright when the psalms were chanted, rising to his tiptoes with face glancing upward. He liked psalms better than salmon, he used to say, but most of all ' little books in quiet nooks.' Such was the man who wrote the biographies of his spiritual fathers, the " Imitatio Christi," and other books, and who made himself part of thousands of lives, in which he still lives."

3. The historical setting of the writer and his work casts curious light on the book, even though it makes scarcely any reference to history and human affairs.

It presents a strange contrast to the contemporary life of the world and the Church. The age was ripe for dissolution on the way to new constructions. The condition of Europe was chaotic. The Ottoman Turks had seized Gallipoli in 1358, twenty years prior to Thomas à Kempis' birth, and after a century of menace and ruinous struggle captured Constantinople in 1453, thus involving the destruction of the Eastern Empire, and threatening Christendom with a Mohammedan conquest. Wars, internal and international, continue—civil war in England between the Houses of York and Lancaster, wars between England and France, revolt in Bohemia. There are surging waves of social unrest. The Black Death and the Oriental Plague are spreading desolation and misery. In the Church there continue strife, confusion, division, and moral decay and religious embitterment and heresy. The seventy years' Babylonian Captivity of the Papacy at Avignon is finishing in the Great Schism ; two rival popes anathematize each other ; a third at Ravenna tries vainly to suppress both at Avignon and Rome ; some of the popes are deposed and condemned for crimes. Great Œcumenical Councils, of Pisa and of Constance (1414–18), fail to bring ecclesiastical unity— the first act of the Council of Constance was to burn Huss, the Bohemian reformer, at the stake ; darkness broods over all. The Councils of Reform, in spite of the efforts of Gerson, are balked. Shameless corruption, worldliness and immorality among Church rulers, lawlessness are rampant, and Europe is distracted with dissensions.

Yet here is a book, the deposit of a long life set in these times of turmoil and disaster for both Church and State, which contains scarce a reference to the maelstrom in the surrounding world ; it shows never a ruffle of the surface from the storm without, never an echo of the wars nor wavelet of the universal strife. Here is the still and peaceful centre of the tempest. It is filled with the gracious air of devout tranquillity, disturbed only by the strivings of a soul in secret conflict with itself under the subduing hand of God.

The author is far withdrawn from the world ; " the world is very evil, the times are waxing late," as wrote the hymnist. Yet the key-note of it is " Peace."

Under his supposed portrait at Mt. St. Agnes (near Zwolle) are inscribed these words of his : " In omnibus requiem quaesivi, sed non inveni nisi in hoexkens ende boexkens," or, to complete it in the Latin, " in angello cum libello "—" I have sought everywhere for peace, but I have found it not save in a little nook with a little book."

Great wickedness prevailed alongside great saintliness in monastic life. A hundred years before the Reformation his writings represent earnest attempts to revive vital religion which were thwarted for the time being. Scholasticism was in a process of decay under the Nominalists. This New Devotion, as a religion of the heart, breathed the air of the coming springtide and gave foretokens of a new epoch in the Revival of Learning and of the Gospel.

Mysticism was for many devout spirits a " way out " of the maze of scholastic philosophy and ecclesiastical dissension. While fulfilling all ceremonial duties with appreciation as well as regularity, and accepting the dogmas of the Church, the mystic transcended the organized system, and pursued the " direct way " up to the High and Holy One. He sought immediate awareness of the supersensible and Perfect in illumination and union of spirit above clear thinking. Many mystics, e.g. Eckhardt, tended to Pantheism. The risk with many was that they would dispense with all mediation, even with that of Christ, in the immediacy of insight.

Thomas à Kempis was a semi-mystic ; he was free from the speculative, pantheistic, rapturous, and was practical and moral in personal relations with God through Christ and His Cross.

4. The title and the purpose of the " Imitatio "—these two hang together—call for exposition.

The familiar title " Imitatio Christi " was not originally given to the work or cluster of four booklets by the author himself. It is not found until the 1494 edition (Nuremberg), and then only as the title of the first Book. It was taken from the rubric of the first Book, which opens, " Qui sequitur me non ambulat in tenebris, dicet Dominus "; " Whoso follows me shall not walk in darkness, says the Lord." It continues, " Haec sunt verba Christi, quibus admonemur, quatenus vitam eius et mores imitemur," etc. The title thus imposed on the first of the four short treatises came to be attached to the whole collection.

The earliest title, probably—at least for three of the four books, the first, second and fourth—was " Ecclesiastica

Musica," " Church Music." This was the generic title for
writings of this character. It is an appropriate descriptive
title. The Church through its worship uttered itself in a
spiritual music—as witness the illustration in which four
Latin Fathers are producing ecclesiastical music in harmony
of spirit. Gladstone said : " All the music of the human
heart is in the Psalms "—the same idea as in this title. Or
perhaps the title was derived from the " Divine Music,"
the " Canor," that sustained the mystic.

The " musical " title answers to the cadence of the language of which it is composed. It was written " metrice," in
rhythm (reflected in Liddon's translation), and is marked
by a musical flow and lilt, a wave-like beat, which in such
compositions comes from the throb of emotion and pitch of
thought cast in words pulsing with corresponding rhythm.

It is pointed in a manner parallel to the pointing of
music : full stop followed by small capital, full stop followed
by large capital, colon by a small letter, the usual sign of
interrogation, and lastly the *clavis* or *flexa*, used in the
musical notation of the period. " The external structure
of the sentence marks its outline and establishes the most
complete harmony between the sentence and the internal
structure of the ideas." It was originally prepared as a
guide in concise directions for novices, as Thomas's function
normally was to receive and train the younger brethren,
many of whom he deeply influenced. With its rhythmical
cadence and musical structure of sentences, its chapters
were apparently intended to be learnt by heart and chanted
or recited.

Its literary style is determined by its original purpose and
by the subdued intensity of the writer's soul. While
seemingly spontaneous, it is a piece of art-mosaic built
together phrase by phrase, the carefully-wrought product
of skilful perfecting in expression. In form it has been
carved, recast and polished in the course of repeated use.
Its style has been called by Lamennais " celestial," the
union of pregnant brevity with the purest sentiment. And
Milman, alongside criticisms on other grounds, emphasized
" its short quivering sentences, which went at once to the
heart, and laid hold of and clung tenaciously to the memory

with the compressive incompleteness of proverbs, and its axioms each of which suggested endless thoughts." Its phrases, while diamond-cut, bear the mark, not of artificiality, but of intensity of spiritual emotion and moral perception, of a refined distinction expressive of the inner qualities of a gracious personality.

5. The antecedent sources, among his precursors, whence he drew can frequently be traced. The " Imitatio " is the creation of Thomas à Kempis, minted in his own soul and bearing his personal mark. Yet, as Dr. Butler says (p. 77), " it was born out of the heart of humanity and is only possible with a long spiritual history behind it. Its greatness consists in the fact that it transcends the limitations of individual life, and becomes, so to speak, impersonal by breathing and living in a universal atmosphere."

While an individual product as a whole, the product of personal experience as well as of history, it yet contains no original language, no fresh moulds, for such experience, " only phrases that time had proved to be a living force in the spiritual life of man. The words that had been the life and death cry of unnumbered millions are recombined into the *logos* of the spiritual life " (Montmorency, 171). This faculty of crystallizing the experience of past generations is no mere mechanical skill but the power first of all to absorb it and transmute it in the fire of his own life.

The Holy Bible is the chief source both of inspiration and of language. Thomas had copied it from beginning to end with neat hand and meticulous care, and had learnt its phraseology as well as assimilated its ideas. Almost every book of the Bible is represented in the text of the " Imitatio." But it is chiefly the Psalms from which he derives his expressions, next the Epistles, and then the Gospels. More than one thousand direct references to the Bible and the Apocrypha are found in his book (cf. Montmorency, 174 ff.). But, beyond direct references, the book is pervaded with the Scriptures, " haunted with Biblical reminiscence," somewhat lost in any English translation which is not expressed in the archaic classic Elizabethan language with its rich cadence.

Next to the Bible, it is in St. Augustine and St. Bernard that we find the chief sources of the " Imitatio." His familiarity with St. Augustine is manifest, at various points in express terms. In his saying, " My heart cannot truly rest nor be entirely contented unless it rest in Thee," we have a clear echo of St. Augustine in his " Confessions " at the beginning, " Thou hast made us for Thyself, and our hearts are restless until they rest in Thee." There is a reference to the memorable scene in the " Confessions " where St. Augustine and Monica, leaning out over the balcony at Ostia, talk with open heart and see the mystic vision of the transcendent life above all earthly limits.

The " Imitatio " also reflects the idea, anticipated in the Apocryphal book, " The Wisdom of Solomon," found in St. Augustine, and reproduced in Dante, of the " weight " of the soul's desire or love, like gravitation, determining its fall or its ascent.

His indebtedness to St. Bernard, the great mediæval mystic, is more manifest. Direct references to him are traced in dozens of expressions; indirect reflections are still more numerous; and more important is the spiritual and mystical influence of St. Bernard, both in style and in religious contents.

Dante's " Divine Comedy " appears to have been known to him. He embodies Dante's principle, that the punishment of unrepented sin is experienced in the operations and consequences of the sin. " In quibus homo peccavit, in illis gravius punietur." A common source might have been the " Wisdom of Solomon " (chap. xi.) : " Wherewithal a man sinneth, by the same shall he be punished." St. Augustine left an epigram to the same effect.

The parallel with Dante, in the process of penal suffering (cf. *supra*, p. 99), is in the " Imitatio " so extensive and detailed as to be a manifest reflection :

" The sins wherein a man has sinned,
    In them shall he be punished with the greater pain ;
    For there the lazy shall be driven with burning goads,
    There the greedy shall be tortured with a thirst and hunger infinite
    There the wanton and the lovers of delightsome things
    In burning pitch and in foul brimstone shall be bathed."

(I, xxiv.)

There seems also to be a reflection of Dante's words, uttered in Piccarda's speech, " In His will is our peace."

The author's spiritual heritage is traceable to Eckhardt —though he is free from Eckhardt's speculative and pantheistic mysticism, asserting moral and spiritual experience as the vital interest—to St. Francis of Assisi, to the St. Victors, Bonaventura, Tauler, Henry Suso, who supplied the ground-plan of the " Imitatio " (cf. Montmorency, 218, 220) and most influentially to Ruysbroek (ditto 221 f.), and Gerard Groote.

6. The structural form of the " Imitatio " follows a definite order of ideas, showing the book to be no promiscuous collection of pious counsels.

It is composed of four tracts or books. In some editions the order of the books has been altered ; but the order must be accepted in which the author is believed to have left them. Underlying these divisions were the three stages of the mystic's ascent to God—(*a*) Purification, (*b*), Illumination, (*c*) Unification with the Divine, as given in St. Augustine.

The first Book contains " Admonitions useful to the Spiritual Life," setting forth the doctrine of the Word, the spiritual type which he who follows Christ must imitate. Earthly desires must be resisted, such resistance bringing humility and peace. To this end familiarity with men and free expressions in speech must be limited. Temptation, while shunned if practicable, must be fought down patiently and humbly. Obedience and service, silence and solitude, help the soul to grow—" Shut thy door behind, and call unto Jesus thy Beloved." Renunciation of the world is imperative—" the world well lost for Christ." Death we must train ourselves to accept, as pilgrims here : " In omnibus respice finem." But " if to die be dreadful, to live long may perhaps prove more dangerous. . . . Study so now to live that at the hour of death thou mayest rejoice rather than fear."

The first book deals with the outer relations of the devout soul. The second sets forth " Admonitions to draw us to the Inward Life." The third—sometimes placed fourth—

presents A Pious Encouragement to the Holy Communion, "De Sacramento Altaris." These three Books lead up to the fourth, to the dramatic conversations between God and the faithful soul, " The Book of Inward Consolation." Here we find the full mystical signification of the " Imitatio."

7. The characteristic notes of the contents of the " Imitatio " are manifest to any careful reader thereof. And, indeed, it is a book to be read, to be absorbed, to be interpreted by the Spirit who beareth witness with our spirits. It is able to speak for itself to all who are good listeners to God. It needs no great amount of comment, which would be intrusive upon the communion of the sanctuary. For this reason, and also because there is not very much to be said about the book needful for its appreciation, we must be content with a short analysis of it in this chapter. We offer here only a few samples of its unsearchable riches.

Which characteristic note in it is to be placed first ? One hardly knows : it is so symmetrical in its spiritual harmony.

One keynote is peace, tranquillity : not the high joyous sense of victory such as we find in St. Augustine and in Bunyan who came out of great tribulation and had washed their robes in the blood of the Lamb—there is no record of Thomas' sins ; but the serenity won by self-discipline such as monastic life could procure, with a quiet joy suffusing it. The secret of our unrest and unhappiness lies in the urgent claim of self, in unbridled longings, and in the specious attractions and relish of the world. " He that leans to things of sense can hardly steal himself away from earthly longings. And when he does so he is but sad, easily angered if a man withstands him."[1] " Therefore peace has no being in the heart of carnal man, But in the burning spiritual soul." " Peace lives ever with the lowly, But in the proud man's heart Envy and constant wrath." " Then will he be content let come what will come ; Then will he not rejoice over what is great, Nor grieve over what is little,

---

[1] The quotations here given are mainly from the edition edited by Canon Liddon (published by Robert Scott, London) because it reproduces the metrical form of the original. Capital letters indicate new musical bars in the original.

Resting wholly, trustingly in God, His all-in-all." " First keep yourself at peace ; Then you can quiet others. The peaceful man is of more use than the great doctor. The passionate turn even good to bad, Lightly believing good of evil. The peaceful man turns everything to good."

Self is the root of all evil, self-insistence, " self-love that keeps us back from the best." " You must give all for all, And not belong to self ; Your self-love harms you more than any other thing." " If I bring myself to nothing, Bruise myself to dust (I am but dust), Thy grace will be kind to me." To escape feverish tumult, Thomas carries self-effacement to the extent of self-contempt, which is not true to the Christian spirit. Yet his altruism, wisely applied, is genuinely Christian. He is not always an individualist ; he is aware of others. He strikes deep into Christian experience when he says, " If thou wouldst be carried, carry another." It is in sharing the struggle of our fellows that we win our own souls. He sees deep also when, showing how temptation might spell opportunity of proving God and ourselves, he .shows how we might overcome temptation by rallying all our powers to the rescue of others, " to succour those who strive and rely on God's grace."

The Cross of Christ, with Thomas à Kempis, stands for renunciation. It figures largely in some portions of his book. But it represents a principle and moral law of life. " There is none other hope of eternal life save in the Cross." But it does not carry the evangelical meaning of atonement for sin through Jesus Christ, though always symbolic of Christ. The Reformation had yet to come, with a return to New Testament founts of the Christian religion. But one thing he realizes, that sacrifice belongs to the essence and true success of life.

The self-indulgent sinner has his Golgotha. He, as much as the Christian, has to endure a cross—self-weariness, the decay of desire and strength, and heart-burnings. Thomas à Kempis has observed this fact. The Cross awaits us all in some form. " Run where you please, you cannot shun it ; For everywhere you take yourself along with you, And always find the cross, within or without, turn where you will." On the other hand the Christian gains support from his cross, and the victory of faith : " Bear the cross willingly, And it will carry you."

The inwardness of bliss—" the kingdom of God is within you "—was one of his ruling ideas. " Venture onward, deep down into a crypt, you will find the altar, and its sacred ever-burning lamp. All His glory lies within, where Christ often comes and gives you His consoling presence— sweet the talk, the intimacy passsing wonderful. Room, then, for Christ, our peace, our health, who opens the seal of the divine mysteries, having built a private chapel in the soul." Herein is scope for true spiritual mysticism.

Two conditions are required for the enjoyment of this spiritual intimacy—purity and simplicity. " By two wings man is lifted above the things of earth, by simplicity and purity. Simplicity must be the keynote of his motive, purity the keynote of his love." Does not St. Paul (2 Cor. xi. 3 R.V.) recall us to " the simplicity and purity which is toward Christ ? " God, therefore, must be the final end of all endeavour. The highest bliss of life is to be " alone with the Alone," in sacred contemplation such as the monastic life provided.

When walking with the brethren, and when it would be borne in upon him that the bridegroom Christ was calling him to communicate with him, he was wont to say, " My beloved brethren, it behoves me to go ; there is One expecting me in my cell." Thus he kept watch upon the heavens open to him, and the sign was not wanting.

The limitations of the " Imitatio " are open to all observers. But one initial demur to it must be repelled. The perfectly accurate statement is made that the true principle of the Christian life is not the literal " imitation " of Christ's actions but the absorption and exercise of the spirit of His life and teaching. Our circumstantial conditions are not identical with His, and we cannot pretend to all the functions and powers which He exercised as the incarnate manifestation of God and the reconciling redeemer of the world—though we cannot agree to the dualistic idea that " His head was in eternity, His feet in time." We realize the immense power of example in conduct, as with the young and with simple people in the Mission Field.

Yet we are not called upon to reproduce Christ's actions in His special conditions in answer to the popular question, "What would Jesus do?" We must, as His disciples, pass through similar experiences to those He endured, and in these we must be transformed into the image of the Master, into the form in which His progressive life unfolded itself.[1]

What is it to be a Christian? The present writer has proposed the answer: It is to have faith in God as Jesus Christ made Him known, to put our trust in Christ as Saviour and be loyal to Him as Lord, to live and serve in the spirit of His life and service.[2]

The title which Thomas à Kempis' book came to assume was incidental. More than Imitation was in mind; his governing interest lay in the enormous dower of vitality and the divine fecundity which come from the love of Christ.

The limitations of the "Imitatio" are due to the mediæval and monastic conditions in which it came into being. Its atmosphere is cloistral; the monastic note is ever recurring. The conception of the godly life is ascetic, enforcing detachment from mundane concerns. "That is the best philosophy, To scorn the world and strive to gain the kingdom in the skies. It is but vanity to look for offices of state." It favours self-absorption. In taking shelter within a monastery the monk escapes the world's perils and temptations; but, as we see in the counsels of this book, he finds himself beset by tempers and temptations peculiar to the cloistral life, ruffled by querulous nagging, friction, petty cabals; he suffers from "accidie," already described in the chapter on Dante's "Purgatorio," "from despondency, tedium, fatigue, dryness of spirit." Weary of the same perpetual round and of the same society as of the solitude of the cell, monks were peculiarly subject—though other devout people in the world are subject at times—to that strange ailment of accidie, a distaste for the things esteemed the holiest, recoil from sacred exercises, and at the same time dismay at this distemper of depression. Too much

[1] Cf. W. M. McGregor's "Christian Freedom," pp. 324 ff; E. Underhill's "Mystic Way," pp. 158 ff. 288, 309; Lindsay's "College Addresses," pp. 157 ff.
[2] "The First Things of Christianity" (London: R.T.S.).

of the same sort of interest, however good in itself, may be asked of human nature.

In this matter Thomas à Kempis shows a fine humanity as well as true insight when he writes : " It is not difficult to despise human consolation when one possesses a higher— that of God. Hard it is, very hard, to do without the Divine as well as the human, and, out of love to God, willingly to endure exile of heart, as one banished from the land of consolation. . . . What marvel is it that he feels no burden who is sustained by the Almighty arms, and led by the Omniscient Guide ? " He missed the family affections which would have helped him here, though he did not know what it was that he was missing. In Thomas a tendency persists to divorce human affections from the Divine, to regard God and man as rivals, saying, " Thou oughtest to be so dead to such affections of beloved friends, that (so far as thou art concerned) thou wouldst choose to be without all human sympathy." Wisely has Dr. Butler remarked, " his religion is a direct relationship to Christ, but it does not lead to a Christ-like relationship with nature and man."

A French writer says that " a man needs to be twice converted—first from nature to grace, and then back again to nature." One shrewd observer has added, " There is in this both philosophy and Christianity. The reason why so many of even the greatest men are not complete in their greatness is that they lack one or other of these two experiences," and he has selected Goethe as representing those who lacked the former conversion, and Pascal—he might also have named Thomas à Kempis—those who lacked the second, the return to nature and humanity.

The social sense, on a wide scale, is palpably deficient in the " Imitatio." Milman (" Latin Christianity," IX, 161 f.) has magnified this shortcoming in severe aspersions. He has, indeed, little consciousness of the community of mankind, no enthusiasm for humanity, and no vision of the kingdom teaching of the prophets and the Synoptic Gospels. We miss the modern social applications of Christian truth and life, the idea of the service of God being one with the service of man. But this is no private defect of his own ;

it is representative of the monastic life of his age. We must be glad to take from him what he has to give us, and it is much. One notices that, in spite of its limited outlook on life, the book finds most of its readers, not among cloistered students, but among men and women in the throng of the world and in the business of life. They recognize its insight into their own truest yearnings, its voice as almost their own, its response to their own secret cries.

The air in this high latitude of the soul is very pure, but it is austere, so rare that some cannot easily breathe it. We recall Walter Pater's description—" those wonderful, inaccessible, cold heights of the ' Imitation,' eternal in their æsthetic charm." Cold, however, it is not. " The bush is bare," but it burns with inner glow, and shines with tender imaginative gleams. Take some lines from his great pæan upon love :

" Love is a great thing. . . . The only thing that makes all burdens light . . . carrying a weight, not feeling it, Turning all bitterness to a sweet savour. . . . It is the child of God, Nor can it rest except in Him " (compare St. Augustine's axiom). " The lover runs and flies and is alive with joy, Gives all for all, Has all in all, Makes light of toil, Would do more than it can, Pleads no impossibility. The noble love of Jesus drives men on to do great deeds, And rouses them to long for what is better." And again, " Love all for Jesus ; But Jesus for Himself."

He rises to " wonderful and eternal heights " in his closing section—in a prayer which is essential " church music " :

" Bless and sanctify my soul with blessing from above,
    That it may be Thy holy dwelling-place, the home of Thine eternal glory,
    And that nothing may be found within the temple of Thy condescension
        (i.e. the soul of man)
    Offending Thy majestic gaze.
    According to the greatness of Thy mercies look on me,
    And hear the prayers of Thy poor servant so long an exile in the region
        of death's shadow.
    Guard, save Thy servant's soul amid the many dangers of a life that soon
        decays,
    And with Thy favouring influence to keep him company, guide him
        along the road of peace unto his native country of everlasting
        light."

St. Augustine saw it from the Ostia window ; Dante aspired
to be " In Patria " ; Bunyan caught a glint of it from the
Delectable Mountains ; Thomas à Kempis has a guide
along the road to his " native country " of everlasting light.

8. Appreciations of the " Imitatio " cannot be numbered,
much less can its influence be measured.  It needs no
laurels ; but one is interested to observe from what diverse
quarters and standpoints tributes have come.  Protestants
vie with Roman Catholics, and non-Christians with both,
in its praise.  Men of letters, statesmen, soldiers, and
philosophers are for once in accord with  theologians in
feeding in this pasturage.   We can cite only a few instances.
Ignatius Loyola, father of Jesuits, read two chapters daily,
either in order or wherever the book opened.   Francis de
Sales encouraged others to read it, saying, " Its Author is
the Holy Spirit."   Pascal said of it, " One expects only a
book, and finds a man."   Ullmann, in his " Reformers
before the Reformation," calls it " the attracting magnet
to countless multitudes."   Lamennais left the Church, but
held by this book which, he says, " has made more saints
than all the books of controversy."   Michelet, as an historian,
depicting the popular miseries of the author's time, writes,
" What must have been the emotions of the people, of the
women, of the unfortunate (everybody was  unfortunate
then), when for the first time they heard the Divine Word,
not in the language of the dead, but as a word that lived,
not as a ceremonial formula, but as a living word from the
heart ; they heard the manifestations of their own secret
thoughts.   Humanity raised its head ; it wished to live."
Samuel Johnson, telling how the world had taken the book
to its heart, observes that he was always struck with this
sentence in it, " Be not angry that you cannot make others
as you wish them to be, since you cannot make yourself as
you wish to be."
Philosophers of opposite schools are also found here
among the prophets.  Leibnitz exclaims, " Happy is he
who puts its contents into practice, and is not satisfied
merely with admiring them."   Comte, the Positivist, read
a chapter daily, discovering new beauties daily in it, though

its use as a means of self-culture is quite separable from its theological ideas (he vainly thinks). His follower, George Eliot, who kept a copy of the " Imitatio " by her bedside, paid a memorable tribute to it in " The Mill on the Floss " (Book IV, Chap. iii.) ; it is used to soothe the ruffled spirit of Maggie Tulliver.[1] Matthew Arnold in his "Essays on Criticism," called it " the most exquisite document after those of the New Testament of all that the Christian spirit has ever inspired," and said of its moral precepts, "they are equal to the best ever furnished by the great masters of morals—Epictetus or Marcus Aurelius."

Soldiers have carried it in their kit like another " Soldier's Pocket Book." General Lord Wolseley on setting out on his military expeditions took it along with the " Book of Common Prayer." General Gordon, who had the spiritual eye to perceive its sound mysticism, bore it everywhere as his companion next to the Bible. And one has been touched to note how often young champions who fell in the Great War took it (some of them took Dante also) to speak to them through the noise of cataracts, deep calling unto deep.

Churchmen have joined in the chorus of " The Ecclesiastical Music." Rev. John Newton, the hymn-writer, was

[1] " The small old-fashioned book, for which you need only pay sixpence at a bookstall, works miracles to this day, turning bitter waters into sweetness. . . . It was written down by a hand that waited for the heart's promptings ; it is the chronicle of a solitary, hidden anguish, struggle, trust, and triumph—not written on velvet cushions to teach endurance to those who are treading with bleeding feet on the stones. And so it remains to all time a lasting record of human needs and human consolations. . . . A strange thrill passed through her (Maggie Tulliver) while she read, as if she had been wakened in the night by a strain of solemn music, telling of beings whose souls had been astir while hers was in stupor. . . . Here was insight and strength and conquest, to be won by means entirely within her own Soul, where a supreme Seeker was waiting to be heard. It flashed through her like the suddenly apprehended solution of a problem, that all the miseries of her young life had come from fixing her heart on her own pleasure, as if that were the central necessity of the universe ; and for the first time she saw the possibility of shifting the position from which she looked at the gratification of her own desires —of taking her stand out of herself, and looking at her own life as an insignificant part of a divinely-guided whole. She read on and on in the old book, devouring eagerly the dialogues with the invisible Teacher, the pattern of sorrow, the source of all strength. . . . She knew nothing of doctrines and systems, of mysticism or quietism ; but this voice out of the far-off middle ages was the direct communication of a human soul's belief and experience, and came to her as an unquestioned message."

powerfully affected by the " Imitation," which helped to turn him from his wicked life.   John Wesley, whose version of it was entitled " The Christian's Pattern," was anti-pathetic to its ascetical note, yet repeatedly acknowledges the profound impression it made on him in his spiritual crisis, and declares it " comprehends all that relates to Christian perfection and the principles of internal worship with which alone we can worship God in spirit and in truth." Dr. Thomas Chalmers edited an issue of the book in the preface to which he argues that, although it does not set forth justification by faith, it sends men to an evangelical standpoint, and lays open the spiritual enjoyment that springs from the cultivation of the graces—revealing the hidden charm which lies in godliness.   It was a copy of this edition by Dr. Thomas Chalmers that Carlyle in 1833 sent to his mother with this commendation, " None, I believe, except the Bible, has been so universally read and loved by Christians of all tongues and sects.   It gives me pleasure to think that the Christian heart of my good mother may also derive nourishment and strengthening from what has already nourished and strengthened so many."   With what wiser word to our readers could we end our present introduction to it ?

# X

# Bunyan's " Grace Abounding " and " Pilgrim's Progress "

IN the Christian Classics to follow, we enter another age, in which we feel more at home, and breathe an atmosphere to which we are generally more accustomed. The essential religious ideas may remain the same, but the spiritual climate is different, the standpoint and religious values are different.

Something, very much, has happened in the interval, opening new regions of mental and spiritual interest, new sources of religious as well as intellectual life, namely the Renaissance and the Reformation. In the Revival of Learning, under Erasmus, Colet and More, the ancient classics and the Christian Scriptures in their original tongue had been rediscovered. In the corresponding religious Reformation, under Luther, Melanchthon, Zwingli, Calvin, and Knox, there had come, with the return to the original founts of faith and life, a notable renewal of rich and powerful Christian experience. From this experience of refreshing grace there sprang literary documents of the soul, with differences of accent, yet of universal value for soul-culture.

We may be surprised that the Reformation itself produced no special classic document of the soul such as would come within the present series of studies. It is not enough to say that it was an age of political and theological controversy. But it naturally took some considerable time before the new motives for life and the new Evangel could be assimilated and brought to expression in confessional writings as the result of reflection.

In this mental and spiritual renewal, most of the manuscripts of Christian experience are naturally Protestant in a broad sense, while a few of the writers abide by the Roman faith, like Sta. Teresa (died 1582), Pascal (d. 1662), and Madame Guyon (d. 1717). Of the former are Bunyan's " Grace Abounding " and the " Pilgrim's Progress," Bishop Lancelot Andrewes' " Private Devotions," Bishop Jeremy Taylor's " Holy Living and Holy Dying," Samuel Rutherford's " Letters," the writings of the Quakers (Friends), George Fox, Barclay, Wm. Penn, John Woolman, followed later by Wm. Law's " Serious Call," John Wesley's " Journal," etc.

When we now take up John Bunyan, we may seem to be breaking off the spiritual succession. He had no conscious connexion with those seers whom we have already had before our minds. While he owed something to Luther, and through him something to St. Augustine, his spiritual experience was quite fresh and independent. Of them all, it is nearest akin to St. Augustine's " Confessions " in passionate experience and in human appeal, as well as in the sense of Divine saving grace.

1. The appeal of Bunyan's chief writings is almost universal wherever the reading of them is permitted. His " Pilgrim's Progress " has, as already stated, been translated into more languages than any other book in the world, except the Bible. The Religious Tract Society alone has translations in seventy languages and dialects. One hundred thousand copies were sold within his own lifetime.

Thomas à Kempis' " Imitatio Christi " has had a wider circulation, mainly because the Protestant elements in Bunyan's book have excluded it generally from the Roman Catholic communion. An attempt was made to adapt it for use within the Roman Church in an expurgated edition in which Giant Pope was cut out. But, even with this excision, it is, as it has been called, the " Sum of Evangelical Theology."

From the opposite, Rationalist standpoint, Froude could say, in line with George Eliot's estimate of Thomas à

Kempis' book, " Bunyan's experience is so truly a human experience that . . . even those who regard Christianity as the natural outgrowth of the conscience and intellect, and yet desire to live nobly and make the best of themselves, can recognize familiar footprints in every step of Christian's journey." The reasons for its wide and permanent appeal are too manifold to be enumerated fully ; many will appear as we proceed ; but one or two initial attractions may here be indicated.

It has a captivating dramatic interest ; it exhibits swift and vigorous action on the part of its personal figures ; in this respect its opening is typical. " As I walked through the wilderness of this world, I lighted on a certain place where was a den ; and I laid me down to sleep, and as I slept I dreamed a dream. I saw a man clothed with rags, with his face from his own house, a Book in his hand, and a great burden on his back. And as he read the Book he wept and trembled, saying, ' What shall I do ? ' "

In this vivid opening our imaginative sympathy is seized at once. It grips instantly like " Robinson Crusoe " by Defoe—who (it may incidentally be mentioned here) a generation later abandoned his early intention to be a Dissenting minister, engaged in business and travel, and owing to his Dissenting pamphlets was pilloried and imprisoned, and whose body was laid in 1731 in Bunhill Fields, London, close to the grave of Bunyan. The same dramatic action is maintained to the close of the story.

Of its power of characterization and its graphic phrases we shall be better able to speak when the story has been recited.

As an unrivalled allegory the " Pilgrim's Progress," with little that is artificial and much that symbolizes genuine human experience, has fascinated both the simple and the wise, both the young and the old. No need to say why it appeals to the young, haunted by the glamour of adventure and the thrill of fight. It appeals to the elderly because through defeated efforts it cheers them on with its assurance of " the final perseverance of the saints which consists in ever new beginnings," the grace of " holding on."

Peculiarly pleasing to both spirited youth and stale age is the air of geniality, the humour of a fresh humanity, that plays through this and almost every product of Bunyan's pen and fancy. It has grim fights with dark powers, but even its fighting scenes have somewhat of the brisk, fair and picturesque Stevenson touch; its champion is a "bonnie fighter." There are desperate situations in the miry clay of sin and the sore conscience that fears hell; but no pessimism ever settles down upon the field of action; rippling sunlight passes in smiles over the landscape; there is sprightly gaiety in the whole adventure of the Pilgrimage as of the "Holy War." There is nothing here of the traditional picture of Puritan gloom and wailings (however characteristic of some later Puritans). The characteristic note is found, not only in the upper chamber in the Interpreter's house, whose window opened towards the sunrising and was named Peace, and in the Delectable Mountains of celestial vision, but in happy Christiana and her smiling boys. "One smiled and another smiled and they all smiled for joy." In Dante the wayfarer receives three smiles from his guide Beatrice as Divine Revelation, one that made all the heavens to laugh. But in Bunyan the consciousness of conquering grace is more frequent; the fresh joy of the Gospel recovered through the Reformation has become dominant. According to the verse prefatory to the Second Part,

> "Some there be that say he laughs too loud;
> And some do say his head is in a cloud."

But his laugh fills eyes that have just ceased crying, and is the very natural human expression of the triumph of redeeming grace.

Augustine had been attracted to the Christian Church by what he called its "non-dissolute hilarity," as Marius the Epicurean in Walter Pater's work is impressed by the sound of singing among the early Christians. The New Testament is full of song. The songs of the pilgrims in all Christian story have their echo in Bunyan.

Another source of this note of joy may here be mentioned. According to Bergson ("Hibbert Journal," Oct. 1911), "true joy is always the signal of the triumph of life"—joy, not mere pleasure. Joy accompanies the achievement of creation, whether that of the mother looking on her infant child, or that of the artist and the man of science over his masterpiece and his discovery; and "the richer the creation the deeper the joy." Bunyan's work manifests this joy. He tells us that he had not deliberately set about a book upon the journey of the race of saints; he "fell suddenly into an allegory" about it; the idea came to him unsought as inspiration has come to prophets and men of genius.

> "Thus I set Pen to Paper with delight,
> And quickly had my thoughts in black and white."

The happy spontaneity with which the story flowed into form evoked the joy of creation that marks his work; not conceit egotistical, but joy over a creation "born from above," of which he was the happy medium.

It is written with no aim at literary effect; as he puts it, "I could have stepped into a style much higher than this, in which I have here discoursed, and could have adorned all things more than here I have seemed to do; but I dare not; God did not play in tempting me; neither did I play when I sank as into a bottomless pit, when the pangs of hell caught hold upon me; wherefore I may not play in relating of them; but be plain and simple, and lay down the thing as it was; he that liketh it, let him receive it; and he that does not, let him produce a better. Farewell, my dear children, the milk and honey is beyond this wilderness."

J. R. Green wrote in felicitous terms: "It is in this amazing reality of impersonation that Bunyan's imaginative genius specially displays itself. But this is far from being his only excellence. In its range, in its directness, in its simple grace, in the ease with which it changes from living dialogue to dramatic action, from simple pathos to passionate earnestness, in the subtle and delicate fancy which often suffuses its childlike words, in its playful humour, its bold character-painting, in the even and balanced power which passes without an effort from the Valley of the Shadow of Death to the land 'where Shining Ones commonly walk because it is on the borders of Heaven,' in its sunny kindliness unbroken by one bitter word, the

'Pilgrim's Progress' is among the noblest of English poems."

2. The times in which Bunyan lived and wrote, the historical events in the political and ecclesiastical life of England which bore upon his career and left their marks deeply on his writings, one may presume to be commonly known to all who are familiar with British history. A brief outline of them here ought to be sufficient.

His life—1628 to 1688—extended through the later reign of Charles I, the period of the Civil War (1642-49), the Commonwealth under Cromwell and Puritan predominance, the Restoration under Charles II (1660–85), and the eve of the Revolution. It was a period of deadly strife in Church and State. The issue between personal autocratic government and the rights of the elected Parliament as an integral factor in national government was being contested and determined. Ecclesiastical conflict over uniformity of worship was equally bitter, first under the Laudian control of the established Church of England, then under the Puritans and the Presbyterians, and again under the Anglicans in the Restoration. The principle of toleration, much less the principle of entire freedom of worship according to individual conviction, was not yet commonly recognized on the side of any of the ruling parties in conflict.

The fight bore sorely upon all earnest and devout men of the time. Under Archbishop Laud many thousands of Puritans had been imprisoned or driven out of the country to America. Under Parliament and the Commonwealth many Anglican clergy had been displaced from their livings —among them Jeremy Taylor, of whom more in another of our present studies. Another of our subjects, Samuel Rutherford, had already (1636) under Laudian bishops been brought before the High Commission Court in Edinburgh and sentenced to silence in confinement in Aberdeen, and soon after the accession of Charles II, in 1660, he was summoned on a charge of treason. Under the Restoration the Uniformity Act (1662) ejected two thousand ministers from their parishes, and Richard Baxter, author of " The Saints' Everlasting Rest " and half a hundred other works, was imprisoned for a time, and in 1685 under James II was tried by the infamous Judge Jeffreys and sent to prison—Baxter who preferred monarchy to Cromwell, who, according to the inscription under his monument in Kidderminster, " in a stormy and divided time advocated unity and comprehension," and who always laboured in line with his memorable declaration, " I am not for narrowing the Church more than Christ Himself alloweth us." George Fox the leading Quaker (Friend) suffered persecution under both the Commonwealth and the Royalist churchmen.

Bunyan was, in 1660, brought before a justice of the peace, Francis Wingate, the original of Judge Hategood in the " Pilgrim's Progress," under a statute of Elizabeth's reign imposing imprisonment on those who frequented conventicles, and was committed to the County gaol at Bedford where, with the break of a few weeks, he was detained till 1672, his first imprisonment thus covering twelve years. During that period a series of repressive measures, besides the Uniformity Act, compelling attendance at the parish Church, were passed against all Dissenters (as they are now called) and put into force—the Conventicle Act (1664) imposing imprisonment and in the case of incorrigibles transportation of attendants at separate assemblies for worship, the Five Mile Act keeping recalcitrant ministers and teachers at a safe distance from towns, and later (1673) the Test Act, excluding from civil or military office under the Crown those who refused the Anglican sacraments, an Act by which they remained excluded from public office and from the Universities until the nineteenth century. Bunyan's second imprisonment for six months, in 1675-6, and his third imprisonment for a short time in the Town Gaol on Bedford Bridge, took place under these Acts.

The pleas of Jeremy Taylor, the Anglican, for " The Liberty of Prophesying " (preaching), of John Milton, the Puritan, for the freedom of the Press, and of Richard Baxter, the Presbyterian, for " Comprehension " in the Church, thus far and for many years failed to heal the breach in the body of Christ's people. Such lamentable divisions and waste of strength and influence in the world it is now our heavy task and joint effort to amend.

3. To come to Bunyan's religious history and his chief writings, which are now our main concern, the two principal documents in the case are his " Grace Abounding to the Chief of Sinners " and the " Pilgrim's Progress." The former is the primary document, his masterpiece. It is pure autobiography, the record of his spiritual experience in personal terms, and so the key to all his other writings. It was written straight out of his own heart and life. His " Pilgrim's Progress " and other books give extended and pictorial form to his own record, with enlargements drawn from wide observation of Christian experience beyond his own.

Both " Grace Abounding " and the " Pilgrim's Progress " (first part) were written while he was a prisoner in gaol for conscience' sake : the former during his first imprisonment (published in 1666) : the first part of the latter during his second imprisonment ending in 1676 (published in 1678). The second part appeared in 1685 when he was free, after he had issued " Mr. Badman," a pendant to the " Pilgrim's Progress." In 1682 came the " Holy War."

Here we might take up the interesting study of Prison-bred Literature—some of the Epistles of St. Paul, the Apocalypse of St. John (the isle of Patmos his prison as well as his Pisgah point of vision), the " Consolations of Philosophy " by Boethius (died 524), the " History of the World " by Sir Walter Raleigh (died 1618), Bunyan's " Grace Abounding " and " Pilgrim's Progress " (first part), numbers of Samuel Rutherford's Letters written from his confinement in Aberdeen, Silvio Pellico's " Ten Years' Imprisonment," in our own time Oscar Wilde's " De Profundis " written in Reading gaol before his final debacle. Dante's Vision was written in an exile which felt to him like imprisonment.

The motive of Bunyan in writing and publishing his " Grace Abounding " was not the impulse to find relief in giving expression to his soul, but the desire to continue ministering from his prison to the spiritual children who had enjoyed, and now sorely needed, his fatherly care. As we learn from the " Preface," it was written to fortify those of his Puritan people who were hard put to it by persecutions and by temptations, much as some of St. Paul's prison epistles were written for the comfort and instruction of gatherings of new-born Christian folk " under the Cross."

" I have sent you here enclosed a drop of that honey that I have taken out of the carcass of a lion. . . . I have eaten thereof myself also, and am much refreshed thereby. Temptations, when we meet them at first, are as the lion that roared upon Samson ; but, if we overcome them, the next time we see them we shall find a nest of honey within them. The Philistines understand me not. It is something a relation of the work of God upon my soul, even from the very first, till now ; wherein you may perceive my castings down and risings up. . . . I can remember my fears and doubts and sad months with comfort ; they are as the head of Goliath in my hand."

John Bunyan (d. 1688) was born in the parish of Elstow, beside the hamlet Harrowden, about two miles from Bedford. His father, apparently originally of French stock, was an itinerant brasier or tinker (not a gipsy), and in due course of years the son followed the same trade. Of his mother little is known.

In the opening paragraph of his " Grace Abounding " he speaks of his pedigree as of " low and inconsiderable generation," and in another writing of his says, " I was brought up at my father's house, in a very mean condition, among a company of poor countrymen." His early education, in reading and writing, was " that of poor men's children," soon lost ; happily his first wife helped him to recall it.

His youthful sins ran on into his early manhood : " I had but few equals (especially considering my years, which were tender, being few) both for cursing, swearing, lying and blaspheming the holy name of God ; they became a second nature to me." Apparently he never had reason to charge himself with unchastity or drunkenness.

We can see that he had a nervous temperament and high-strung sensibilities, often inducing morbid moods of exaggerated self-recrimination. Even when about nine or ten years old, he was, he says, scared with horrible dreams and terrified with dreadful visions, haunted by the apprehension of devils labouring to draw him away with them, afflicted

with thoughts of the torments of hell-fire, so that he almost
wished he was one of the devils, to be a tormentor and not
tormented.  The sight of others' piety offended him ; and
he was at the same time shocked and horrified at the sight
of professors of religion sinning.

He recalls with thankfulness to Divine providence several
escapes from death he had, as from drowning, and from
being hurt with the poisoned fang of an adder, whose sting
he abstracted with his own hand.

While still a youth of sixteen (c. 1644) he was called out
under a levy as a soldier, evidently, as Dr. Brown has shown
(against Froude), in the Parliamentary army.  He relates
little directly of his soldier-life, beyond telling how, " when
I was a soldier, I, with others, was drawn out to go to such
a place to besiege it ; but, when I was ready to go, one of
the company desired to go in my room ; to which, when I
consented, he took my place ; and, coming to the siege, as
he stood sentinel, he was shot into the head with a musket-
bullet and died "—another case of Divine sparing mercy.

His soldier-life was of about two years' duration.  While
little is reported, it left its mark deeply engraved in his mind.
The thought and imagery of war runs through much of his
published writing.  It not only dominates the entire " Holy
War " in Mansoul, but it comes out in the famous fights in
the " Pilgrim's Progress," as with Apollyon in the Valley of
Humiliation, Giant Despair in Doubting Castle, Giant
Maul ; and some of his most vivid characters are soldier-
figures, such as Valiant-for-Truth and Greatheart.  To
Bunyan, as Mark Rutherford says, courage was the root
of all the virtues.

His soldiering was over in 1646 with the disbanding of the
army.  When twenty he married his first wife, who before
her death in 1655 bore him four of his six children.

She, of whom we know almost nothing, brought him no
material possession, but memories of a godly father and
certain holy books, "The Plaine Man's Path-way to Heaven,"
by Arthur Dent, a parish minister in Essex, and " The
Practice of Pietie," by Lewis Bayly, former Bishop of Bangor.
The former was written entirely in the form of a dialogue,
with conversations between various men who represent

types—worldling, ignoramus (cf. Bunyan's Ignorance), theologian, etc.; the latter contains a long "colloquie" between Christ and the soul. His indebtedness for spiritual influences to these two books was profound, and he probably also drew from them his first lesson in the use of dialogue, afterwards so liberally employed in his writings and his sermons.

The ordeal of Bunyan's soul commenced soon after his marriage, and lasted for about four years. It was at first an uneasiness about external doings, indulgence in sports on the Sabbath, mischievous ringing of church bells, dancing, the use of strong language in cursing and swearing, profaning the Holy Name. But ere long the war had its arena in the depths of his soul, which was a very cockpit for fights with Apollyon and all sorts of mocking demons.

It was the veritable Devil, he was sure, who contended for his soul. Many of the dark shapes with which he wrestled were merely spectres of the mind, concrete projections of current beliefs. Yet for him the Devil was no phantom, but as actual a personal power as he was for Luther when flinging an ink-bottle at him. "Sometimes I have thought I should see the devil, nay, thought I have felt him, behind me, pluck my clothes."

Incidentally, it would be interesting to study comparatively the diverse conceptions of the Evil One formed by different writers. Professor Masson did so in his "Three Devils"; but there have been more than three. We think of Milton's majestic figure of Satan, Goethe's astute, sardonic, intellectual Mephistopheles in "Faust," the amused, amusing, mischief-making De'il of Burns, the haunting and tormenting Devil of Bunyan as Apollyon and as Diabolus, all these to be placed alongside Lucifer in Dante's "Inferno" and the earliest type in the Adversary of Job.

It would have astonished Bunyan to learn from modern psychology, in the person of Royce, that the tempter really "was a sort of inverted conscience, busily insisting upon whatever was opposed to any pious intention." Insistent ideas held his mind with mesmeric fascination; words haunted him until he was (as William James puts it in his "Varieties of Religious Experience," p. 157) "a victim of

verbal automatisms." Hence the " voices " which he, like
others, believed he heard. Macaulay in his " Essays " wrote
of " fearful disorders " in Bunyan's state of mind, seeing no
deeper than the surface thereof. Bunyan admitted later
that he had sometimes been distraught and unbalanced.
But, despite morbid impulses, his reason was sound ; it was
his vivid imagination working on accepted beliefs that
visualized ideas.

Texts of Holy Scripture were the chief weapons with
which the diabolic tempter, who seems to have known " his
Bible" amazingly, smote him down ; with these again, as the
" sword of the Spirit," the False Accuser is dislodged from
one ground of assault to another. His soul is torn between
different texts. He sees the amusing side of this mêlée.
One day, " Lord, thought I, if both these Scriptures would
meet in my heart at once, I wonder which of them would
get the better of me ! " (" Grace Abounding," par. 213). Dr.
Glover shrewdly observes here : " This is proof of sanity.
One great difference between sane and insane lies in this
power of seeing two things at once, of responding to the
thought or impulse and its corrective. Bunyan is never
swept out of himself by any voice or impulse " (p. 122).

The record of his conflicts, alternations of deep gloom and
passing blinks of sunshine, oscillations between despair and
faint hope, continuing with scarcely any abatement, is
heart-rending. Was there ever a soul more fiercely put to it ?

A spell of moral reform, Sabbath-keeping and church-
going, left him only a formalist. When playing cat one day
a voice " suddenly darted from Heaven into my soul, which
said, ' Wilt thou leave thy sins and go to heaven, or have
thy sins and go to hell ? ' At this I was put to an exceeding
maze," but not changed. Under reaction he felt, " I had
as good be damned for many sins as damned for few," and
went on with the game. Rebuked for swearing by some
women, he corrected the habit, took to Bible-reading, and
was passed as good. Still bell-ringing, he was fearful the bell
might fall and kill him, yet remained standing by to watch
others carry on ! It is notable how often in the " Pilgrim's
Progress " bells are set ringing, bells of joy as in Beulah.
He overheard some poor women talk of their sins and of the

soul's new birth ; he did not know what it was they meant, "though I was now a brisk talker myself." The Ranters, perfectionists who thought they were free to do as they liked, had dealings with him, in vain. True, he "was never out of the Bible," but he was distressed by his lack of faith, and tempted to experiment in working a miracle of faith. In a "kind of vision" he saw some godly poor people in the sunshine on a mountain compassed by a wall, in which was a gap. The mountain he took to be the Church, the sun the face of the merciful One, the wall the Word of God, the "gap" Jesus Christ. His soul desired greatly to enter. But the passage was so narrow that "there was only room for body and soul, but not for body and soul *and* sin." Is not this the source of the Gate at the narrow entrance to the Pilgrim Way ? He was afflicted by the doubt whether he was one of those "elected" to be saved, by predestination. How could he tell ? He might as well leave off striving. A verse was borne in on him—"as if it talked to me"—saying, "Did ever any trust in the Lord and was confounded ? " He could not find it in the whole Bible. Later he found it was in the O.T. Apocrypha (Eccles. ii. 10) ; but at any rate the substance of it was in the sacred canon. He feared the day of grace was past for him—had he committed the sin against the Holy Ghost ? "Yet there is room" broke in comfortingly on his mind. He wished Christ would say to him "Follow Me." He envied the converted, "who carried the Broad Seal of Heaven" upon them. "But the Lord let me go for many months and shewed me nothing." He had a first talk with the Rev. John Gifford, the Bedford minister —of whom more later ; but that good man thought too highly of his state, thus deepening his self-conviction. Through unbelief he had his "shoulder to the door to keep Him out," even when crying, "Lord, break it open." He was inwardly "tender," and went "gingerly," though it was through a "miry bog." "I was lost if I had not Christ. I wanted a perfect righteousness," only to be found in Him (par. 84). Much of this reappears in Hopeful's account of his conversion on the Enchanted Ground.

The message of God's love, backed by the Song of Love (Canticles), came so home to him that "I thought I could have spoken of His love even to the very crows that sat upon the ploughed lands before me. . . . I said in my soul, ' I would I had a pen and ink here, I would write this down before I go any further ; for surely I will not forget this forty years hence.' But, alas ! within less than forty days I began to question all again." A voice followed him, saying, " Satan hath desired to have you," sounding " so loud within me that once I turned my head over my shoulder, thinking verily that some man behind me had called me." This—which is now designated an " audition," like the children's voice to Augustine—is doubtless the personal source of Christian's experience in the Valley of the Shadow of Death, where he did not know his own voice, but had blasphemies whispered in his ear which seemed to proceed from himself.

Next his mind was beset with questionings as to the very being of God and the truth of the Gospel. Yet he was relieved to find that his innermost soul did not consent to these unholy doubts. He says with fine insight, " By the distaste they gave unto my spirit, I felt there was something in me that refused to embrace them." Even when a preacher, Bunyan knew such dismay in moments of doubt (see par. 157).

When he heard others speak of the sin against the Holy Ghost, the Tempter provoked him to desire to commit that sin, and he was so pressed to utter the word against the Holy Ghost that " often I have been ready to clap my hand under my chin, to hold my mouth from opening " (par. 104). He wished he were a dog, a horse, a toad, which had no soul to perish in hell and no sin like his.

" My heart was at times exceeding hard ; if I would have given a thousand pounds for a tear, I could not have shed one ; no, nor sometimes scarce desire to shed one." We remember Dante's denizens of the Inferno, there " all for lack of one sorry tear." But Bunyan's case is rather like that of the newly bereaved whose sorrow is so dry that sometimes they are staggered at their own apparent hardness and inability to shed tears.

He persisted in praying. Remember how in that most fearsome time in the Valley of the Shadow of Death, against the flame and smoke belching from the mouth of hell with hideous noises, Christian's sword (Scripture) was useless, and he had to " betake himself to another weapon, called ' All-Prayer,' " while yet the fiends continued their shrieks.

But, though Bunyan persisted in prayer, " I thought I felt the tempter behind me pull my clothes . . . continually at me in time of prayer to have done ; break off, make haste, you have prayed enough . . . fall down and worship me."

Yet he hankered after God, and at times had heart-affecting apprehensions of God and the reality of the Gospel —" I should cry with pangs after God that He would be merciful unto me."

But again he would be " daunted by such conceits as this, ' How art thou deceived ! ' " The Tempter jeered at him— " You are very hot for mercy, but I will cool you ; this frame will not last always ; many have been as hot as you, but I have quenched their zeal . . . I will cool you insensibly, by degrees, by little and little. What care I, saith Satan, though I be seven years in chilling your heart, if I can do it at last ? Continual rocking will lull a crying baby to sleep. I will ply it close, but I will have my end accomplished " (par. 111).

Then, again, he had blinks of sunshine—a " sweet glance," as he finely puts it—from certain Scriptures : " He hath made Him to be sin for us, who knew no sin, that we might be made the righteousness of God in Him. . . . If God be for us, who can be against us ? " (par. 114). " These words were but hints, touches, and short visits, though very sweet when present ; only they lasted not, but, like to Peter's sheet, of a sudden were caught up from me to Heaven again."

" One day, as I was travelling into the country, and musing on the wickedness and blasphemy of my heart . . . that Scripture came to my mind, ' He hath made peace by the blood of His Cross ' (Col. i. 20). By which I was made to see, again and again, that day, that God and my soul were friends by this blood ; yea, I saw that the justice of God and my sinful soul could embrace and kiss each other through this blood. This was a good day to me ; I hope I shall not forget it " (par. 116). Here we may see the personal experience suggesting his description in the " Pilgrim's

Progress " of Christian's sight of the Cross which loosed his burden of sin, so that it fell instantly into the empty grave.

Now comes help from Christian guides, of which thus far he had received little. In the " Pilgrim's Progress " there appear opportunely, at successive stages, human helpers for Christian, and in the second part for Christiana, such as Evangelist, Help, the Interpreter, Greatheart. Bunyan himself had hitherto almost no close direction except from the Scriptures. These, through ignorance and false methods of interpretation, had often been wrested from their context and proper application, becoming the textual source of much distress. If only he had enjoyed enlightened counsel, explaining himself to himself, and therapeutic healing for his unnatural maladies ! Yet in that case could he have written so much in the " Pilgrim's Progress " to interpret and heal the minds of others ?

The first human helper who came to his rescue was the Rev. John Gifford. " Holy Mr. Gifford " (as he was called), the original from which the figure of " Evangelist " was drawn in the " Pilgrim's Progress," had been a man of dissolute life, then had been profoundly converted, and became minister of the church in Bedford, from 1650 to 1665.

He had studied medicine, had entered the Royalist army, in which he became a major, had been embroiled during the Commonwealth in the Maidstone insurrection, was made a prisoner by Fairfax's men and condemned to death. On the night before his execution his sister was allowed by the courtesy of Fairfax to visit him in prison. While the sentries were sleepy after the battle, she managed to get him safely past them and away into the country, where he lay in ditches and thickets for some days until he reached London. Thence he went to friends in Bedford, where ere long he found it safe to practise his old art of medicine. He " abode still very vile and debauched, being a great drinker, gamester, swearer " ; he was notorious in the town for his scandalous life, and his persecuting hatred for the Puritans made his name and person a terror as well as an infamy. One night, after having lost heavily at gaming, and being near suicide, he was put into a rage, a " dumpish fit," " thought many desperate thoughts against God," but while reading a godly book was seized with a sense of sin which held him for a month. " At last God did so plentifully discover to him by His word the forgiveness of sins for the sake of Christ that all his life after, about the space of five years, he lost not the light of God's countenance, no, not for an hour, save only about two days before he died " (Brown, 83).

The conversion of such a conspicuous sinner at first brought the " godly to a stand in the case." But, instead of hiding in shame, he cast in his lot with the extreme Puritans, and after a time he became minister of the Non-conformist congregation and for a time the parish minister of St. John's in Bedford.

Gifford, who had narrowly escaped the City of Destruction, helped John Bunyan in his escape. Evangelist comes to his rescue three times in the " Pilgrim's Progress,"—as Christian has dragged himself out of the Slough of Despond, when Evangelist directs him to the wicket gate ; again when the thunder and lightning of Sinai (the Law) have brought him to sore plight and Evangelist directs him back towards the gate ; and once again at the gates of Vanity Fair.

Something, but not all, of the help Mr. Gifford brought Bunyan is told in " Grace Abounding." We saw how Mr. Gifford's first talk with Bunyan had been unsatisfying (G.A. 78), while inducing deeper convictions. Now, he says (G.A. 118), " I sat under the ministry of holy Mr. Gifford, whose doctrine, by God's grace, was much for my stability. This man made it much his business to deliver the people of God from all those false and unsound tests that by nature we are prone to. This was seasonable to my soul."

Luther was his next helper. " I did greatly long to see some ancient godly man's example, who had writ some hundreds of years before I was born," who had " gone down himself into the deep," and had not written merely what others had felt. " God, in whose hands are all our days and ways, did cast into my hand one day a book by Martin Luther, his Comment on the *Galatians* : so old it was ready to fall piece from piece if I did but turn it over. The which I found my condition, in his experience, so largely and pro-foundly handled, as if his book had been written out of my own heart." [1]   It debated the rise of temptations to blasphemy, desperation, and such like as he knew ; and doubtless it helped Bunyan by its teaching of justification by faith apart from meritorious works.   " I do prefer this book of Martin Luther upon the *Galatians* (excepting the Holy Bible) before all the books that ever I have seen, as most fit for a wounded conscience."   (We recall that Luther said that he preferred the " Theologia Germanica " above all books except the Bible and St. Augustine's " Confessions." So far at least Bunyan entered into the spiritual succession of Classics of the Soul.)   " Now I found that I loved Christ dearly ; my soul cleaved unto Him."

But his spiritual deliverance was by no means complete ; he suffered sorely from reactions.   He had still to keep up the old fight.

For " the space of a year," he says (though his chronology is not accurate) he was urged by the Tempter to sell Christ (G.A. 134 ff.).   In his meticulous scrupulosity, he could not eat his food, nor stoop for a pin nor cut a stick, without hearing the devilish voice, " Sell Christ for this, sell Him for that."   He defiantly replied, " I will not, I will not, for thousands of worlds."   Still insisted the voice, " Sell Him, sell Him."   At last one morning in bed, almost out of breath, the " thought passed through my heart, ' Let Him go if He will,' and I thought that I felt my heart consent thereto. . . .   Down I fell, as a bird that is shot from the top of a tree into a great guilt and fearful despair."

The conviction that he has committed the unpardonable sin against the Holy Ghost stays with him, he says, for two years (again his chronology is exaggerated).   Though there are occasional words of hope from Scripture and glimpses of Divine grace—the Tempter " leering and stealing away as though ashamed " while the light of the Son of God suffering for sin breaks kindly upon him—the sin of Esau,

[1] We may wonder how it was that Luther's Commentary in English dress was in circulation among the godly common people of Bedford.   The present writer has a copy of an English translation published in 1786, in Paisley, Scotland, by subscription, and the appended list of subscribers to it gives some 1,800 names classified under the heading of trades, nearly all of them the common trades ; over 1,200 are weavers, many are blacksmiths, tailors, shoemakers and the like.

who sold his birthright and found no place for repentance, and the blasphemy against the Holy Ghost, obsess his thoughts. Through many paragraphs he compares his guilt with others, with David and with Solomon—but they were only under the Law and had not had Christ presented to them—with Peter, who denied the Lord, and with Judas.

He was tempted again to adopt " false opinions " about the Resurrection and the gravity of sin. " Methinks Satan will use any means to keep the soul from Christ." He was driven into deeper despair by reading " that dreadful story of that miserable mortal, Francis Spira, his dolours, his gnashing of teeth, his tears and prayers, especially that frightful sentence of his, ' Man knows the beginnings of sin, but who bounds the issues thereof ? ' It rubbed salt into my wounds. It was as knives and daggers to my soul." [1]

The spiritual struggle struck his very body to the point of tottering, brought a " clogging heat " to his stomach, and made him feel as though, like Judas, he would " burst asunder." What cut his heart was, " My sin was point-blank against my Saviour." Yet he had " flying fits " in which Divine grace would call to him, and Scripture assurances would overtake him. " My life hung in doubt before me, not knowing which way I would tip." Salvation, like the issues of the Great War, seems a hairbreadth escape— " saved as by fire "—and in that hairbreadth it is the final spiritual pull that counts and decides : in a single word, it is God.

At long last peace came to his distracted soul, though the old tremblings oft vibrated through the assurance of faith. It came to him like a voice—for he had heavenly voices as he had diabolic—" This sin is not unto death " ; it shot sweetly into his soul, " I have loved thee with an everlasting love." It came declaring, " He is able to save to the uttermost," " My grace is sufficient." The die was cast, the surrender was made, the tumultuous forces long

---

[1] Francis Spira, an Italian lawyer, who died shortly before Bunyan's time, played traitor to the Protestant faith, and conformed to the Roman Church for selfish expediency. His biography, reciting his deathbed conversations, exhibits the desperate, morbid melancholy of soul he endured *in extremis* as a betrayer of his true faith:

at work in him were rearranged under control of Jesus Christ as the centre of gravity.

John Bunyan was received into membership in the Bedford Church in 1653 by " Evangelist," the Rev. John Gifford. He left no record of his action and experiences, unlike St. Augustine, when thus welcomed into the Christian fold and fellowship. We gather that, as one of the former " town-sinners," this turn in his life caused wonder. He had to endure slander under accusation of unchastity. With vehemence he could declare (G.A. 315 f.) " I know not whether there be such a thing as a woman, but by apparel and common fame, except my wife." His record and ministry shamed these slanders.

His career from this point onward must be very briefly summarized. He removed in 1655 from Elstow to Bedford. In the same year his first wife died—of his second wife, whom he married in 1659, we know little—and his minister, John Gifford, passed away. In the same year, 1655, his brethren, he relates, " desired me with much earnestness that I would be willing sometimes to take in hand in their meetings to speak a word of exhortation to them." His word came with much power and much acceptance, and he had hundreds of opportunities of preaching, even in parish churches, while toleration lasted.

But with the Restoration in 1660 came insistence on uniformity of worship. We have already dwelt sufficiently with the Royalist Acts which caused his arrest and successive imprisonments and with his prison-writings, including " Grace Abounding," and the first part of the " Pilgrim's Progress."

In prison—prisons were terrible in those days—he made tagged laces for the support of his family, and preached to his fellow-prisoners.

In a continuation of " Grace Abounding " he gives an account, often racy and sometimes heart-piercing, of his trial in court. His trial scenes in the " Pilgrim's Progress," as in the " Holy War," are vivid, as in Vanity Fair before Judge Hategood, drawn (as already stated) from Francis Wingate, the Bedford Justice who tried his case. The prospective penalties—whip, pillory, perhaps transportation beyond seas—pressed acutely on his family affections and on his shrinking sensibilities.   Parting with his wife and his blind child cut him to the quick.[1]   Facing the possible gallows, he was afraid of himself rather than of hanging. He suffered from the *fear of fear*, such as our boys felt in the Great War, not fear of the enemy, but anticipatory fear lest they should lose courage when the onset came, though when it came they forgot both fear and danger.   Bunyan feared lest he should scramble up the ladder with symptoms of quaking, and so give the enemy occasion to reproach the way of God because of his pale face.   "But, if God did not come in (thought I), I will leap off the ladder even blindfold into Eternity, sink or swim, come Heaven, come Hell ; Lord Jesus, if Thou wilt catch me, do ; if not, I will venture in Thy name " (G.A. 338).   After all he never had to come to such a sore pass.

During the intervals between his periods of imprisonment, and when he was finally released, he found a widening call as a preacher, and drew immense numbers to hear him. In London crowds gathered at 7 a.m. to listen to his message. It was not always calm weather in his own soul ; he still had seasons of doubt and distress through which the thunders of the past reverberated.   " I went myself in chains to preach to them in chains."   On the other hand his popular success tempted him to take pride in praise.   But he had the self-possession to recall how he owed all to the enabling grace of God whose instrument he was.   His native wit flashed in his self-rebuke—" Is it so much to be fiddle ? " It was God's Spirit who played on him and made the music —an ancient metaphor of which doubtless he had never heard.

It is not our concern here to consider him as a preacher. Enough to mention his natural force, his shrewd and homely thrusts at conscience, his tenderness of touch in handling tender hearts, his wit and humour, his dramatic use of imaginative dialogue, his intimate knowledge of human

---

[1] " Poor child ! what sorrow art thou like to have ?   Thou must be beaten, must beg, suffer hunger, cold, nakedness, and a thousand calamities, though I cannot now endure the wind should blow upon thee. . . .   But I must venture you all with God " (G.A. 328 f.).

nature as also of the Bible.   Like St. Augustine, he had
gone through distracting complications of mind, tortuous
turns, now this way, now that way, and had suffered from
the clash of the two wills, hating the sins that yet he
practised, crying from the bottom of his heart for the
decisive power that would lift him free from the suction of
the subsiding past.   He had the two keys of St. Peter held
by the Angel-warder in Dante, one with which to open
hearts and diagnose conditions, the other with which to
assure of Divine absolution for sin.   He had experienced
the power of both.

After a comparatively short period of service as minister
in Bedford, he died in London in 1688, and his body was
buried there in Bunhill Fields, near the grave of Daniel
Defoe.   Close at hand the body of George Fox, Quaker,
was to be laid two years later, as also that of the Wesleys'
mother in 1741 ; and just over the road in the future Wesley
Chapel the body of John Wesley was, a little over a century
after Bunyan's death, to be enshrined.

4. The general conception of the Christian life as a pilgrim
journey was not derived by Bunyan from others' writings—
though considerable elements in the " Pilgrim's Progress "
have anticipations in or resemblances to parts of Spenser's
" Faerie Queene " (description of the Celestial City) and
in Bishop Patrick's " Parable of the Pilgrim," published in
1665 during Bunyan's first imprisonment.

The idea of life as a pilgrimage is as old as ancient
wanderers like Abraham, who set out to seek the " city
which hath foundations, whose builder and maker is God,"
who confessed that they were strangers and pilgrims (Heb.
xi. 13 ff.).   Bunyan, who " was never out of the Bible,"
found the idea there, but doubtless also he drew the idea
of the Road from the roads he had so often travelled as an
itinerant brasier.

A comparison with Dante seems at first sight incongruous ; yet both deal with the great adventure of the soul
as a pilgrim from darkness to light and from death in sin to
life in God.   Dante's journey is set in the worlds beyond
death, while Bunyan's is cast in this present world.   Yet

both deal with the same eternal realm of experience (cf. Brown, 291 f.).

Milton's " Paradise Regained " was published in 1671, and Bunyan might have read it or have heard accounts of it as the work of another Puritan.   There is no comparison between the two ; but it is notable that both are dramas of the recovery of the soul, and mark the nature of Christianity as a gospel of recovery.   There are many dramas of decline and fall, generally pagan dramas, with an exception in " Paradise Lost " ; but great Christian dramas reflect the distinctive Christian message of the recovery, rise, and triumph of the penitent and believing soul.

The " Pilgrim's Progress," with " Grace Abounding," has given Evangelical Christianity much of its hold on the English-speaking world, and, along with the work of the Wesleys, has enforced the doctrines of Grace, especially justification by faith.

The pilgrim-idea of this life is not the modern point of view ; people to-day think of this present world as a place, not to be got through, but to live and work in, planting the Kingdom.   The very opening words of the " Pilgrim's Progress " are thus somewhat alien to modern thought, and perhaps the allegory has therefore lost currency among young people.   Yet, after all, the reality ever true is the escape of the soul from the world, the flesh and the devil.

5. Bunyan shows, as St. Augustine showed in signal measure, the gift of observation, an eye for the sights and sounds and common interests of human beings.   The scenes he depicts were such as he knew.   From his window in the prison on the bridge he could probably see the ruins of Bedford Castle, Cainhoe Castle was only a few miles off, and these may have suggested the Castle of Despair.   A cross stood at the centre of Elstow village.   Vanity Fair is just a reflex of fairs common in his day in many towns and villages which he must have seen, especially the great fair at Stourbridge, near Cambridge, like that of Novgorod in Russia, which lasted for weeks.

He has a singular power in characterization.   He has the dramatic instinct in making his characters speak for themselves and so at once reveal themselves. "As he wrote, he fairly saw his men, and identified himself with them. Such a faculty is the outcome of experience and imagination. He had himself been Ignorance, for he too was a 'brisk talker.' He had looked down the street where Atheist lived. Worldly-Wiseman had tried to let him a house in the village of Morality, where (as he justly remarked in 1678) houses stood empty and were to be had at a reasonable rate. By-Ends—and that half-brother of his mother's, the Mr. Two-Tongues, who was the 'Parson of our parish,' holding on in spite of the Uniformity Act, like his much-harassed contemporary the Vicar of Bray—the old gentleman, Mr. Legality, and the 'pretty young man, his son Civility with the simpering looks'—Bunyan had known them all " (Glover, 133).

A few deft strokes and the character stands forth distinctive. Mr. G. B. Shaw has compared Bunyan, one of his favourite authors, with Shakespeare in this respect. Put the latter's hero and coward, Henry V and Pistol, beside Mr. Valiant and Mr. Fearing ; "Bunyan's coward stirs your blood more than Shakespeare's hero, who actually leaves you cold and secretly hostile."

The vitality of his characters is all the more remarkable in that they are generally ideal qualities personified. Dante's figures, we saw, are historical persons idealized. Yet the former have as much flesh and blood as the latter. Unlike Dante, but like the New Testament, Bunyan shows no mortal antipathies in his treatment of persons from whom he or his work had suffered.

Bunyan's women are notable achievements in portraiture ; he excels in pictures of domestic life. He is as chivalrous to women as Dante, from whose Hell they are mostly absent. Says the Puritan : " I read not that ever any man did give unto Christ so much as a groat ; but the women followed Him and ministered to Him of their substance. It was a woman that washed His feet with tears, and a woman that anointed His body to the burial. They were women that wept when He was going to the Cross, and women that followed Him from the Cross, and that sat by His sepulchre when He was buried. They were women that were first with Him at His resurrection-morn, and women that brought tidings first to His disciples that He was risen from the dead. Women, therefore, are highly favoured, and show by these things that they are sharers with us in the Grace of Life."

He shows a keen sympathetic insight and tenderness in dealing with the frail and with all who through weaknesses are struggling for what is good, and a trenchant judgment for the false and the pretentious.

His story has dramatic unity. While lacking in school culture, his writings are marked by simple purity of style free from mannerisms, by verve, terse terms, the spontaneity of genius, and all the qualities which we have already observed in him as a preacher.

Such confessional histories of the soul, presenting the critical stage in personal experience, are apt to close with that crisis or with the call to life-service and with settlement in a system of things, as works of fiction are apt to end with marriage. But Bunyan conducts us the whole way, to the very end of our human pilgrimage, and expounds things new and old through all the decades of our life's experience. He carries us from the system of perishable things, through the gate, by the Cross, over the hills of difficulty, through valleys of despair, past by-paths, across green pastures and mounts of vision, to the last adventure of the River. He goes with us along the " long last mile " of the journey of life, pathetically and somewhat darkly reflected in Dr. McLean Watt's verse (in " The Tryst ") :

"Carry me over the long last mile,
   Man of Nazareth, Christ for me !
Weary I wait by death's dark stile,
   In the wild and the waste where the wind blows free :
      And the shadows and sorrows, come out of my past,
         Look keen through my heart,
         And will not depart,
      Now that my poor world has come to its last.

" Lord, is it long that my spirit must wait,
   Man of Nazareth, Christ for me ?
Deep is the stream, and the night is late,
   And grief blinds my soul that I cannot see ;
      Speak to me out of the silence, Lord,
         That my spirit may know
         As forward I go
      That Thy pierced hands are lifting me over the ford."

In spite of all that daunts or dashes the heart, the dominant note to the very end is the joy of triumph. When the gates of the Celestial City open to admit the pilgrims, we are allowed a glimpse within : " Which, when I had seen, I wished myself among them."

# XI

# William Law's "Serious Call":

## JACOB BEHMEN AND JOHN WESLEY

### I. WILLIAM LAW AND HIS "SERIOUS CALL"

WILLIAM LAW has a distinct share in the goodly
fellowship of the prophets. He received good
seed from Tauler and Ruysbroek, and a rich dower from
the "Theologia Germanica" and the "Imitatio Christi."
What he gave to John Wesley and others in spiritual impact
we shall see later.

He left small record, in any of his books or otherwise, of
his own spiritual history, beyond his discovery of that
native genius among mystics, Jacob Behmen, or Böhme,
and the enlargement of vision which he attributes to that
discovery. Byrom, the quaint sedulous recorder, who did
for William Law something like what Boswell did for Samuel
Johnson, left us reports of interviews and conversations,
and Christopher Walton collected a mass of later biographical
material. But we have no means of knowing through what
experimental "mystery" his feet were set in the way of
life, although there are significant records of his continual
combats with himself in subduing all things to the obedience
of Christ, as well as of his controversies over what he believed
to be the truth. His writings do not strictly belong to
confessional literature. Yet few books surpass his "Serious
Call," as well as his "Spirit of Prayer" and "Spirit of
Love," in searching exposition and insistent enforcement
of personal spiritual experience.

He is commonly and rightly cited as chief among English
mystics. But the "Serious Call to a Devout and Holy

Life " is not a mystical work; it was written before his interest in mysticism had developed and his mind had come to be dominated by Behmen, when he had nearly reached the " five-barred gate " of life. It is a serious, forceful, and rather stern summons to practical obedience to the law of Christ in the whole sphere of life. Like Jeremy Taylor's " Holy Living and Holy Dying," though in another mode, it is a regulative directory for the conduct of a thoroughly Christian life, while at the same time tinctured with a warm sense of humanity.

It needs little introduction or exposition. It will speak for itself quite clearly, if people will only read it with an earnest mind. There is little in the author's career to cast light upon it—and we are not here writing a series of complete biographies; enough that we convey some understanding of the man as he was, and whet an appetite for the book.

William Law (1686–1761), son of a prosperous grocer in King's Cliffe, near Stamford, Northamptonshire, entered early into a Christian heritage and made it his own. When a student in Emmanuel College, Cambridge, at the age of nineteen he drew up rules for the guidance of his life which show his devout and conscientious spirit, forecasting chapters in his " Serious Call." The first of the eighteen rules cuts deep—to keep in mind " that I have but one business upon my hands, to seek for eternal happiness by doing the will of God "; then fitly follow such as these— to remember that " the greatness of human nature consists in nothing else but in imitating the Divine nature "; to avoid idleness, and all excess in eating and drinking; " to call to mind the presence of God whenever I find myself under any temptation to sin, and to have immediate recourse to prayer."

Elected to a Fellowship in Emmanuel College and entering Holy Orders in 1711, he was deprived of his Fellowship and sacrificed prospects of preferment in the Church of England by the scrupulous position he took as one of the Non-jurors on the accession of George I. He obstinately declined to take the oath of allegiance to the Hanoverian house, remaining faithful in sympathy with the exiled Stuart dynasty.

Realizing the melancholy outlook for his career he sent a tender message to his anxious mother, saying that the concern which he fears his action must cause her " is the only trouble I have for what I have done. . . . My education had been miserably lost if I had not learnt to fear something worse than misfortune." He thus deliberately forfeited benefices in the Church. Misguided loyalties characterized many Jacobites.

Where he lived for ten years after his ordination is not known ; but he was busy with his pen, by which he achieved his notable influence.

A High Churchman, as well as a Tory, he engaged in public controversies with Latitudinarians in the person of Dr Hoadly, Bishop of Bangor, with Mandeville whose " Fable of the Bees " gave a naturalistic explanation of the moral life with a cynical defence of selfishness, and with supporters of the theatre in its then corrupt condition which Law reprobated as wicked beyond all possible cure. In each case his argument was set forth with telling force, while his standpoints were sectional and in some things came to be superseded. With these and other later controversies we are not here concerned.

Happily he turned to his real field of interest, to works of personal religion. His first treatise on practical religion, " Christian Perfection," published at the age of thirty-seven, made a deep impression on his generation in spite of its sombre estimate of human nature and austere attitude to the world. Among books of its class in the eighteenth century it stands second only to his later book, " The Serious Call." John Wesley, who with other early Methodists greatly profited by it, complained to Law that his standard of perfection was higher than man could attain. Law, who was no perfectionist in the modern sense, replied, " We shall do well to aim at the highest degree of perfection if we may thereby at least attain to mediocrity." Christian perfection, he says, consists in nothing but " the right performance of necessary duties of life according to the laws of Christ . . . living in such holy tempers and acting with such dispositions as Christianity requires."

In this book he begins to employ a device which he

elaborates more carefully in the " Serious Call," namely, sketches of imaginary characters as illustrations of his instruction. " Patronus is fond of a clergyman who understands music, painting, statuary, and architecture. He is an enemy to the dissenters, and loves the Church of England because of the stateliness and beauty of its buildings ; he never comes to the sacrament, but will go forty miles to see an altar-piece. He goes to Church when there is a new tune to be heard, but never had any more serious thoughts about salvation than about flying." " Matrona has been this fifty years eating and drinking, dressing and undressing, paying and receiving visits. She has no profaneness, and, if she has no piety, it is owing to this, that she never had a spare half-hour in all her life to think about it. She envies her daughters, because they will dress and visit when she is dead." There is also the widow Julia, who cannot spend her time alone without foolish novels to support dull hours like drams drunk in private. And there is Junius, the orthodox churchman who reads all confutations of atheists, deists and heretics, and passes as pious, yet has no taste for books of devotion, confessing " he does not understand their flights."

About a year later (*c.* 1727)—the year in which he founded a school for fourteen girls in his native King's Cliffe—he became an inmate of the household of Mr. Gibbon in Putney on the Thames as tutor to his son Edward, who was to become the father of the great historian Gibbon. He later accompanied his pupil to Emmanuel College, Cambridge, which had suspended him. Macaulay has described the parasitic dependence, and some great novelists have portrayed the pliant character, of unbeneficed clergymen who found a cramping corner as domestic trencher-chaplains or family tutors in the houses of county gentlemen or merchant magnates. Unlike that depreciated class, William Law gained a place of honour in the family of the Gibbons, and became the centre of a friendly circle. He was the spiritual director of Miss Hester Gibbon, the daughter of the house, who later joined him in his house of retreat in King's Cliffe, and of others, like Byrom and John Wesley, who gathered to that Putney grove. Here Law remained for

about twelve years. Gibbon the historian later wrote this
brief tribute to him : " In our family William Law left the
reputation of a worthy and pious man who believed all that
he professed, and practised all that he enjoined." How his
early influence on Wesley came to be marred must be left
over to a later paragraph.

The " Serious Call," the book of his with which we are
here chiefly concerned, was written during his residence in
the Gibbons' household in Putney. What induced him to
write and publish it is not manifest. We remember that,
like Jeremy Taylor, and in another way like John Bunyan,
he was deprived by ecclesiastical and political stress from
public ministrations in the Church, and we may well assume
that he also found such a sacred fire burning in his breast
that he must give it public utterance in the printed page,
and call his generation to serious religion.

The apathetic and rationalist religion of his age was a
challenge to his earnest and conscience-bound spirit as a
Christian man. The great soul of his contemporary Bishop
Butler burned hot for a positive and living Christianity underneath the somewhat cold exterior of his " Analogy " and his
" Sermons." A little later in Germany Schleiermacher in
his " Speeches," under impact from Moravians and English
Methodists, passionately challenged men of culture thus :
" You know that you have not only deserted the temple of
the Highest, but that you have ceased to worship Him in
secret, and that you look on your religion as if it were an old-
fashioned costume such as often continues to be worn among
the common people after it has been discarded by the upper
classes." The religion he saw consisted in assenting to
certain (questionable) doctrines, without consequent moral
obedience.

William Law's " Serious Call " stands out boldly against
such an indifferent and rationalist background. He was
branded by some contemporaries as an " enthusiast," the
favourite vituperative missile of the " moderates " of the
barren eighteenth century. He, a man of high intellectual
endowment, while adverse to some forms of " enthusiasm "
in his age, accepted the term. As he wrote in a later
controversy, " enthusiasm is as common, as universal, as

essential to human nature, as love is. No people are so angry with religious enthusiasts as those who are the deepest in some enthusiasm of another kind, like those who would travel over mountains to salute the dear ground that Cicero had walked upon," or fops and beaux whose ardour is kindled by tailors. Enthusiasm is not blamable in religion, when it is approved in other spheres of life.

In his " Serious Call," while enthusiastic and (as we say) " meaning business " in the practice of the Christian religion, he was governed by sanity and common sense, though his demands in religious exercises were austere and perhaps excessive. It, the masterpiece of all his writings, said the sceptical historian Gibbon, " is still read as a popular and powerful book of devotion. His precepts are rigid, but they are founded on the Gospel ; his satire is sharp, but it is drawn from the knowledge of human life ; and many of his portraits are not unworthy of the pen of La Bruyère." Dr. Johnson wrote : " When at Oxford I took up Law's ' Serious Call,' expecting to find it a dull book (as such books generally are), and perhaps laugh at it. But I found Law quite an overmatch for me ; and this was the first occasion of my thinking in earnest of religion after I became capable of rational inquiry." The book which influenced early Methodists, which generated a religious interest in the mind of Dr. Samuel Johnson, and which has won warm appreciation from the detached mind of Leslie Stephen, is proved to have a truly catholic appeal.

We cannot reduce to a brief summary the contents of the " Serious Call." It calls most emphatically for the application of Christian principles to the entire field of human life. It explains why from diverse worldly considerations, natural desire, social diversions, public or scholarly ambitions, idleness and self-satisfaction, men " live below their nature "—or, as we might say, fail to achieve their higher potentialities. The great question is whether we resolutely intend to fulfil the requirements of the Gospel call in constant regulated devotions, in all tempers and in all business, in the use of money, of leisure, dress, sleep, and social advantage, as well as in the enjoyment of all lawful comforts. Much is said as to the vain pride of worldly ambitions and selfish satisfactions, and, on the other side, of the true happiness and peace of a life completely devoted to God, of times and methods of prayer, of the practical help derived from the singing of sacred song, of the power and personal benefit of intercessions, of the practice of humility, and of false and true education of sons and daughters.

To select a few samples of his keen observations, he insists on equal moral and Christian laws for the " professed " and for the ordinary lay disciple, urging that " all Christians are called to the same life of holiness. . . . A man is not to be reasonable and holy because he is a priest, or a father of a family ; but he is to be a pious priest, and a good father, because piety and goodness are the laws of human nature." We are to do justly, not merely upon occasions when it is easy and creditable to do so, but " from such a living principle of justice as makes us love truth and integrity in all its instances, follow it through all dangers and against all opposition : as knowing that the more we pay for any truth the better is our bargain, and that our integrity becomes a pearl when we have parted with all to keep it." He reminds us of some points in our study of Dante's Vision about disordered love when he says : " The lowness of most people's virtue, the imperfections of their piety, and the disorders of their passions are generally owing to their imprudent use and enjoyment of lawful and innocent things." He reminds us of the " Imitatio Christi," which he had well studied, when, asked how a certain saintly character could be an example to us in different conditions, he replies that we can imitate such as we " imitate the life of our blessed Saviour and His Apostles. . . . It is their spirit, their piety, their love of God, that you are to imitate, and not the particular form of their life." He is in touch with the *Aufklärung* or Illuminationists when he says that " the religion of the Gospel is only the refinement and exaltation of our best faculties," although the fallen nature of man is one of his basic ideas. " The greatest spirits of the heathen world, such as Pythagoras, Socrates, Plato, Epictetus, Marcus Aurelius, etc., owed all their greatness to the spirit of devotion, being full of God." He sounds the evangelical note when he says : " The Christian's great conquest over the world is all contained in the mystery of Christ upon the cross. . . .   Unless our old man be crucified with Him, the cross of Christ will profit us nothing."   As to social values of moral conduct, he shows unusually deep insight when he urges that civil society is injured, not only by cheating and dishonesty, but by " pride and sensuality," and by the lack of spiritual influence.   As one might say, we are guilty of robbing men as well as God when we refrain from living the thoroughgoing Christian life.   The spiritual view of man and society is not only fundamental but creative. Fallen and redeemed spirits " are baptized into a fellowship with the Son of God, to be temples of the Holy Ghost, to live according to His holy inspirations, to offer to God the reasonable sacrifice of an humble, pious and thankful life." First and last William Law is a practical director, and in religious thought he is almost a pragmatist.   In his view our highest devotion lies in our " tempers of duty, reverence, love, honour and gratitude to the Benefactor of mankind," and in the charitable service of others.

The racy, incisive, and often quietly satiric characterization of the imaginary figures whom he sketches as illustrations of specific types of character is one of the distinctive features of the " Serious Call."   Dante employed historical or mythological persons to exemplify typical virtues and vices. Bunyan sketched ideal characters, good and bad, as factors in his story.   William Law, while he tells no story, often gives concrete embodiment to his description of distinctive characters in the form of imaginary personalities.   They are etched with keen wit and shrewd insight into human nature, into the psychology of men and women who seek a compromise between the Christian and the worldly or selfish life, into mixed motives in religion, and into the glad sacrificial devotion of faithful Christians.   These sketches are marked by careful drawing, and by considerate compassion for human frailties.   They have been used and might well be still used as subjects for Christian instruction in classes.

We have room here only for brief mention of some of these character-sketches.   Callidus, the prosperous tradesman, consumes his meals in a hurry, would say grace if he had time, gains sleep at night by driving business out of his mind with the use of strong spirits that make him drowsy, and makes ejaculatory prayers " in tempestuous weather because he has always something at sea." He could not have carried on but that he got out into the country at every week-end for refreshment—a forecast of the modern week-ender who in this way escapes religious claims. There are Flavia, and Miranda, as representative women. They are minutely characterized. Flavia, the genteel and orthodox lady of moderate fortune, spends half her time in bed or in visiting, in plays and in assemblies. She keeps in the fashion of the time. She dispenses her charities among the poor, although many of them she finds to be cheats. She gathers all sorts of people in her Sunday afternoon receptions, and gives audience to social lampoons. Her sister, Miranda, William Law's ideal Christian woman, is depicted fully—the devotion of herself, her time and her fortune, to God, in her exercises of prayer and her use of the Scriptures, in her charities and in her tender help for the quarrelsome, the poor, and the frail and old. She is the embodiment of Christian compassion.

Similar character-sketches are given of Fulvius, the learned neutral (cf. Dante's neutrals in his " Inferno ") ; of Flatus, the restless man, who passes from one interest to another—dress, gaming, hunting and foreign travel ; of Feliciana, Eugenius, and a dozen other representatives of ethical or religious qualities.

Chief among these is William Law's ideal of the parish clergyman, under the name of Ouranius. " In a poor country village every soul is as dear to him as himself, because he prays for them all as often as he prays for him-self. . . . When he first entered into holy orders, Ouranius had a haughtiness in his temper, a great contempt for all foolish and unreasonable people ; but he has prayed away this spirit. . . . At his first coming to his little village, it was as disagreeable to him as a prison, and every day seemed too tedious to be endured in so retired a place. He thought his parish was too full of poor and mean people that were none of them fit for the conversation of a gentleman. He kept much at home, writ notes upon Homer and Plautus, and sometimes thought it hard to be called to pray by any poor body when he was just in the midst of one of Homer's battles. . . . But now he is daily watching over the weak and infirm, humbling himself to perverse, rude, ignorant people, desiring to be the servant of all. He now thinks the poorest creature in his parish good enough and great enough to deserve the humblest attendances, the kindest friendships, the tenderest offices he can possibly show them. He thinks there is no better conversation in the world than to be talking with poor and mean people about the kingdom of heaven. He presents every one so often before God in his prayers that he never thinks he can esteem and serve those enough for whom he implores so many mercies from God." There is more in like vein, in a chapter (xxi.) on "The Benefit of Intercession."

The events in the later period of Law's life can be briefly summarized. After the break-up of the household of the Gibbons at Putney, he returned in 1740 to his native village of King's Cliffe. Three years later his house became the home of Miss Hester Gibbon and of Mrs. Hutcheson, whose husband at his death had committed her to Law's care and spiritual direction. Together they tried to carry out the precepts of the "Serious Call," in early rising, frequent devotions, and almsgiving. Out of their combined incomes of £3,000 they devoted £2,700 to charities, often indiscriminate and profuse. Beggars and other vagrants were attracted to the village from many quarters, and the rector and parishioners made open protests, but in vain. As Dean Inge says : " A saint who could never resist the impulse to liberate imprisoned canaries from their cages, to fall a prey to the nearest cat, was not the best financial adviser for two rich and not very clear-headed women. In all other ways Law's life was most exemplary."

Dr. Alexander Whyte, whose incomparable and sympathetic life-sketch and selection of extracts from all Law's writings has made us all his debtors, has described the faithful and punctilious consecration of William Law to prayers and studies. " When at any time he felt a temptation to relax his rule of early devotion, he again reminded himself how fast he was becoming an old man, and how far back his sanctification still was, till he flung himself out of bed and began again to make himself a new heart before the servants had lighted their fires or the farmers had yoked their horses." And Dr. Whyte adds: "He religiously reserved a certain spot, first of his bedroom and then of his little study, for secret prayer. He never allowed himself to do anything common on that spot, till he came to find that just to kneel in that spot was a real and sure assistance toward a spirit of prayer." One may be allowed to say now without breach of confidence that Dr. Whyte himself, his intimate friends knew, kept likewise a particular spot in his study sacred to such private devotions.[1]

## 2. Jacob Behmen and William Law

The mysticism of Jacob Behmen (1575–1624) held possession of William Law's mind and coloured his writings for the last twenty-five years of his life. His early interest in mediæval mystics like Tauler and the " Theologia Germanica " indicated his natural attraction to what he called " spiritual " writers. But it was the " Teutonic philosopher," as the unlearned cobbler of Görlitz was called, who quickened that natural interest to an enthusiasm. As the Classic under review in this chapter, the " Serious Call," appeared prior to this enthusiasm, little more need be written here of Behmen than what will suffice to promote the study of Law's later mystical books.

If out of the chaos and complexities of his writings Behmen could have composed an orderly and progressive whole, and if he had drawn together into some sort of continuous autobiography his frequent, incidental and winsome reflections on his own experience, we may well believe that one of the most illuminating and distinctive classics of the soul would have resulted.

[1] The very day that the present writer was penning the above paragraphs he happened to be reading Sir A. T. Quiller-Couch's story, " Sir John Constantine," and found these words : " The great Sir Henry Wotton, as he returned towards Eton, said to a friend that went with him, ' How useful was that advice of an old monk that we should perform our devotions in a constant place, because we so meet again with the very thoughts which possessed us at our last being there.' "

The story of this son of a cattle-herd, of this shoemaker, who had no more schooling than what enabled him to read and write, and who with original genius, though not without stimulus from Eckhardt, Paracelsus and Protestant mystics, became a great speculative and creative thinker, studied by Sir Isaac Newton and Hegel, is a strange and baffling phenomenon.  He relates how his soul, when overwhelmed in dark waters, was lifted out of the depths and moved to hazard all upon an appeal to God.  " My whole spirit seemed to me suddenly to break through the gates of hell, and to be taken up into the arms and the heart of God. Then, with all reverence I say it, with the eyes of my spirit I saw God.  I saw both what God is, and how God is what He is.  And with that there came an incontrollable impulse to set it down, so as to preserve what I had seen.  Some men will mock me, and tell me to let these high matters alone.  So I have often said to myself.  But the truth of God did burn in my bones till I took pen and ink and began to set it down.  Do not mistake me for a saint or an angel. My heart is full of evil.  In malice, in lack of brotherly love, and all manner of infirmity I am like all other men."

Again, " when the Spirit of God is taken away from me, I cannot even read so as to understand what I have myself written.  I have every day to wrestle with the devil and with my own heart, no man in all the world more.  I have no more light than thou hast.  I marvel every day that God should reveal both the Divine Nature and the Temporal and Eternal Nature for the first time to such a simple and unlearned man as I am.  But what am I to resist what God will do ?  What am I to say but, Behold the son of thine handmaiden !  I have often besought Him to take these too high and too deep matters away from me, and to commit them to men of more learning, and of a better style of speech. But He always put my prayer away from Him and continued to kindle His fire in my bones."

When the first visionary manifestations of the supernal realm were borne in upon him, he, like Mohammed in his early days as a herdsman, was perturbed and perplexed.  Without thought of making them public, he felt constrained to write them down in fragments as a " memorial."  The MSS.,

lent to a sympathetic nobleman, were copied, and came into
the hands of the ignorant and arrogant Lutheran minister
of the parish, who induced the Town Council to order him
to leave the town.   Then the magistrates permitted him
to remain, but commanded him to " stick to his last."
Always to the end a devout Lutheran, he bowed to the
authorities, and for five years he refrained from book-
writing.   Then after long musing the interior fire became so
vehement that he felt bound to give utterance to the word
of the Lord.   Other persecutions followed, driving him
into voluntary exile in Dresden, to find happily a few
friends.   His sufferings, as well as his amazing spiritual
teaching, rallied sympathizers among enlightened men.
When he died near fifty years of age, they graved on his
tombstone a cross with symbols of a lamb, an eagle, and a
lion, and his last words—" Open the door and let in more
of that music."   The rabble removed the cross ; but in
1875 a monument was erected to his honour, a great number
of shoemakers as well as scholars being present.   When we
know the story along with the writings of Jacob Behmen,
we can the better understand the Apocalypse of St. John
on the heights of the prison-isle of Patmos.

The Theosophy of Behmen, derived by immediate apprehension of reality (he believed) and not by processes of
theoretical reasoning, outranged theology and sought to
show the ultimate essence and developing order and meaning
of the universe.   His stupendous conceptions winged by
eagle imagination burst the bonds of common modes of
expression ; they cast themselves in a terminology all his
own, in writings sometimes obscure in their form and their
transcendentalism, yet through all that seems incongruous
labouring towards a consistent system of thought.   It is
not our business to deal with his cosmic speculations, which
often forecast Hegelianism—his conceptions of the Eternal
Abyss as pure Will in which all things lie potentially, of the
development of distinctions within Deity, of the eternal
procession of the Son and the Spirit, the Son as the actual-
ization of the Divine nature and the Spirit as the bond
between the Father and the Son, of the principle that things
become and are known as what they are only by division

and contrast (" Yes " vs. " No," day vs. night, good as
against evil), of the dark principles in God and the function
of evil on the way to good, of the order of the angelic world,
and much else of the kind.

Bishop Martensen, in his studies of and selections from
Behmen, urges that, as the outcome of his theosophy,
Behmen " reveals to us the LIVING GOD, the God of Goodness, the Eternal Love, God in His inmost being as most
kindred with man, even as man in his inmost being is still
kindred with God," in contrast with the Athanasian creed
which " but displays an abstruse God of mere thought, in
whom there is nothing sympathetic for the heart of man."

William Law, like many others who have read Behmen
with profit, left aside most of the theosophic system of the
naïve " Teutonic philosopher," and seized upon his more
vital spiritual mysticism.   He says that he was put into a
" perfect sweat " when he first read Behmen's speculations,
but that soon he caught glimmerings of the seer's practical
meaning and message which came upon him like a refreshing
shower of rain.   Law was always severely and narrowly
antagonistic to academic learning.   Here in Behmen he
found the untutored mind, enlightened of God, who taught
the wisdom of God in love and experimental power.

According to spiritual mysticism in Behmen and others,
as in William Law, everything in nature is a " signature "
or symbol of some Divine equivalent in an invisible world.
There is not merely an illustrative analogy between the
natural and the spiritual world ; the natural world (as we
should say) is the mask of the spiritual realm.   In Behmen's
words : " The visible world is a manifestation of the inner
spiritual world, a copy of eternity, wherewith eternity hath
made itself visible."   Hence came the sacramental view
of life, of the processes of nature.   Behmen came closer to
Christian experience when he dealt with the atonement,
redemption, and regeneration.   The imputed righteousness
of Christ applied to Christian believers is often blindly
accepted.   But a merely historical faith in ancient acts of
grace is vain, producing only nominal Christians who still
live their natural life.   " Faith is a strong desire, a hunger
and thirst after Christ and the Spirit of Christ," who " tinc-

tures " our will with the Divine will and guides it to God. It is not a mere theory with Behmen, a most practical Christian. If, he says, " thou dost once every hour throw thyself by faith beyond all creatures into the abysmal mercy of God, into the sufferings of Christ, and into the fellowship of His intercession, then thou shalt receive power from above to rule over the world, and death, and the devil, and hell itself."

It was this teaching that dominated the later mind and writings of William Law—see " The Spirit of Prayer " and " The Spirit of Love." Behmen gave him no new information, but drew out his deep and lasting religious impressions, and, without adding entirely new revelations, showed him the profound significance of Biblical revelation.

" Next to the Scriptures," wrote William Law, " my only book is the illuminated Behmen. For the whole kingdom of grace and nature was opened in him." One of the chief ideas of Law, consonant with Behmen, was that, as man was made in the image of God, God was potentially present in every man. The inwardness of the kingdoms of heaven and of hell so obtained in his mind that what was requisite was an inward Saviour, " a Saviour that is God Himself, raising His own Divine birth in the human soul." There could be no wrath in God against fallen man requiring the precious blood of His Son to pacify Him. The only wrath in the case is in man's fallen soul, and the precious blood of Christ was poured out to quench that fiery wrath and " kindle a birth of light and love."

" No son of Adam is without a Saviour, or can be lost, but by turning away from the Saviour within him." " Every man has an open gate to God in his soul." Yet we must not make a possible saint of the natural man. Nothing is safe in religion but a personal regeneration which " leaves nothing for corrupt human nature to feed upon."

As to personal assurance of salvation, the important thing is that we should be aware that we are alive and growing. Delightful religious sensations must be classed with outward blessings such as health, as allurements to piety, and not be counted among authentications of personal religion. As Fénelon in the same period said, " those who love God only out of regard to happiness love Him just as a miser loves his gold, a voluptuous man his pleasures."

William Law embodied in his later writings the suggestions he received from Behmen, and applied them practically, as in " The Spirit of Love." One may agree with Dean Inge in saying that it is, from the mystical standpoint, the masterpiece of William Law. There is much of like value in " The Spirit of Prayer," from which we take the following typical passage:

" This pearl of eternity is the Church, or temple of God within thee, the consecrated place of divine worship, where alone thou canst worship God in spirit and in truth. In spirit, because thy spirit is that alone in thee which can unite and cleave unto God, and receive the working of His Divine Spirit upon Thee. In truth, because this adoration in spirit is that truth and reality, of which all outward forms and rites, though instituted by God, are only the figure for a time, but this worship is eternal. . . . In the holy service of this inward temple . . . the holy mysteries of redemption are celebrated, or rather opened in life and power. There the Supper of the Lamb is kept; the bread that cometh down from Heaven, that giveth life to the world, is thy true nourishment; all is done and known in real experience, in a living sensibility of the work of God in the soul. There the birth, the life, the sufferings, the death, the resurrection and ascension of Christ are not merely remembered, but inwardly found and enjoyed in the real estate of thy soul, which has followed Christ in the regeneration. When once thou art well-grounded in this inward worship, thou wilt have learnt to live above time and place. For every day will be a Sunday to thee, and wheresoever thou goest, thou wilt have a priest, a church, and an altar along with thee."

This is not the ancient Biblical allegorism, which served its day in the absence of the historical method. It comes much nearer Dante's view, that there is a natural correspondence between things experienced in different spheres of life, in the seen and the unseen. William Law, a High Churchman, had no sympathy with Quakers as such, with any who are content with a silent or formless worship.

In his own words, " body and spirit are not two separate, independent things, but are necessary to each other, and are only the inward conditions of one and the same being " (" Spirit of Love "). To put it in our own terms, outward acts of concerted worship are sensible signs and valuable exercises of the inner religious spirit ; they give definiteness and stability to ideas and emotions which tend to become faint and vague if left without concrete expression. But they have validity just because they are derived from and symbolical of the essential and eternal realities in the inner life. In the above passage, which offended Wesley because he misapprehended its bearing, Law was expounding the inner essential realities of the temple which are the original of organized Church observances.

### 3. WILLIAM LAW AND JOHN WESLEY

It is a far cry from Behmen to John Wesley ; yet William Law held close relationships with both. Wesley (1703-91) was profoundly influenced in his early religious life by Law, as by Thomas à Kempis' " Imitatio Christi," and by Jeremy Taylor's " Holy Living and Holy Dying." His attitude to Law and Law's writings was at first cordially sympathetic, that of a disciple to his spiritual director, but later critically antipathetic, that of a disciple who under a distinctive experience and with a different temperament is driven to take an independent course. Divisions within the Christian Church can never be justly appreciated —independently of wilful schism and of theological and ecclesiastical controversies—unless regard is paid to such diversities in spiritual experience and in temperament, as also in traditions and in national conditions ; they are largely a matter of *spirit*, of *ethos*, which is more vitally distinguishing than doctrine or Church order, and which is not reducible to mechanical reorganization by forced measures.

These divergent attitudes correspond broadly, on the one hand, to the two phases of Law's teaching, first that of practical experimental religion, and next that of mystical vision to which the mind of Wesley was entirely alien, and, on the other hand, to the two stages in the spiritual career of John Wesley, the early formal exercises of self-effort to acquire salvation, and the subsequent experience of immediate salvation through supernatural grace by faith alone. John Wesley should rightly have an ample chapter to himself if we were here dealing with his incomparable " Journal," and with his life-work, which left an immeasurably deeper and more lasting impression upon the mind and life of Europe and America than anything William Law ever did or wrote.

Yet Wesley's " Journal,"[1] although one of the great treasures of Christian literature, does not strictly come within the compass of Classics of the Soul. After he has got well under weigh as a Gospel believer and has found his *métier*, he records practically nothing of his inner spiritual experience and personal emotions. His preaching, as he travelled up and down the country (chiefly on horseback) through forty years of amazing activity, aroused intense religious emotion among multitudes ; but in his " Journal " his eyes look outwards, not inwards. " It is not so much the story of Wesley's inner life as the record of his dealings with other people." It might almost seem as though his soul in its settled complacency endured no conflicts, no wounds, no alternations, such as we have observed in many saintly souls.

The portion of his record that calls for notice falls within his early manhood and within the period covered by his relationships with William Law.

John Wesley and his brother Charles had their early spiritual interests, acquired at home in the Epworth Rectory, intensified by William Law's " Christian Perfection " and " Serious Call," along with his personal influence. They paid visits to him while in Putney and sought his spiritual counsel. When John Wesley, after completing his curriculum and enjoying his Fellowship in Oxford

---

[1] Here it is interesting to note how, according to the original preface, " it was in pursuance of an advice given by Bishop Jeremy Taylor in his ' Rules for Holy Living and Dying ' that I began to take a more exact account of the manner wherein I had spent my time, writing down how I had employed every hour." From these notes, in twenty-six bound volumes, he selected and transcribed his " Journal."

University, was invited to go as a Missioner to Colonists and Indians in Georgia, America, he took counsel with his mother and with William Law, who both favoured the undertaking. Every one knows how powerfully Susanna Wesley impressed and how thoroughly she exercised her many children in vital religion. As he had been rescued at the last moment from the burning of the Epworth parsonage, " saved so as by fire," she accounted him a chosen vessel of the Lord, and therefore the subject of special spiritual nurture. Her method was regulative and even Spartan. She supported his acceptance of Mission work overseas in Spartan terms : " If I had twenty sons, I should rejoice that they were all so employed, though I never saw them more."

The mothers of illustrious men would form a good subject for separate study—from the Roman mother of the Gracchi, Helvia the noble-minded mother of the Stoic teacher Seneca, Monica the mother of St. Augustine, down to Susanna the mother of the Wesleys, and others outside our present survey.

This methodical and austere religious training at home had its sequel in Oxford in the so-called " Holy Club " whose members met frequently for self-improvement in Biblical knowledge, conversations with young students, the visitation of prisoners, poor families and the workhouse, the rescue of freshmen from bad company, and generally the promotion of a sober studious life. The term " Methodist " had been applied, generations earlier, to certain sectaries marked off by plain preaching and sedate ways, and was now taken over as a nickname for this " new method " of the Holy Club. Observe that their ultimate aim was the salvation of their own souls, and that they sacrificed all the luxuries and some of the common necessaries of life, until John Wesley's constitution was nearly undermined by self-mortifications.

This ascetic and serious religious interest laid him open to, and was intensified by, the teaching of William Law with its challenge to the thorough obedience of Jesus Christ. He had made much of churchly observances, and William Law appealed to him as also a High Churchman. Law's

influence  did  not  *make*  his  religion  legalistic,  though  it
did  not  lead  him  into  the  freedom  of  faith :  hence  the
rupture  that  followed  later.

Wesley  tells  us  that  he  went  out  to  Georgia  in  order  to
save  his  own  soul  and  to  learn  the  meaning  of  the  Gospel
by  preaching  it.   On  board  ship  on  the  Atlantic  his  mind
was  impressed  by  the  serenity  of  Moravian  brethren  in
the  midst  of  a  storm.   His  " Journal "  tells  of  his  labours
and  his  disappointments.   As  a  Ritualist  he  established
a  confessional  with  kindred  practices,  of  which  he  wrote
long  afterwards :  " Can  High  Church  bigotry  go  farther
than  this ?   And  how  well  have  I  since  been  beaten  with
mine  own  staff ! "   Sometimes  unwise  in  his  aggressive
way,  baffled,  and  deeply  humbled  in  mind,  he  soon  returned
home.   He  was  ill  at  ease  on  the  voyage.

" I  went  to  America,"  he  confesses  in  his  " Journal "
(24 Jan., 1738),  " to  convert  the  Indians ;  but  O !  who  shall
convert  me ?   I  have  a  fair  summer  religion.   I  can  talk
well ;  nay,  and  believe  myself  while  no  danger  is  near ;  but  let
death  look  me  in  the  face  and  my  spirit  is  troubled.  . . .  I
think  verily,  if  the  Gospel  is  true,  I  am  safe :  for  I  not  only
have  given,  and  do  give,  all  my  goods  to  feed  the  poor ;
I  not  only  give  my  body  to  be  burned,  drowned,  or  whatever
God  shall  appoint  for  me ;  but  I  follow  after  charity  (though
not  as  I  ought  yet  as  I  can)  if  haply  I  may  attain  it.  . . .
Whoever  sees  me  sees  I  would  be  a  Christian.   Therefore
I  have  been,  I  am  content  to  be,  a ' by-word,  a  proverb
of  reproach.'   But  in  a  storm  I  think, ' What  if  the  Gospel
be  not  true ?   Then  thou  art  of  all  men  most  foolish.
For  what  hast  thou  given  thy  goods,  thy  ease,  thy  friends,
thy  reputation,  thy  country,  thy  life ?   For  what  art
thou  wandering  over  the  face  of  the  earth ?—A  dream !  a
cunningly-devised  fable ! '

" O !  who  will  deliver  me  from  this  fear  of  death ?   What
shall  I  do ?   Where  shall  I  fly  from  it ?   Should  I  fight  against
it  by  thinking,  or  by  not  thinking  of  it ?   A  wise  man  advised  me  some  time  since, ' Be  still  and  go  on.'   Perhaps
this  is  best,  to  look  upon  it  as  my  cross ;  when  it  comes,  to
let  it  humble  me,  and  quicken  all  my  good  resolutions,
especially  that  of  praying  without  ceasing ;  and,  at  other

times, to take no thought about it, but quietly to go on, in the work of the Lord."

In London he almost immediately met and had spiritual converse with Peter Böhler, one of the Moravian missionary brethren for whom he had already acquired a high regard. Böhler, ten years his junior, urged upon his distracted mind the acceptance of salvation through free grace by faith alone, teaching him that salvation is sudden and the assurance of it is faith, and enjoining him meanwhile to go on preaching and to " preach faith alone till you have it, and then because you have it you will preach faith " (a very Pragmatic injunction). Böhler goes on his way to the Carolinas. Wesley, while preaching here and there, still shrinks, as throughout his life he shrinks, from unreasoned emotional experiences.

Then within a few weeks, on 24 May, 1738, in his thirty-fifth year, as he records in his " Journal," " In the evening I went very unwillingly to a society in Aldersgate St., where one was reading Luther's preface to the Epistle to the Romans. While he was describing the change which God works in the heart through faith, I felt my heart strangely warmed. I felt I did trust in Christ, in Christ alone, for salvation ; and an assurance was given me that He had taken away my sins, even mine, and saved me from the law of sin and death." Tempted by doubts from lack of transports of joy, he learns that " God sometimes giveth and sometimes withholdeth them," and " I found all my strength lay in keeping my eyes fixed on Him, and my soul waiting on Him continually."

This passage in the " Journal " is the *locus classicus* in his spiritual history and in the annals of Methodism. He counted the occasion his spiritual birthday.

He declared that until that date he had never been a Christian. He wrote : " I who went to America to convert others was never myself converted to God," but in an apparently later footnote he says, " I am not sure of this." His judicious brother Charles, the hymnist, deprecated such extravagent statements as likely to discourage many earnest people. John a year later writes, " I am not a Christian at this day ; for a Christian is one who has the fruits of the Spirit, which (to mention no more) are love, peace, joy. But these I have not." But here he has sunk into a moment of depression. He was not always self-consistent, and his judgment of men and things was occasionally at fault. In his old age he wrote, " When fifty years ago my brother Charles and I, in the simplicity of our hearts, taught the people that unless they knew their sins forgiven they were under the wrath and curse of God, I wonder that they did not stone us. The Methodists know better now." At another time he says, with more discrimination, that formerly he " had only the faith of a *servant*—now, that of a *son*."

He was an intensely religious man, seeking eternal life under favour of Christ, for many years before he passed through the sharp evangelical experience after the Augustinian type. The question is, not whether he was a Christian, but how much of a Christian he was. It is a mistake to impose a specific evangelical crisis upon all as a condition of Christian life. This is to narrow the scope of the Gospel and to exclude many from the kingdom whom God has not excluded. Dr. Chalmers received a re-quickening when more than half-way through his noble ministry, and, like Chalmers, Wesley thereafter was a new man in spiritual power.

Wesley, in his zeal, exaggerating his new experience, turned upon his former master William Law with censorious correction and rebuke, opening a long-lasting rift between them.

John Wesley's letter to William Law, his former master, runs thus : " It is in obedience to what I think the call of God that I, who have the sentence of death in my own soul, take upon me to write to you, of whom I have often desired to have the first elements of the Gospel of Christ. If you are born of God, you will approve of the design ; if not, I shall grieve for you, not for myself. For as I seek not the praise of men, so neither regard I the contempt of you or any other.

" For two years I have been preaching after the model of your two practical treatises, and all who heard allowed that the law was great, wonderful and holy ; but when they attempted to fulfil it they found that it was too high for

man ; by the doings of the law no flesh could be justified.
. . . I might have groaned to death had not a holy man of
God (Böhler) directed me, saying, ' Believe and thou shalt
be saved.'

" Now how will you justify it to our common Lord that
you never gave me this advice ? Why did I scarcely ever
hear you name the name of Christ, never so as to ground
anything upon faith in His blood ? If you say you advised
other things as preparatory to this, what is this but laying
a foundation below the foundation ? Is not Christ the
First as well as the Last ? If you say you advised this
because you knew that I had faith already, you discerned
not my spirit at all. Consider deeply and impartially
whether the true cause of your never pressing this upon
me was this, that you had it not yourself." In closing
Wesley warned Law, on the authority of Peter Böhler,
whom he called a man of God, that his state was a very
dangerous one ; and asked him whether his extreme rough-
ness and morose and sour behaviour could possibly be the
fruit of a living faith in Christ.

William Law's reply runs thus :

" Rev. Sir,—Yours I received yesterday. As you have
written that letter in obedience to a Divine call, and in
conjunction with another extraordinary good young man,
whom you know to have the spirit of God, so I assure you
that, considering your letter in that view, I neither desire
nor dare to make the smallest defence of myself. . . . But
now, upon supposition that you had here only acted by
that ordinary light which is common to good and sober
minds, I should remark upon your letter as follows : How
you may have been two years preaching the doctrine of
the two practical discourses, or how you may have tired
yourself and your hearers to no purpose, is what I cannot
say much to. A holy man, you say, taught you this :
' Believe and thou shalt be saved,' etc. I am to suppose
that till you met this holy man you had not been taught
this doctrine. Did you not above two years ago give a
new translation of Thomas à Kempis ? Will you call
Thomas to account and to answer it to God, as you do me,
for not teaching you that doctrine ? Or will you say that

you took upon you to restore the true sense of that divine
writer, and instruct others how they might profit by reading
him, before you had so much as a literal knowledge of the
most plain, open, and repeated doctrine in his book ?  You
cannot but remember what value I always expressed of
à Kempis, and how much I recommended it to your meditations.  You have had a great many conversations with
me, and I daresay you never was with me half an hour
without my being large upon that very doctrine which you
make me totally silent and ignorant of.  How far I may
have discovered your spirit and the spirit of others that
may have conversed with me may perhaps be more a
secret to you than you imagine.  But granting you to be
right in your account of your own faith, how am I charge-
able with it ?  I am to suppose that you had been meditating
upon an author that of all others leads us the most directly
to a real living faith in Jesus Christ ; after you had judged
yourself such a master of his sentiments and his doctrines
as to be able to publish them to the world with directions
and instructions on such experimental divinity, that after
you had done this you had only the faith of a Judas or a
devil, an empty notion only in your head ; and that you
were thus through ignorance that there was anything
better to be sought after ; and that you were thus ignorant
because I never directed or called you to this faith.  But,
sir, à Kempis and I have both had your acquaintance and
conversation, so pray let the fault be divided betwixt us,
and I shall be content to have it said that I left you in as
much ignorance of this faith as he did, or that you learnt
no more of it by conversing with me than with him.  If
you had only this faith till some weeks ago, let me advise
you not to be hasty in believing that because you change
your language and expressions, you have changed your
faith.  The head can as easily amuse itself with a living and
justifying faith in the blood of Jesus as with any other
notion ; and the heart, which you suppose to be a place
of security, as being the seat of self-love, is more deceitful
than the head.  Your last paragraph, concerning my sour,
rough behaviour, I leave in its full force ; whatever you can
say of me of that kind without hurting yourself will always

be well received by me." Other letters in rejoinder were exchanged, but they are of no moment for us, although one short passage imports another of our Classics into the case.

Law writes : " If you remember the ' Theologia Germanica ' so imperfectly as only to remember something of Christ our Pattern, but nothing express of Christ our Atonement, it is no wonder that you can remember so little of my conversation with you. I put that author into your hands, not because he is fit for the first learners of the rudiments of Christianity. . . . but because you were a *clergyman*, that had made profession of divinity, and had read (as you said) the (my) two practical discourses. . . . The book contains the whole system of Christian faith and practice, and is an excellent guide against all mistakes both in faith and works. What that book has not taught you, I am content that you should not have learnt from me."

The larger measure of blame for this dissension between two godly Anglican clergymen is, it is curious to note, ascribed to John Wesley by Tyerman the Wesleyan in his biography of Wesley, and to William Law by Overton the Anglican in his biography of Law ! Readers will see for themselves wherein Wesley's letter, while animated by a pure motive, was offensive, especially to his senior and former spiritual director, and at the same time how caustic and cutting was the reply of the skilled controversialist William Law, while keeping within the bounds of formal courtesy.

Why should we recall this dissension ? Not for the unholy satisfaction of discovering the foibles of the saints, the infirmities which show them to be akin with ourselves. These letters are cited because in a concrete case they bring to a focus certain psychic, temperamental sources of division within the fellowship of faithful men ; and because they reflect different conceptions of the experimental process by which men become Christians. One conception of it urges the efficiency of religious education (such as Horace Bushnell taught in his " Christian Nurture "), spiritual tuition in faith and practice as the agency of the Spirit by which, through gradual percolation, the soul is quickened and cleansed ; the other urges the necessity of a revolutionary and somewhat phenomenal change standardized under the term conversion. From the psychological point of view there is no fundamental difference between the two experiences, however different the duration, the phases, and the compass thereof. A different emphasis is laid on this or on that factor in the process. But what radically matters in becoming a disciple of Jesus Christ is, not the mode or other phenomena of the experience, but the vitality of the soul, and its direction of heart and will to God and to the needs of fellowmen.

It will generally be admitted that William Law's books were not such as to meet the immediate needs of those lying under heavy conviction of sin ; they had other uses, in accord with his own experience and observations. Law and Wesley each spoke as he saw and felt, each presenting an aspect of the " truth as it is in Jesus."

Both William Law and John Wesley underwent a re-quickening of personal religion in the course of their Christian ministry. In the case of Wesley it was, as already indicated, an evangelical renewal ; in the case of Law it came later in the form of mystical illumination, which gave him more penetrating insight while limiting the public able to appreciate him. When this mystical development became pronounced in Law's writings, Wesley was further estranged from his old master and published an Open Letter to him for the benefit of Christians generally, which Whitefield and other friends condemned as not only injudicious but un-Christian. While yet under the counsel of Law, he had read the German Mystics, but later he wrote to his brother Samuel, " I think the rock on which I had the nearest made shipwreck of the faith was the writings of the Mystics." He called them " one great antichrist." Dangerous enemies to Christianity, " they stab it in the vitals." The whole of Behmen's teaching is " sublime nonsense, inimitable bombast."

Thus far and no farther was he able to penetrate into " The Beyond that is Within," into the supernal realms discovered by intuitive insight beyond clear reasoning. But, for one thing, like many others since his day, he was un-

aware of the true meaning of mysticism, and thus overlooked the difference between speculative mysticism (much
of which might be called " clotted nonsense ") and spiritual
mysticism, sane and free from unnatural rapture.  For
another thing, Wesley (as one of his best biographers says)
" had all the eighteenth-century confidence in sense and
reason.  Although it was his religious mission to bring new
warmth and light to the religious life of England, yet he
shared the general distrust of enthusiasm, of any conduct
that could not be defended by reason."  When Anglican
brethren charged him with " enthusiasm " he replied :
" The reproach of Christ I am willing to bear ; but not the
reproach of enthusiasm—if I can help it."  Eminently
practical, he was impatient of any religion that could not
give a clear account of itself.  The preacher who roused so
many to excitement was himself collected, logical, and
masterful in the enforcement of plain truths.

Yet, making allowance for his temperament and special
experience, he seems inconsistent in his attitude to quietism and mysticism in that he published a Life of Madame
Guyon the quietist, and in his " Christian Library " of fifty
volumes he made ample extracts from mystical treatises.
On the other hand, Luther's " Commentary on The Epistle
to the Galatians," the book which served Bunyan so well
in his dire crisis, and which is a classic among Protestant
documents, he condemned as " shallow, muddy and confused " because it is " deeply tinctured with mysticism,
and hence often dangerously wrong."

Equally puzzling is the deep offence given to Wesley
by Law's beautiful interpretation of the temple as symbolic of worship in spirit—" This pearl of eternity is the
Church, or temple of God within thee." . . .—quoted
above (p. 210).

Law on his side could be uncompromising and peremptory.
He once wrote to Wesley in reply to a question : " You
would have a philosophical religion ; but there can be
no such thing.  Religion is the most plain, simple thing
in the world : it is only, We love Him because He first
loved us."  This answer reveals Law's distaste for human
learning, while himself a learned scholar, and also his

stiff severity of tone. Deep down under forms of controversy they really came close together.

In spite of the rift John Wesley always paid cordial tribute to what he counted the best in William Law, both in "The Serious Call" and in "Christian Perfection." He did so incidentally in private, often in his preaching, and likewise in his letters. In one of these he says that Law's "treatises must remain, as long as England stands, almost unequalled standards of the strength and purity of our language, as well as of sound practical divinity." He used "The Serious Call" as a textbook for the highest class in his school at Kingswood. He publicly stated that all Methodists were greatly profited by these two books.

He remained a resolute clergyman of the Anglican Church to the end of his ministry of half a century, while organizing "Methodist Societies," preaching agencies, and more good work than can be told, and all this time his catholicity of spirit grew and found voice. As thus: "The distinguishing marks of a Methodist [are they strictly distinguishing, or rather characteristic?] are not his opinions of any sort. His assenting to this or that scheme of religion, his embracing any particular set of notions, his espousing the judgment of one man or another, are all quite wide of the point. . . Is thy heart right, as my heart is with thine? I ask now no further question. If it be, give me thy hand. Dost thou love and serve God? It is enough. I give thee the right hand of fellowship."

The geniality of Wesley grew through daily contact with all sorts of people, in contrast with the austere detachment of Law, who lived for study in comparative solitude. Wesley's sense of humour, which appears more freely in his "Letters," is very slightly evidenced in his "Journal." Sometimes it appears, by mere suggestion, "extra-dry" humour: as, in describing a hostile mob that threw stones at him, he adds that "a very large gentlewoman sat in my lap and screened me, so that nothing came near me." (He does not tell by what special providence the large gentlewoman was protected, or whether she received some stones intended for the chivalrous gentleman!)

Living among average humanity through fifty years of

itineracy he must have encountered humorous situations and characters, including early Methodists of the type of Mrs. Poyser in George Eliot's "Adam Bede." But he shows no natural appreciation of the humours of life. In his interviews and dealings with casuals and critics, repeatedly he shows "a very pretty wit," usually with a satiric edge, as when he says : "I talked with a warm man who was always very zealous for the Church when he was very drunk, and just able to stammer out, 'No gown, no crown.' He was quickly persuaded that, whatever we were, he himself was a child of the devil. We left him full of good resolutions, which lasted several days."

The best-known example—in a passing tilt between a Calvinist and Wesley an Arminian—may here be added. On a journey "I overtook a serious man with whom I immediately fell into conversation. He presently gave me to know what his opinions were, therefore I said nothing to contradict them. But that did not content him. He was quite uneasy to know 'whether I held the doctrines of the decrees as he did ; ' but I told him over and over, 'We had better keep to practical things lest we should be angry at one another.' And so we did for two miles till he caught me unawares and dragged me into the dispute before I knew where I was. He then grew warmer and warmer ; told me I was rotten at heart and supposed I was one of John Wesley's followers. I told him 'No. I am John Wesley himself.' Upon which . . . he would gladly have run away outright. But being the better mounted of the two I kept close to his side and endeavoured to show him his heart till we came into the street of Northampton " (20 May, 1742). A queer scamper in which each in turn tries to shake off the other, and Wesley, the better mounted of the two, preaches to the fugitive as they ride at full speed !

Wesley was usually more profitably engaged in his long and constant rides ; it was on horseback that he did much of his extensive reading.[1] By such means he indefatigably maintained his literary and scholarly culture.

[1] "Near thirty years ago " (" Journal," April, 1770) " I was thinking, ' How is it that no horse ever stumbles while I am reading ? ' (History,

In a letter on " Christian Perfection " as taught in Methodist Societies, in reply to an inquiry from " a pious and sensible woman," we can observe reflections of William Law's early book on that subject (see *supra*, p. 197). " By Christian perfection I mean, (1) Loving God with all our hearts. Do you object to this? I mean (2) A heart and life all devoted to God. Do you desire less? I mean (3) Regaining the whole image of God. What objection to this? I mean (4) Having all the mind that was in Christ. Is this going too far? I mean (5) Walking uniformly as Christ walked. And this surely no Christian will object to " (" Journal," 27 June, 1769). All true, though these five points are not all distinctive one from another. But it was well that Wesley had already explained that they " *laboured* to distinguish themselves " by such marks, without claiming to realize them perfectly. So we may say the perfection of " those called to be saints " lies in integrity of purpose and fullness of endeavour after union with God and with fellowmen through oneness with Jesus Christ in spirit and in service.

Wesley once met a " serious man " who said to him, " Sir, you wish to serve God and go to heaven. Remember you cannot serve Him alone. You must therefore find companions or make them. The Bible knows nothing of solitary religion." Which recalls Thomas à Kempis' maxim, " If thou wouldest be carried, carry another." The good word of that " serious man " resounds through Wesley's stupendous life-work—which it is impossible to survey here—and through his " Journal." His religion was not " solitary." We may apply to him Matthew

poetry and philosophy I commonly read on horseback, having other employment at other times.) No account can possibly be given but this: because then I throw the reins on his neck. I then set myself to observe ; and I aver that in riding over one hundred thousand miles I scarce ever remember any horse (except two, that would fall head over heels any way) to fall, or make a considerable stumble while I rode with a slack rein. To fancy, therefore, that a tight rein prevents stumbling is a capital blunder. . . . A slack rein will prevent it if anything will. But in some horses nothing can."

Wesley does not draw a moral as to human nature—the wise management of those under us by trusting much to themselves for the prevention of stumbling !

Arnold's words in his memorial in " Rugby Chapel " to his
father, Dr. Arnold:

> " Therefore to him it was given
> Many to save with himself. . . .
>
> Langour was not in his heart,
> Weakness not in his word,
> Weariness not on his brow."

Wesley's " Journal " is one of the primary documents
descriptive of the general condition of the people of England
in the eighteenth century.   That is not our present theme.
But, it falls to be said here, two of the dominant religious
tides and concrete movements running from the eighteenth
through the nineteenth century had their core in John Wesley's " Journal " and John Henry Newman's " Apologia pro
Vita Sua " ; namely, the Evangelical Revival generating
social reform, the other the Anglo-Catholic revival with its
spiritual enrichment of the Church along with its Romeward
reaction.

Incidentally it is interesting, and appropriate to the
general purport of this volume, to note that these two had
fontal connections.  Newman, also, was deeply influenced
by William Law in his formative years, both directly by
reading his early writings, and indirectly through Thomas
Scott, the Bible commentator, who owed a vital religious
impulse to Law, and who rendered the same to Newman
while an Oxford undergraduate.   Scott tells how, " carelessly
taking up Law's ' Serious Call,' I had no sooner opened it
than I was struck with the originality of the work and the
spirit and force of the argument. . . .  I was convinced
that I was guilty of great remissness and negligence ; that
the duties of secret devotion called for far more of my time
and attention than had been hitherto allotted to them ;
and that, if I hoped to save my own soul and the souls of
those that heard me, I must in this respect greatly alter my
conduct, and increase my diligence in seeking and serving
the Lord.   From that time I began " to amend.

Newman, in his " Apologia " (cap. i), after telling how a
work by Romaine made him conscious of his "inward conversion (of which I am still more certain than that I have
hands and feet)," he proceeds to pay honour to " the writer

who made a deeper impression on my mind than any other,
and to whom (humanly speaking) I almost owe my soul—
Thomas Scott. I so admired and delighted in his writings
that, when I was an undergraduate, I thought of making a
visit to his parsonage in order to see a man whom I so deeply
revered." But death interposed. He studied his writings,
including his " Commentary." What impressed Newman
(he says) was his " bold unworldliness and vigorous independence of mind. He followed truth wherever it led him.
. . . It was he who first planted deep in my mind that
fundamental truth of religion, the doctrine of the Holy
Trinity. . . . For years I used almost as proverbs what I
considered to be the scope and issue of his doctrine, *Holiness
rather than peace*, and *Growth the only evidence of life*."

Therein lay some of the primary germs of Newman's
life-course—" following truth wherever it led," and the
spiritual principles of holiness and growth. His " Apologia,"
while one of the great documents in religious literature, cast
in confessional form—see Appendix, Kindred Classics in
Brief—is chiefly engaged with a controversial, often
teasing, yet fascinating vindication of his life-course from
the Church of England to the Church of Rome. But it is to
be noted at this early stage of his spiritual pilgrimage that
the most creative elements in his personal experience came
from evangelical sources such as Romaine and Thomas
Scott. And this evangelical *sap* was preserved in Newman's
work, and the Anglo-Catholic movement of later days.
It brought refreshing life to the Church, despite Newman's
flight to Rome and despite the recrudescence of mediæval
theories and practices.

To return to Wesley's co-ordinate influence in the world—
which he took as " my parish "—Augustine Birrell declares :
" You cannot cut him out of our national life. No single
figure influenced so many minds, no single voice touched so
many hearts. No other man did such a life's work for
England."

Let another give his estimate of the spiritual aspect of
Wesley's " Journal," namely, Sir William Robertson Nicoll.
" It is pre-eminently the book of the resurrection life lived
in the world. It has very few companions. It stands out

. . . clear, detached, columnar. It is a tree that is ever green before the Lord. It tells us of a heart that kept to the last its innocent pleasures and interests, but held them all loosely and lightly, while its Christian, passionate peace grew and grew to the end. To the end these are, not diminishing, but increasing : the old zeal, the old wistfulness, the calm but fiery revealing eloquence. John Wesley was indeed one of those who attained the Second Rest—of those who, to use his own fine words, are ' at rest before they go home : possessors of that rest which remaineth even here for the people of God.' "

## XII

## Tolstoy's " Confessions "

IN Tolstoy we find ourselves in a new generation, which manifests a different inspiration and is working out a new order of values for life. A new standpoint in religion has been reached. The centre of gravity has shifted from a future heaven to the kingdom or reign of God in the application of Christian principles within the sphere of human society. Another vision has come, the vision of a cleaner earth and a closer heaven.

Tolstoy is included among these studies, not only because his " Confessions " must be placed in the front rank of documents of the human soul, but because he is representative of the modern social aspect and application of Christianity. The process of his own spiritual history arises and moves within the action of social conditions and forces and is bound up with significant socio-political movements. Here the Christian life is conceived and interpreted in terms of the commonweal, or at least of the individual in his relation to the community. In this respect Tolstoy is unique in the succession of seers in our present purview.

### I

It has always been difficult for men of the Western world to enter into the mind of the Slav, peculiarly difficult to ascertain and characterize the native spirit of Russia ; it is now more difficult than ever. To understand Tolstoy we must think of Russia before recent revolution ending in a debacle confused and obscured the situation. Here, accordingly, we take our stand in the past century.

The sacred fire of freedom has for long generations burnt

fervid in the soul of Russia. The world generally saw, and we were all struck by, the autocratic imperialism, the bureaucracy, the military and secret police, the gag on the mouth of the press, the multitudes of exiles to Siberia, the subjection of Finland, the pogrom in which the Jews were baited. But all that was only the outside of the case. Organized government had imposed itself on the people, and was not evolved out of their own life.

A responsible Russian writer (Berdyaev) declared that " imperial power was always an external, not an internal principle in the mind of the unimperialistic Russian people. It did not grow out of them, but came to them from the outside. And that is why power frequently produced the impression of something foreign—a sort of German power."

In fact, the citizens have mostly wished to be free to live their own lives, and have had little interest in the state. They indeed have been lacking in the desire for order, and showed little capacity for organization until the Unions of Towns and Zemstvos (County Councils) came. As the same writer said, " it is as if the Russian people did not wish a free empire—did not so much wish freedom in their empire as freedom from empire, freedom from all care of earthly management. The Russian people does not wish to be a dominating superior ; its nature is passive, rather gentle, ready to obey—more like that of a wife than that of a husband. Passive, receptive in its relation to imperial matters and power—such is the character of the Russian people and of their history. There are no limits to the meek patience of the long-suffering people."

" There is not in the world a country whose population is more distrustful of the directing element than Russia," says the Russian writer, Alexinsky, ex-deputy of the Duma (" Modern Russia," p. 89). " This suspiciousness of the Russian peasant extends even to persons who are sincerely resolved to devote their labour and their energies to the people "—as illustrated during the cholera epidemic of 1902, when " peasants destroyed hospitals and barracks prepared for those stricken with the disease, beat and killed doctors and nurses."

We hoped the world-war would demand and develop the

capacity for organization. But it seems that it was just this somewhat easy-going love for a let-alone freedom that left the Russian people to be mastered by autocrats and again by revolutionaries; and the latter can be as despotic as the former, for both are organizations of force. Maxim Gorky, writing two years after the war, said that Tolstoy, "national in the most complete sense, embodied in his great soul all the defects of his nation, all the mutations we have suffered by the ordeals of our history."

The Russian mind is said to be full of paradoxes and surprises, and to be unfathomable. But this may be true partly because Russia is an overgrown child and the child-mind is paradoxical and unfathomable. Russia has not yet discovered herself. The child-mind of the people is coming to self-consciousness.

The plain Russian of the country—to go back before the Revolution to Tolstoy's time—has to our eyes a stolid, heavy, unkempt look. The people spread over the wide expanse of country are still close to primitive nature, showing much that is naturistic and instinctive, for better and for worse. They are still responsive to the cry of the earth, to the cry of the forest, to the cry of the wolf, to the weird things of the night, and to the winds of the impenetrable winters and the lone, wide steppes. They have hauntings of old tremors, of the unseen, of change, and demons, and death—and of angels singing from the skies to the shepherds. They have keen sensibilities, both of physical sense and of spirit, and can break into raw rage, deeds of violence and sensuality, or can be lifted to a high pitch of heedless heroism and enthusiasm. The lights and again the shadows follow close on each other over their faces. With keen feeling and vivid imagination, they are subject to moods of sadness, sometimes desperate melancholy and occasionally gloom, and so are subject to despair in private troubles as also in politics; the clank of fetters runs through their writings. Yet they are not on the whole gloomy, but rather light-hearted, passing easily from sobs to laughter and lively talk in the tavern or the fair, so that they seem often wilful.

Russian novelists have shown a notable power of psychological analysis, worked out with much elaboration, minuteness, and candour regarding themselves. " Russia is the nation which, above all other great nations in our day, has the most tragic destiny, suffers most deeply " ; and her great writers, with so deep a compassion, fathom the abysses of suffering, although a few, like Gogol, can be cheery if not gay. As Stephen Graham depicts them, from his partial angle, they show a naive simplicity, faith, and yet eager questioning, open to all they can see or learn.

They are hospitable, both in social relations and in their minds. They are rich in pity for all suffering, as they also are great sufferers—what glory they have found in suffering ! They have a great tenderness for even the wrongdoer, accept him or her as part of the inevitable order of things, and do not condemn, so that they often seem lax in their moral attitude. They have a sense of the pathetic destinies of mortals, touched with Oriental fatalism.

They have a quick sense of wonder and mystery : the skies are still peopled ; the vast, rolling country has helped to give them a sense of vastness, of the magnitude of things. " Every common bush is aflame with God." They are therefore subject to what we could call superstition, and to the panics that accompany it ; but it is not superstition to them, it is sincere belief in the unseen. Pilgrims abound, as do ikons.

They can, especially when highly educated, become the most antagonistic to Church and creed—intellectual nihilists. But even when materialistic, they are always touched with mysticism. Like the people of India, they are deeply religious, and of religion they are not ashamed, talking of it freely in trains and taverns.

Their Church services are rich, impressive beyond all others, with the most inspiring, poignant, heart-searching, subduing music, full of hauntings of winds and seas, tragedy and triumph.

They are among the most definitely Christian people anywhere, though pagan remainders still show through, and naturalistic feelings survive. The Church (Orthodox) may seem fettered, but within it all the Christian sentiments of love, brotherhood, suffering borne patiently, abound.

Patience, endurance, kindness—such qualities more than balance their well-known defects.

Count Leo Tolstoy (1828–1910) remains an authentic Russian voice. There have indeed been other national voices, and new voices, expressing different elements in the modern Russian life and mind. But he embodies personally the older native spirit of the people, reflects in his utterances and conflicts the indigenous dispositions of the Russians, even though they in general would not agree with his final judgments upon religion, social conduct, and the State.

The economic and social conditions of Russia to-day are of recent growth and are not found reflected in Tolstoy's outlook. The industrial proletariat of the cities and the capitalists and the bourgeoisie of the mercantile middle classes were foreign to his interest. The Russian society he knew comprised chiefly the class of nobles and landowners to which he belonged, the civil bureaucrats who ran national affairs, the military who were the instruments of the rulers, and the vast multitudes of peasants who had been emancipated from serfdom. With political revolutionaries he had no kinship ; revolutionaries and autocrats were alike alien to his mind, equally dangerous. On the other hand he, like the Russian unspoilt by Westernism, disliked all government, and desired the freedom of simple human relations, and common toil and service. In this as in other ways he represented the characteristic spirit of the home-grown Russian (cf. Alexinsky's " Modern Russia," 347, 349).

## II

Tolstoy delivered his mind in one of the great documents of the human soul, " My Confession," amplified in " My Religion," written with concentrated energies of heart and thought when at the age of fifty he emerged from a tremendous inner struggle lasting five years and found a faith and a foothold in life. Almost all his works were self-revealing fragments of a great confession—" Youth," " War and Peace," " Anna Karenina," " Resurrection."

" My Confession " may be ranked with St. Augustine's " Confessions," and even with Bunyan's " Grace Abounding " and other classics of the soul. It is more modern in that it shows the reaction of his sensibilities on the social order. His inward spiritual crisis is essentially one with the politico-social crisis.

Psychologically considered, his inner history follows the main stages common to many soul-histories. There is the traditional faith, with conventional life, disturbed in youth by contact with a wider world and by hunger of mind and soul for life in its fullness, for reality, for the truth. Then there is the moral discord, the lapse into evil ways, the sway of sense, the glamour of world-interests in human enterprise and fame. There are ever-recurring visitations of conscience, recoil from the things enjoyed, unrest, distraction between opposing dispositions and aims. Then comes disenchantment, despondency, occasionally touched with hopes and pledges that swiftly pass. Then, in a desperate struggle through much turmoil and gloom, the baffled and almost exhausted spirit takes its decision, gets its moment of insight in which a few vital things become clear and sure, and all the confusion of the soul-storm passes into settled peace.

His "Confession," while in essence kindred with the experience of other living spirits, has an individual character, distinctive features. He is characterized by introspective egoism, lack of humour, headstrong wilfulness, yet vacillation, humanist sympathies yet fundamentally aristocratic pride. There were always, not only in his spiritual transition, two sides to his nature, two Tolstoys.

The distinctive quality of his experience springs, not merely from his personal idiosyncrasies, but from his Russian temperament and from the social and political conditions in Russia in which he lived. His course of experience shows " the immense pressure of the Russian social order upon his over-sensitive soul," and the transitional movement in the Russian nation.

The leading external facts in his career may be quickly summarized. Born in 1828 at Yasnaya Polyana in South Central Russia, of a noble titled family of landowners, we find him destined to a legal career, studying at the universities of Kazan and then of St. Petersburg. A keen student of literature, an ardent sportsman, a resident of Moscow, he goes off as a soldier to his brother in the Caucasus, fights in the Crimean War, enduring the terrible siege of Sebastopol (" War and Peace " illustrates his horror of war, his later war against war).   He leaves the army, settles on his estate, devotes himself to educating and assisting the peasants under him, travels across Europe, marries, continues to write books and keep up intercourse with the kindred and literary friends of his own class.   Incidentally, he organizes relief for the famine-stricken.   Later he relinquishes his property in land and in book copyrights, having adopted views of peaceful anarchism.   Owing to his teaching he is practically excommunicated as a fanatic by the Holy Synod of the Orthodox Church, his books being prohibited in Russia. He leaves house and family by stealth with crazy socialist notions, and in 1910, aged eighty-two, dies before he can be brought home again.

Such a career affords scope and material for a distinctive inner drama.

We select the most vital and significant passages in " My Confession " with additions from other works, e.g. " Anna Karenina," in which Levin reflects Tolstoy at a critical stage in his career, and " Resurrection," in which Nekhludoff represents the author after he has found the new life.

He starts by telling that he was christened and educated in the Orthodox faith, but as a university student of eighteen he found he had discarded all religious belief.   Comrades of his own social standing had done the same.   He had read Voltaire without any sense of shock at his mockery of sacred things, and later he read Rousseau and philosophical books. The old practice of prayer and church-worship was abandoned.   Spasms of serious thought and relenting recurred— mark the two sides of his nature, pagan and spiritual—and he suffered from a surge of conflicting moods.   " I desired with all my soul to be good ; but I was young, I had passions, and I was wholly alone in my search after goodness."   He drew up good rules of conduct—witness his Diary—but they were swiftly forgotten.

Such was his life for ten years.   When a soldier, he indulged in gambling (involving heavy burdens of debt), sensuality, vanity.   He exaggerates, in recalling these years from a later date, when he says : " I put men to death in war, I fought duels to slay others, I lost at cards, wasted my substance wrung from the sweat of peasants, punished the latter cruelly, rioted with loose women, and deceived men. Lying, robbery, adultery of all kinds, drunkenness, violence, murder I committed. Yet I was none the less considered by my equals a comparatively moral man." His intellectual companions in the great cities had a theory justifying this sort of life—it was development, self-realization.

He was ambitious for fame as a writer and for the reward in money and power, and shared in festivities with other writers and thinkers. He and his literary friends disputed, quarrelled, yet praised each other in turn for the returned words of praise. But often he concealed under a mask of indifference or pleasantries those yearnings for something better that formed the real intent of his life. He was secretly disgusted with mankind and with himself. Such was his life for some six years.

He travelled through Western Europe, and saw in Paris a man guillotined; he was revolted at the useless punishment which passed as justice. He returned and settled in the country, organizing schools for the peasantry. The serfs had just been emancipated, and he was appointed an arbitrator.

All the time his mind was seeking escape from the contradictions of life, escape from the leash of self-love. Despair might have overtaken him then, as it did fifteen years later, but that he married, and found in family life safety from temptations.

The circumstances of his happy family life kept his mind away from the search for the meaning of life, engaged as he was in increasing the means of life for the sake of his household. He enjoyed the seductions of authorship, enormous monetary rewards and great public applause. " In this way fifteen years passed."

He tells how for the next five years he had recurring periods of strange perplexity and a stoppage of life, feeling lost and dejected. He found it was no chance indisposition. These questions persisted : " What's it for ? What does

it lead to ? "    He tried to satisfy himself by recalling that
he had his estates to look after, his peasants to help, and
that his writings had fame among the great ones.  But
what did it all amount to, what was it all for ?  His life
had come to a standstill.  If a fairy had come and offered
him anything he cared to have, he would not have known
what to ask.  He went on living, walking as it were auto-
matically, and found it impossible to go back, impossible
to close his eyes or avoid seeing that there was nothing
before him but suffering and real death, annihilation.  He,
a healthy, fortunate man, with happy home, estate, respect
of friends and praise, felt he could no longer live.  In sound
mental state, he yet hid a cord from himself in his room lest
he should hang himself, and ceased going out to shoot lest
he should turn the gun on himself to end it all.

One may import at this point some remarks, based on
other writings of his, upon the haunting sense of death as
the grand evil that during most of his life overshadowed his
mind and oppressed his spirits.  In the procession and feast
of human life he sees quiveringly, in almost the same form
as Sakya-muni saw, how mortals are seized now by misery
in misfortune, now by old age that follows close on youth,
and again by death that ends the banquet of life before it has
been well tasted.  Repeatedly he gives us the " very psychology of death "—in his " Youth," in his description of the
deaths of his mother and his grandmother, in his war-stories
(describing the soldier's fear of death while still healthy and
daring), in " Anna Karenina," " Ivan Ilyich," " The Power
of Darkness," etc.  In " My Religion " he asks : " Is it
not senseless to labour at what, however much you try, can
never be finished ?  Death will always come before the tower
of your prosperity can be completed, and will triumph."

This is not, as it might seem, a morbid feeling in Tolstoy,
who was healthy and courageous.  It is the melancholy that
has often haunted pagans of acute sensibilities and engaged
in imaginative thinking, which are the psychic source of
pessimism.  It is the pensive foreboding of one who has a
keen gusto for life, a strong sense-nature for pleasure and
the pride of glory, who has a vast pagan capacity for enjoyment, and who poignantly realizes that the " feast of life is

too brief," with deep abhorrence of "losing the power of enjoyment." Blended with it is that very different melancholy of the Christians which has its origin, not in the triumph, but in the renunciation of the flesh (cf. Lloyd, "Two Russian Reformers," 222 f., 243 f.).

It seemed to him as if life were a foolish, spiteful joke that some one was playing off upon him for his own amusement, watching him live for forty years and rise to the summit and then like an arch-fool have nothing at the end but oblivion. When he had been intoxicated with life, it was easy to go on, but in sober, mature hours all seemed a stupid fraud : "I could give no reasonable meaning to any single action or to my whole life."

Then he relates the Eastern fable about a traveller in the steppes who is attacked by a furious wild beast. To escape he begins to descend into a waterless well, but sees at the bottom of the well a dragon with jaws waiting to devour him. Not daring to get out again nor to leap to the bottom, he clings to a twig in a crack on the side of the well. He sees two mice, one black, the other white, gnawing at the stem of the twig ; he knows the plant will give way and he must perish inevitably. He looks round and finds some leaves on the plant with some drops of honey on them ; he reaches them with his tongue and licks them. "So I, too, clung to the twig of life, knowing that the dragon of death was inevitably awaiting me, ready to tear me to pieces. . . . I tried to lick the honey which formerly consoled me, but the honey no longer tasted sweet, and the white and black mice of day and night gnawed at the branch by which I hung, and I saw the dragon clearly. This is no fable, but the unanswerable truth intelligible to all."

Two drops of honey still diverted his eye from the cruel truth : his wife and family—but they, too, were mortal, must either see the terrible truth or live in a lie ; and his art—but art only adorns life, and, when life had lost its attraction for himself, how could he make it attractive to others ?

Terror at what awaited him seized him, and "terror was even worse than the position he was in" (cf. the "fear of fear" in Bunyan)—that hypnotism of the fear of life which spoils the momentary sweetness of the honey. We might call it the fascinating horror of the tempting precipice. The idea of suicide captured his mind; a rope-noose or a bullet would instantly free him. But somehow he could not put the idea into execution; the instinct of life still ruled him; and as a perishing man he sought safety from destruction.[1]

The question that burdened him was the simplest that a human being can ask : Why should he wish and do anything ? What will come of all his striving ? He felt sure that there was some misunderstanding, that his state of mind was unnatural, that he must have overlooked something.

" I sought everywhere," he exclaims, in all branches of knowledge among men in the learned world which he knew. He tried science, but science only told him of chemical elements, and agglomeration of infinitesimal particles in their interaction and laws, and development, with ultimate decomposition; but it failed to tell him what he was burning to know—the ultimate meaning of life. He tried philosophy and read what wise men had said from Socrates and Buddha to Schopenhauer. They only gave him back his own questions in other terms.

He turns from the world of learning to seek the clue in life itself, and studies men around him, at first those of his own high social class and culture. Among that upper social class he finds four ways of meeting the situation, four ways of escape. One way is through ignorance, men and women being blind to the evil and absurdity of life, licking the honey without being aware of the dragon and the mice; but he had seen and known the realities, and could not

---

[1] Compare, in R. L. Stevenson's " Ebb Tide," the baffled effort of Herrick to drown himself. The shock of the immersion brightened his mind. In such a little while he would be done with the random, prodigal business. He kept swimming on. " Why should he delay ? Here, where he was now, let him drop the curtain, lie down with all generations of men in the house of sleep. It was easy to say, easy to do. To stop swimming : there was no mystery in that, if he could do it. Could he ? And he could not. He was aware instantly of an opposition in his members, clinging to life with a single and fixed resolve, sinew by sinew. . . . The door was closed in his recreant face. He must go back into the world and amongst men without illusion. He must stagger on to the end with his pack of responsibility and his disgrace."

again shut his eyes. A second way is that of the intelligent epicurean, who makes the most of the pleasant things of life, dulls his imagination, and tries to forget the dark things of sickness, old age and death. But he could not blind his imagination or forget. The third means adopted by a few is the exercise of strength and energy in destroying themselves—the logical means of escape taken by an increasing number of those intellectual men in his own class, but possible only to the rare men who are strong as they are logical; he had thought this the worthiest way of escape but had shrunk from it, though he wished he could adopt it. The fourth way of meeting the problem is to see the evil and absurdity of life, the stupid joke of it, but to drag it out in going on with dining and sleeping, as though waiting for something to turn up—a policy of mere weakness. " To this class of men I myself belonged," he confesses dolorously.

Why, then, did he not take the bold course of the third type of men and kill himself ? He could not give a reasoned answer. Life had endowed him with reason, and it ought surely to be reasonable, but how ? Men who felt the futility and inanity of life still went on living—why ? Was it a mere instinct of life that made them persist in going on, or only cowardice ? No, there must be something else behind it, some secret, some value, which he failed to discover.

He had, he came to realize, been seeking the key to life's meaning in the narrow circle of the rich, learned and leisured class to which he belonged ; and they had failed to enlighten him.

At last it dawned on him that the millions of the common people had been overlooked like cattle. His mind now turns to the peasants, to the simple, the unlearned, the poor. They have their sorrows and hardships ; but they go on living. What is the secret of their life ? They see a meaning in life.

What beliefs do they seem to live by ? They believe in a God who is three in one, in angels and devils, and such like. Their creed he cannot accept while he keeps his reason. Yet they realize the value of life as his intellectual class do not ; their faith is the sap of their life. So then, as we should state it, faith nourishing life bears witness to some reality beyond the grasp of pure reason. Intellectual argument is not the limit of truth. Faith seems irrational, but reason must bow before the facts of experience and yield to the demands of the human soul (this in our terms, not Tolstoy's). Faith gives a practical solution to the actual problems of life, and so must be assumed, beyond our present understanding, to hold touch with something that reason cannot as yet understand. As Tolstoy said at this point, " Faith is the force of life. If a man lives, he believes in something. If he did not believe that there was something to live for, he would not live."

The practical efficiency of faith (in our own terms) shows that he must recognize the shadowy nature of the finite and must relate all finite life to the Infinite.

All great religions into which he looks show the same thing. He studies them, and sees their rival claims ; and in all of them he finds the sense of the Infinite as the key to the meaning of life. Some infinite God, the divine quality in the human soul, the moral values in good and evil—these they all attest as the very terms on which men live.

Accordingly, he draws near to the believers among the poor, the simple, the ignorant, the pilgrims, the peasants, who show no pessimism and surmount privation, suffering and death. Two years he spends in observing them.

He comes to see that, in declaring life meaningless, it was only his own life and that of his class of which it was true. It was not true of human life on the whole, on the broad scale of common humanity.

He discovers that it is by living, and not mere thinking, that we find the truth and the worth of life, that arguments for the being of God may fail to satisfy the reason, while the heart bears witness to the Infinite Divine who gives meaning to our passing lives.

Still doubting, he prays to Him whom he sought, that He would have mercy and help him. There comes no reply to his cry.

But " He is," he cries, and instantly life arises strong in his soul, with the joy of strength. This is the triumphant voice that rings out of the darkness of doubt, " This is He, He without whom there is no life. To know God and to live are one. God is Life." " Live to seek God, and life will not be without God. And stronger than ever rose up life within and around me, and the light that then shone never left me again." " So gradually and imperceptibly I felt the glow and strength of life return to me. And strangely enough this power of life which came back to me was not new. . . . I returned, as it were, to the past, to childhood and my youth."

As he had learnt faith from the peasants and the simple-minded classes of Russia, he was tempted to return to their religious forms of worship in the Church. He went in among the various Christian communions, Old Believers, Dissenters of various orders, besides the Orthodox Church. He took Communion once again, but he was repelled by the theory imposed. He came to the conclusion that ecclesiastical organizations with their theological theories, each banning the other, are not the source of the practical force of spiritual faith.

He simplifies the traditional creed : declares the vital thing to be faith in God, love of the law of God, living for God.

He finds, and he teaches, that to be happy a man must have something to live for, that he must love all and give himself and his whole life to making life good for everybody. What had always stirred his heart most in the New Testament, the substance of Christ's teaching, was the doctrine of Christ which inculcates love, humility, self-denial, and the duty of returning good for evil. The symbolic booklet, " Where Love is God is," contains the soul of his religious faith based on Christ's words, " Inasmuch as ye have done it unto one of the least of these my brethren, ye have done it unto me " (Matt. xxv. 40).

Simplification of life becomes a ruling principle of his action. Simplicity and reality had been ideals of his youth. Now they reclaim his mind. He has simplified vital religion : it is faith in God, love for God and the soul, tender affection for all brother-creatures and warm humanity.

He carries his religious principle into action. He renounces, as he says, the life of his class, for he has found that it was not life, but only the semblance of life, that its superfluous luxuries make it impossible to understand life ; it is not among the parasites, but among the simple labouring people of the country that life reaches its true meaning. " To the ' vanity ' of the intellectual *élite* Tolstoy opposes the ' simplicity ' of the life of those who till the soil." " He declares ' the truth of the mujiks ' to be ' the sole truth of God and humanity.' " He glows with appreciation of the man in the ranks, of the normal man.

We do not follow him in making this the one ruling law of conduct, in glorifying manual labour, and urging that we should not consume more than we produce, much less in his renunciation of personal property, and in the asceticism which has often been the natural rebound from the life of the sensual or the sybarite. If he had lived in the Middle Ages, Tolstoy would probably have become a monk. None the less the principle of simplification is a much-needed message for to-day.

In the above spirit, he vehemently opposes all violence between man and man, the use of force in withstanding evil, and therefore all war. The realities of war have been pictured by Russians, as by Tolstoy in " War and Peace," and Russian thinkers captured by a great idea are ridden by that idea. We have been learning afresh the unutterable horrors which human ambition and hate can wreak upon mankind. But Tolstoy was unpractical in the application of his ideas and lacked saving common sense. He did not see life whole and steadily. It is well to simplify life under some vital and universal principles ; most of the great prophets, like Jesus Himself, have been simplifiers ; but Tolstoy never caught sight of the complexities of organized life. He took little concern, in spite of his later brochure, " What Shall We Do Then ? " in organized projects for the reconstruction of civilization. He would abandon the products and even any system of civilization. In keeping with the traditional Russian mind already described, he had a deep distaste for organization of any kind and therefore for any government, and, in spite of his ardent social sympathies, is fundamentally individualistic and antagonistic to socialism as a form of dominating control.[1]

As little does he see Christianity whole and steadily—see the whole breadth of even the teaching of the Gospels (St. Paul was for him anathema). He bases his ruling views upon the Sermon on the Mount.[2] He takes its terms in literalistic manner, and treats them as if they were infallible, reducing all else in the Book to accord with his particular interpretation of them. Yet he ascribes no inspired function or divine status to Jesus as ground for accepting His teaching as infallible on certain points. Even his conception of the Deity is vague, and almost impersonal. In rejecting other portions of the Gospels, he proceeds on no sound critical method or even scholarly knowledge. He accepts just what has appealed to his individual mind. Wherein he is Christian, he is intensely so. But he is Christian only in part. The pagan and the Christian hold precariously together from the first to the last.

One vital Christian principle Tolstoy did, indeed, see and most powerfully project in his last great work of fiction, " Resurrection " (1899), as never so clearly before. It is, in our current terms, the principle of atonement or redemption by self-identification with the lost. The immensity of that stupendous work makes any intelligent summary difficult to compass. Much in the story, so piteously poignant and captivating as art, is realistically repellent, in Russian frankness devoid of softening glamour. In scenes depicting moral corruption and vain ugly suffering Tolstoy is arguing that in the present cruel conditions of society the whole system of punishment under which weak

[1] Maxim Gorky (" Reminiscences of Tolstoy," 1920, p. 39) says Tolstoy's " misty preaching of ' non-resistance to evil,' the doctrine of passivism, all this is the unhealthy ferment of the old Russian blood, envenomed by Mongolian fatalism and almost chemically hostile to the West with its untiring creative labour, with its active and indomitable resistance to the evils of life. What is called Tolstoy's ' anarchism ' essentially and fundamentally expresses our Slav anti-Stateism, which, again, is really a national characteristic, ingrained in our flesh from old times, our desire to scatter nomadically."

[2] Corrective of Tolstoy, for a suggestive analysis of the Sermon on the Mount, see Clutton Brock's " What is the Kingdom of Heaven ? " and for an illuminating exposition of its place in Christ's teaching as a whole see Oman's " Grace and Personality."

and misguided people suffer to their degradation is both unfair and futile, all the more since very often they are the victims of the men who condemn them.  Incidentally he fiercely assails both state government and law courts, the Christian Church and its sacraments.

In brief outline, Prince Nekhludoff—in the main Tolstoy's reflection—sits on a jury which has to deal with a charge of murder against a profligate woman whom he recognizes in horror as the girl whose one-time innocence he had heedlessly besmirched.  In vain he tries to salve his conscience on the plea that " everybody does the same."  *Then* tender love had issued in the dangerous kiss ; later his moral tastes had been vitiated, though holding his place in society, while she, Maslova, had lost herself.  At the Easter Mass his former tender feeling towards her had revived for a little, but " the dreadful animal man " regained control over him and then over her, in a second kiss which (Tolstoy makes clear) was essentially murder.  Though innocent of the charge, the court condemns her to Siberia on a technical ground. He resolves to make himself known to her and implore her forgiveness.  She spurns his pretence of penitence, thinking he takes this measure only to save what she calls his " dirty soul."  Defeated in his proposal to deal honourably by her, he decides to follow her to Siberia.  Stripping himself of his éclat as an army officer and a landlord, and his place as the head of a family, he proceeds, through much that is repugnant to him, to join her in her ugly conditions in exile. When she discovers that his care for her is genuine and not subtle self-seeking she is touched, moved and gradually awakened.

" His atonement does not wear itself out ; he will pay the ultimate price in deeds, not in words.  And because of the sincerity of his soul-struggle, the woman herself begins gradually to believe in something beyond that comedy of brutality which had been called her life.  Her outlook widens to meet the contraction of his.  In this poor bruised being there springs up the desire for sacrifice.  The man who had everything thinks only of giving ; she who has nothing is equally desirous to give.  And slowly, and in conscious sympathy with the movements of Nature, which are so close to the moral movements of the human soul, these two stricken beings, united by a common sense of sin, drag themselves weary into the sanctuary of ' Resurrection.' And there is no consciousness on his part of a great renunciation " (Lloyd). He and she, cleansed of natural passion, redeem each other through the atonement of his sacrificial devotion. She says, " As we shall go and make atonement so shall we in common wear the cross."

Here Tolstoy touches the more profound springs of human hope and recovery, and approximates the expression of Christian experience. Nekhludoff, indeed, is moved to action by the five commandments of Jesus as expounded in Tolstoy's " My Religion," and in the end the power to redeem has its source only in a man's own soul. The practical directory for life is just the old monastic rule of poverty, chastity and labour. But, at any rate, in contrast with Ibsen, who enjoined self-realization at any price free from duties, Tolstoy preaches the gospel of meekness, self-sacrifice, love and the brotherhood of man. And, although an individualist and " peaceful anarchist," he has become a pervading force in support of social justice upon restricted lines in the Christian spirit.

## XIII

## Marcus Aurelius in Walter Pater's "Marius the Epicurean"

WE have before us here, not one of the well-worn sheep-walks between the entangling thicket and the secure fold, but one of the devious paths by which some *feel* their way through twilight in response to a voice they scarcely recognize as that of the divine "Assistant." The avenue of their approach to the Eternal is through wholesome emotions under impress from Nature in its wonder and mystery or from humanity in its restless quest for the life abundant. They are not, as others, the children of wrath through sin, but the children of Nature, awaking out of the stupor of nature to seek some ideal perfection, some authentic wisdom, some adventurous task, some independent spiritual life freed from bonds of flesh or fear, and some hold upon abiding Reality such as comes not within the scope of nature. Or as humanists, with nothing that is human alien to them, they seek self-development in some mode of spiritual culture, a religion which (in the words of William Law) "is only the refinement and exaltation of our best faculties." But they, after their kind, have their sorrowful disappointments in their quest of the "fair" and true, finding a conflict between soul and sense, between the dream and the reality, and finding under all an incapacity to sustain their own strength, the need of some gift of grace and some guarantee of eternal life-values. Hence their stress of inner travail and their spiritual progression.

A representative of this distinctive type of life must be included in such a book as this if it is to be as comprehensive as its limits will allow. Walter Pater's "Marius the

Epicurean " is chosen for this purpose, both because it embodies, in an æsthetic reception of spiritual experience, the craving for beauty and joyousness in the fullness of life, and (in the words of Dr. Gosse) it " has already become part of the classic literature of England."

I

In " Marius the Epicurean " Marcus Aurelius is one of the central figures ; he plays an important part among various factors in the development of the subject ; and, in discourses recited as also in action recorded, his thought and character are set forth in their nobility and weakness. The final value of his moral principles is placed in the discriminating light of dawning Christianity as it penetrated decadent paganism. It is on this account that his immortal book is treated here, not in a separate chapter, but in combination with Walter Pater's work. It must ever be prized among classics of the soul and used for its cultural value in the Christian life, while not belonging to the literature of Christian experience.

Some may be struck with the apparent anomaly of placing in this Christian company the work of a Roman Emperor who maintained the persecution of Christians. During his regime Polycarp and Justin Martyr and many others were put to death. But, without exonerating him of all responsibility, we must in justice remember that he did not initiate a persecuting policy and was only enforcing the law as head of the Roman State. The policy of the Government was generally tolerant of diversity in religious beliefs and customs. But it repressed rites which were understood to promote gross immorality, as Britain has done in India. Slanderous calumnies long prevailed, Christians being maligned as guilty of incest and the consumption of human flesh in their secret assemblies and dark " mysteries "— even Fronto, an early preceptor of Marcus, echoed these cruel rumours. Again, the Government required of all citizens certain outward evidences of loyalty ; the Roman gods were emblems of the State, and emperors were raised to the rank of deities ; all the people, Romans and inhabitants of subject lands, whatever their religion, were obliged to attest their allegiance to Rome by doing certain acts of homage to the gods, by burning incense on their altars, and by swearing " by the genius of Cæsar." It was not on ordinary religious grounds, but for political reasons—for the security of the State which was under the protection of the gods and for the prevention of sedition among secret societies—that this recognition of the authority of the State was required. Christians regarded the Roman gods as false, and their own faith as the sole truth, and they refused to perform the required act of homage to paganism. They were branded as " atheists "—they had no image in their meeting-places ; and they were suspected of treasonable purposes in their secret assemblies. During the second century strenuous efforts were made to resuscitate the old national religion for the public welfare. The numerous calamities that befell the empire were ascribed to neglect of the gods. Hence some of the best emperors were severe in repressing dangerous cults, just because they took serious concern for the commonweal.

But usually no attempts were made officially to hunt out the Christians. There were a good many of them in the military ranks, e.g. Cornelius in the story of " Marius the Epicurean." It was only when an outcry was raised against them as rebels or pestilently superstitious that Roman authorities took action according to the law. Marcus Aurelius was responsible only thus far, that he allowed the law to take its course. In his " Meditations " he makes only one passing allusion to the Christians, to their in-difference to death, which appeared to him due to sheer obstinacy and perversity. He, in fact, knew little of what was true about Christianity, and its supernatural elements would not have appealed to his philosophic mind.

His early education had been " bookish," and, owing to a delicate constitution and weak health, he had been kept at home and much given to the contemplative life. The adopted son of Antoninus Pius, Marcus succeeded him in 161, dying in 180 while not yet sixty years old. He was deeply religious, and strictly followed the Stoic philosophy of life in line with Epictetus. No need to give an account of Stoicism as a Greek speculative philosophy. In Rome it had become a practical method of life and a religion. In brief, it conceived of God theoretically as the universal Reason pervading all that is, the world-soul, of which a divine spark is alike in gods and men. But the primary element in all things was a fiery ether changing into other elements in perpetual flux. And a vague pantheism dominated its conception of God, who was strictly impersonal yet often spoken of as if personal, and it left room for the many gods as modes of the One.

Though a Stoic, Marcus Aurelius often rose above Stoic traditional conceptions in his effort to enter into fellowship and union with the Divine Will for victory over the world. Of his lofty ethical teaching more falls to be cited in the survey of " Marius."

The title given originally to his book was not " Meditations," but Marcus Aurelius " To Himself." Walter Pater in " Marius " entitles it " Conversations with Himself." It consists of self-communings, reflections, examinations of conscience, and moral judgments enjoined on himself, jotted down in spare silent moments under cover of his tent during his military campaigns. The manuscript was preserved apparently by accident. There is no evidence that this occasional journal was composed for other eyes than his own. Here the emperor confesses himself to himself. In the opening chapter he confesses how much he had learnt from his adoptive father Antoninus Pius, from his preceptors, such as Diognetus, Rusticus, and Fronto, and from his mother, who " taught me to have regard for religion, to be generous and open-handed, and not only to forbear from doing anybody an ill turn, but not so much as to endure the thought of it." And he adds, " all these things could never have been compassed without a protection from above and the gods presiding over fate." The self-communings that follow may be esteemed the more highly in that they come from a ruler, a general, and *the* " heathen saint." How far will they carry Marius " groping for the keys of the heavenly harmonies " ?

## II

Walter Pater (1839-94), who established a new literary tradition in English, left the impress of himself in his writings and in his academic influence, and, in his natural reticence, left little other record of his personal history. The family tradition that on the paternal side he was of Dutch extraction seems to be an unverified inference from the fact that certain Paters came over from Holland in the time of William of Orange. For two or three generations the sons of the family had been brought up as Roman Catholics, the daughters as Anglicans. Walter's father, who practised medicine in Shadwell in East London, had withdrawn from the Roman Church without adopting any other particular form of faith, and Walter was brought up within the Church of England. Whether this double thread in his family history offers us some clue to his complexity and hesitation of mind, it is certain that he early evinced a marked taste for decorous solemnities in symbolical ceremonies. His biographers (e.g. Wright, Benson) report that this bias, leading him to contemplate taking Anglican orders, was augmented by a visit to Hursley where Keble impressed his young mind with the claims of the religious life. Two of his later Studies, " The Child in the House " and " Emerald Uthwart," contain some autobiographical elements. They illustrate his native disposition, sensitive to impressions and tranquilly dreamful.

In Canterbury, at King's School, the old ecclesiastical city stimulated and expanded his imaginative sympathy with sensuous emblems, the beauty of form and melody, as accessories of religion. The first definite acquaintance with art came through Ruskin, whose " Modern Painters " he read in 1858 when in his twentieth year. In the same year he entered Queen's College, Oxford, with an exhibition from Canterbury, four years later took his degree, and in 1864 became Fellow of Brasenose College, with which he was to be identified for the rest of his life, save for occasional visits to Germany, France and Italy, and a short term of residence in London. The events of those thirty studious years were, besides his university lectures and friendships, his reviews in magazines and his books, chief among them being " Studies in the Renaissance " (1873), " Marius the Epicurean " (1885), " Appreciations " (1889), " Plato and Platonism " (1893).

The influence of Goethe and of Winckelmann in his earlier Oxford days gave direction to his Hellenic interests and helped to define the intellectual problems which were to distract him. In the stress between two different strains in his mind he craved, on the one hand, clear insight into transcendental reality and ultimate truth, and, on the other, apprehension and æsthetic enjoyment of beauty in all its modes of expression as symbolic of things most sacred. He was in touch with Benjamin Jowett (misunderstanding unfortunately marring their intercourse) and T. H. Green on the one hand, and with Swinburne, Burne-Jones and the Pre-Raphaelites on the other.

In the humanist spirit of the Renaissance he lost faith in the Christian religion, and even expressed definite hostility to it. He left no written record of his personal religion. But in a book review he singled out for quotation a passage in which he saw his own case mirrored : " The day on which I perceived my faith come to nought, the day on which I lost hope in God, I shed the bitterest tears of my life. Do you suppose that in those hours one does not feel the frightful discomfort of an existence with no moral basis, without principles, with no outlook beyond this world ? " (Pater's " Appreciations," p. 228).

But in course of time he gradually recovered a large measure of religious faith, as his philosophy " progressed from scepticism to an idealism rooted in experience." Like many others of a speculative turn of mind who had been impatient of accepted traditions, he " found that there was far more truth in the accumulated treasures of human thought, simple and in many ways contradictory as they appeared, than he had originally believed." In acknowledging the gift of a copy of Amiel's *Journal*, he wrote to its translator, Mrs. Humphry Ward, saying that, although not capable of ordinary tests, " the supposed facts on which Christianity rests seem to me matter of very much the same sort of assent we give to any assumption in the strict sense

moral." It was under the moral test, as also through
æsthetic appreciation, that he regained the practical attitude
of a devout Christian. His mind was kin with that of
Pascal (the subject of his last essay) in his pronouncement,
" The human reason alone is an unsatisfactory instrument,
and, if truth is to take up its abode in us, it will not be by
the gate of mere argument." He, too, like Pascal, was
" holding the faith steadfastly, but amid the well-poised
points of essential doubt all round him and it." He became
a regular attendant at St. Austin's, at St. Albans, Holborn,
and at other High Anglican Churches, and received the Holy
Communion. He had not proceeded quite thus far, however,
when he wrote " Marius."

" Marius the Epicurean," to which Walter Pater devoted
full five of the best years (1880–85) of his life, was conceived
as (in his own words) " an Imaginary Portrait of a peculiar
type of mind in the time of Marcus Aurelius. I think that
there is a . . . sort of religious phase possible for the
modern mind, the conditions of which phase it is the main
object of my design to convey." It represents the transition
from a pure and wistful pagan state of mind to the threshold
of Christian faith. The materials out of which the history
and spiritual progress of Marius are constructed were drawn
from outstanding events and movements at the centre of
the Roman empire in the second century. In religious and
intellectual movements there was much in common between
that period and the latter half of the nineteenth century,
and Walter Pater, as we have indicated, was caught in the
flux of " sensations and ideas." In chapter xvi. he remarks,
" that age and our own have much in common—many
difficulties and hopes. Let the reader pardon me if here
and there I seem to be passing from Marius to his modern
representatives—from Rome, to Paris and London." It is
this that helps to give the book its modern appeal, all the
more since the " imaginary " Roman is so envisaged and
depicted as to acquire personal actuality.

In the process, at the same time, Pater is projecting a
reflection of his spiritual career at its critical stages. He
is said (Wright, xxxv.) to draw to a considerable extent
upon the mental development of his friend, Richard C.

Jackson, in whose palatial library Pater found and studied
the books which supplied his knowledge of the age of Marcus.
But (he admitted) he drew also upon his own life.   The
sketch of Marius, as also of Flavian, comprises a blend of his
own mind with that of his friend.   In spite of his native
reticence and self-effacement he confesses himself within
the limits of a work of true literary art.[1]


## III


No outline can convey an adequate impression of the
book, not only of the ancient learning woven into the historical sketch, but of the artistic colour, the delicate suggestiveness, the tender, restrained emotion, the sympathetic
understanding, the rich diction, and the skilful composition
of effects in the total presentment.

Marius, at the outset, appears as a Roman youth of noble
family living with his widowed mother in an old country-
house, at once villa and farm.   The traditional religious
outlook gives the setting to the story.   He is keenly sensitive
to the mysterious powers, fears and awe of nature, with an
instinct of devotion, a scrupulous conscience, and a sympathetic interest in symbolic religious usages, floral pro-
cessions, sacrifices, and the cult of the ancestral and guardian
spirits of the place.   The spell of his religion, not only in
comely ceremonies, but as a part of the very essence of home,
meant, for him, so far as he was beginning to realize what
things meant, the effort to procure some sort of protection,
" an agreement with the gods."   One thing alone distracted
his tender nature—a certain pity at the bottom of his

[1] Discriminating readers have " felt that Marius was not so much an
ancient Epicurean, or even the perennial type of the æsthetic moralist,
as the protagonist of a certain tendency which the author held to be
vital in the thoughtful life of his own age ; or, perhaps, a lyrical personage
feigned for purposes of self-explanation. . . . Normally, of course, we have
no right to confuse the sentiments of the creative artist with those which
he puts into the mouth of his creature ; but with Pater and Marius the
case is somewhat exceptional.   In the whole manner and method of its
composition ' Marius ' is an exposition and defence of a mode of life which
not only stirred the author's deepest interest and sympathy, but, as we
know from the circumstances of his own career, was an actual and effective
ideal to him " (Greenslet, 75, 118).

heart for the sacrificial victims and their looks of terror under butcher hands. It is the first intimation of pain—with more to come in due time—as an element in life.

His mother—the father now ten years dead—fosters the sense of sacred presences about him at " White-Nights " (their home) and of the sacredness of all life. He destroys snares for catching birds, and she tells him : " A white bird, a bird which he must carry in his bosom across a crowded public place—his own soul is like that." Such are her kindly offices and her pensive remembrance of her dead, who abide ever in close neighbourhood to the living, that " Marius, even thus early, came to think of women's tears, of women's hands to lay one to rest in death as in the sleep of childhood, as a sort of natural want." She becomes to him " the very type of maternity in things, its unfailing pity and protective-ness, and maternity itself the central type of all love." It falls to him to perform the inherited priestly offices of the family, and the grave ritual answers to his native predisposi-tion. He enjoys long days of open-air exercise, and absorbs the sights and sounds of wholesome nature ; yet he is " apt to be happy in sacred places." At the same time, as in the old Italian religion, he is subject to gloomy, haunting menaces, a vague fear of unexplored evils dogging his steps, fear of coiled serpents, fear of the supernatural, and fears cast by the moral judgment. Living much in the realm of the imagination, with keen humane sensibilities, and " something of an idealist," he represents the ancient conflict between naturistic paganism and meditative idealism.

Suffering from a boyish sickness, he is sent to a temple of Æsculapius among the hills of Etruria, where a college of priests in a sort of religious hospital employ certain medical secrets and ceremonials of a sacramental character to pro-mote health of body as one with moral and spiritual well-being. The serpent that symbolizes the healing power of Æsculapius (as in the badge of our Army Medical Service) visits his night-dream ; a young priest instructs him to meditate much upon and keep round him beautiful visible objects for the sake of purity of vision ; and through a panel opening upon a long valley a vision is given him of mystical unseen realms.

The death of his mother away from home leaves him alone, with eternal gratitude to her, but with wounds of heart, and a serious consciousness of the dire realities of things visible and the poignant sense of final separation. This crisis makes him a " questioner," and tempts him to seek youthful delight in self-expansion, adventure, and the pursuit of fame. It is the " preliminary exercise for a larger contest."

The first among the tests which are either to confirm or to upset his early faith and loyalties meets him at school in Pisa, in the shape of devoted attachment to a senior pupil, Flavian, who helps him in his studies. The latter, the son of a freedman, gifted, fascinating, eager for pleasure without afterthought, ambitious and bound to succeed without restraint from conscience, has lapsed into unbelief. " How often afterwards did evil things present themselves (to Marius) in malign association with the memory of that beautiful head, and with a kind of borrowed sanction and charm in its natural grace ! To Marius, at a later time, he (Flavian) counted for as it were an epitome of the whole pagan world, the depth of its corruption, and its perfection of form." But something fastidious and wholesome keeps Marius undefiled. He is learning that " education largely increases one's capacity for enjoyment."

It is often in " truant reading " that education conveys idealizing power. And so it was with Marius and his school-mate, when they read together " The Golden Book " of Apuleius, with its pathetic symbolic myth of Cupid and Psyche, which is recited fully in Pater's version. The ancient story signifies that we must not seek to see the full face of the object loved nor analyse its secret elements, but, if we are to retain it, must enjoy it without speculation. Its effect upon Marius, in keeping with Dante's first sight of Beatrice, is to stimulate " the ideal of a perfect imaginative love, centred upon a type of beauty entirely flawless and clean." Its effect upon Flavian is to " stimulate the literary ambition," and make him a trained student of words. Here he reflects Walter Pater himself in his methods of literary expression : with scrupulous conscience in writing, he must " weigh the precise power of every phrase and word, to the exclusion of everything that is but middling, tame or only

half-true even to him," working on the axiom that the first
thing is to be forcibly impressed, that (in R. L. Stevenson's
more homely words) " to know when one's self is interested
is the first condition of interesting other people."

The speedy death of Flavian—" a pagan end "—intervenes and pierces the soul of Marius with the tragic pains of
actual life and with a deepened sense of final separation.
The scene is depicted with a fine reserved intensity, in
contrast with the vehement outburst of St. Augustine when
the sudden death of a young comrade startled him into a
serious mind.  The plague brought by the army from the
Orient seized Flavian ;  he strove to finish a poem ;  but
delirium supervened.  Marius " almost longed to take his
share in the suffering. . . . He lay down beside him, faintly
shivering, to lend him his own warmth, undeterred by the
fear of contagion."  He whispered, " Is it a comfort that
I shall often come and weep over you ? "  " Not unless I be
aware, and hear you weeping."  Surely this is not (as Mr.
Benson has called it) " untrue to nature," since the reply is
true to the lower Epicurean nature.  Marius is amazed that
he cannot be near the corpse without fear in attending to
the last tender offices of friendship.  Deeper still is the
silence, the alienation, the sense of distance, that has come
between them.  This is " another of the pains of death."

What comes after ?  " To Marius the earthly end of
Flavian came like a final revelation of nothing less than the
soul's extinction."  This new period in the movement of the
history opens with the Latin words of the Emperor Hadrian
to his soul.[1]

> " Dear wanderer, gipsy soul of mine,
>     Sweet stranger, pleasing guest and comrade of my flesh,
>     Whither away ?  Into what new land,
>     Pallid one, stony one, naked one,
>     No more to jest as you used to ? "

This deadening blow to his former faith drives him into
solitude and resentment against the blindness of nature.
His vigorous intelligence saves him from falling a prey to

[1] " Animula, vagula, blandula Hospes comesque corporis, Quae nunc
abibis in loca ?  Pallidula, rigida nudula ; nec ut soles, dabis jocos ? "

theosophic "mysteries," from professional mystics with their pretence of "secrets unveiled." He will have no illusions, no disguise of facts as they are. He tries the teaching of Heraclitus, with its theory of a "perpetual flux" of things and of souls, nothing being real except phenomenal change, and each one being the measure of all things to himself. He finds it a "philosophy of the despair of knowledge."

Michelet described metaphysic as "the art of bewildering oneself methodically." Marius is in search of a practical world-wisdom, having, like Aristippus of Cyrene, suspended the search for whatever may lie behind "the flaming ramparts of the world." He joins company with Aristippus in the Cyrenaic philosophy, thus "retracing in his individual mental pilgrimage the historic order of human thought." All things are but shadows, and we can never know what is real behind them, however strongly we desire a vision of a wholly reasonable world. Our beliefs are largely a matter of choice, selected from the theoretic ghosts of bygone impressions. We live in fleeting moments of experience, like day-dreams, "between two hypothetical eternities." The true wisdom of life is to take the utmost these moments can yield us of what is best. Suppose all things are fleeting shadows—well, take what is *here and now* for its value to us.

This Epicurean principle may, in Pascal's words, be "pernicious for those who have any natural tendency to impiety or vice." But the blood of Marius is still pure. He has no tang for crude pleasures in the old "Epicurean stye." The best to be made out of what is here and now is to "adorn and beautify our souls, and whatever our souls touch upon—these wonderful bodies, these material dwelling-places through which the shadows pass together for a while, the very raiment we wear, our very pastimes and the inter-course of society." What is to be desired is, "not pleasure, but general completeness, fullness of life, and insight as conducting to that fullness—energy, variety, and choice of experience, including noble pain and sorrow even, loves such as those in the exquisite old story of Apuleius (Cupid and Psyche in the Golden Book), sincere and strenuous forms of the moral life, such as we find in Seneca and Epictetus—whatever form of human life, in short, might be heroic, impassioned, ideal : from these the ' new Cyrenaicism ' of Marius took its criterion of values."

He is resolved also " to add nothing, not so much as a transient sigh, to the great total of men's unhappiness, in his way through the world " ; that, too, is something that the present moment holds in trust for us.

This life will involve restraint as against indulgence, and a life of industry, only possible through healthy rule, keeping clear the eye alike of body and soul.  It may become a kind of religion :  " to offend against it brings with it a strange feeling of disloyalty, as to a person."

Here Marius has reached a principle of life that in great degree coincides with the main principle of the Stoics, and inwardly prepares him for the next stage, his contact with the great Stoic saint, Marcus Aurelius.

Marius is now summoned to Rome, to be near the person of the philosophic emperor as virtually an amanuensis.  In all the buoyancy of his nineteen years he goes greatly expectant.  His impressions of the country are finely described, touched with haunting reminiscences.  Mark the sympathy between the scenes of nature and his inward states.

On the way he meets and travels with Cornelius, a young knight of the Twelfth Legion.  A person, like a book, falling in our way at an opportune moment, often counts for more than an episode.  Little could either of the two young men, each knightly in his own way, guess what is to eventuate for both of them from this new friendship.  Marius observes in Cornelius the expression of earnest soldierly discipline (*ascesis*) and blithe manliness, a distinctive atmosphere and inner serenity, some kind of new chivalry.

Rome, as Marius finds it, is the scene of gay splendour over an ovation to the Emperor upon his return from successful war with barbarians along the Danube, and also the scene of superstitious fears.  It is a time of diverse disasters in the empire after long peace.  Wars recur on the north with German and Sarmatian tribes—Quadi and Marcomanni—taxing the strength of Marcus, whose predilections favour peace.  The war with the Parthians in Syria under his brother-emperor, Lucius Verus, ends in a triumphal ovation in Rome ; but the conquering legions have brought from the Orient the dreaded plague, which now carries death and dismay through town and country. Earthquakes, floods bringing famine, and the burning of cities contribute to the general panic. Prophecies of an impending conflagration of the world alarm the credulous.

These and other calamities and fears have stimulated the spread of superstitions, and even demanded the sacrifice of a human victim. Strange foreign religions, Oriental " mysteries," the cult of Isis, receive sanction and favour, along with the old Roman religion, in ceremonial solemnities. " A blending of all the religions of the ancient world has been accomplished. High and low address themselves to all deities alike without scruple, confusing them together when they pray." For the general security, lights, flowers, and incense are placed on every altar.

Marcus Aurelius is presented here under these conditions, first in the religious triumphal procession and again in private intercourse, with singularly vital and vivid charm, verisimilitude, and tender understanding. Fragile in person, modest in bearing, benignant in countenance, demurely thoughtful in pontifical abstraction of mind, almost inhumanly impassible, this philosopher who is emperor and reluctant warrior cares not for the Divine honours which his venerating people would fain offer him as another Augustus—cares not (it is his own word) to be " Cæsarized." Yet his " peculiar character, at once a ceremonious polytheist never forgetful of his pontifical calling, and a philosopher whose mystic speculations encircled him with a sort of saintly halo, had restored to his person, without his intending it, something of that divine prestige."

" Dignify thyself with modesty and simplicity as thy ornaments," was a Stoic maxim he made his own. As the Roman Stoics taught, the true dignity of man, of any man, lies in his share in the Divine dignity ; for the vital principle of every soul is part of the Deity. It must, therefore, be kept inviolate, not dishonoured by unnatural passions and abnormal desires ; it must not be disturbed by or made subject to " things " which it cannot rationally determine ; it must be independent of things indifferent, indifferent to things without which a man may yet be entirely virtuous. Nature is one with the Order of Reason " sweetly disposing all things "; what is soundly natural is practically reasonable, and the world in itself is faultless. Life, then, is to be according to nature, according to reason. And men are to live together, as cosmopolitans, as fellow-citizens in the commonwealth of humanity, and show the benignity and benevolence which follow from these and kindred principles.

Marcus Aurelius' discourse before the Roman Senate upon the occasion of the ovation is a cento of aphorisms from his " Meditations," skilfully woven into a progressive unity by Walter Pater. Its total impression is lost when we condense it. It is almost wholly a soliloquy *de contemptu mundi*, coming strangely from an emperor's lips in his crowning hour.

Change, impermanence, stares at us wherever we look into the face of the world. " The world, and the thinker upon it, are consumed like a flame . . . Therefore will I withdraw myself from all affections. Are you in love with men's praises ? What judges they are ! Would you survive death in the memory of those who are on the wing but for a while and extinguished in their turn ? Leaves in the wind followed by other leaves in other generations, what is common to them all is but the littleness of their lives. Folly ! to be lifted up, or sorrowful, or anxious by reason of things swept away in the perpetual flux of things ! Think of infinite matter, and of destiny, and the jot you are in it. Everything is losing its substance and ever becoming something else." See it in the mutations of empire and succession of rulers and wise men—Chaldean, Greeks, Romans : Alexander the Great who used the lives of others as though his own should last for ever—he and his mule-driver alike now— Scipio, Tiberius, Hadrian, Pythagoras ; again in great fortunes, and misfortunes, of men's strife of old, nothing left but the dust of their battles. " Ah ! and thy life's breath is not otherwise, as it passeth out of matters like these into the like of them again."

" For the one soul in things, taking matter like wax in the hands, moulds and remoulds—how hastily !—beast, and plant, and the babe, in turn," all in dying still remaining within the order and changes of nature. Would we wish it otherwise? Nature is good and wise. Shall we be agitated and desolate?

"If there be things which trouble thee, thou canst put them away, inasmuch as they have their being but in thine own notion concerning them." Death, for example—detach it from the notions and appearances that hang about it; see it as it is, an effect of nature, which should affright none but a child, and a thing profitable also to nature. "Thou hast made thy voyage and touched the shore : go forth now. Be it into some other life : the divine breath is everywhere, even there. Be it into forgetfulness for ever ; at least thou wilt rest from the beating of sensible images upon thee, from the passions which pluck thee this way and that like an unfeeling toy, from those long marches of the intellect, from thy toilsome ministry to the flesh."

Count not how long you have been a citizen of this wide city, nor repine. "That which sends thee forth is no unrighteous judge, no tyrant, but Nature, who brought thee hither ; as when a player leaves the stage at the bidding of the conductor who hired him. Sayest thou, 'I have not played five acts'? True! but in human life, three acts only make sometimes an entire play. That is the composer's business, not thine." Even if the full play contains five acts, a player withdrawn at the third act may already have proved his worth. (Here one recalls a sentence from " The Wisdom of Solomon," iv. 13—" Being made perfect in a short time he fulfilled a long time.")

The discourse is introduced and viewed in its bearing on the mind of Marius the Epicurean, in its effect on his spiritual travail. Over all the serenity of the emperor, Marius detects " the cloud of some reserved internal sorrow, passing from time to time into an expression of fatigue and effort, of loneliness amid the shouting multitude. . . ." Marcus shows more than the common Stoic tenderness for all men as fellows-citizens of one city, for the eternal shortcomings of men and women. But his charity of judgment is based on the Stoic principle that when men sin it is because they know no better, being "under the necessity of their own ignorance," thus missing the truth that sin is an act of the moral will and not a matter of the instructed understanding.

Under the supremacy of the soul the Stoic is superior to perturbations of the emotions, and suffers no injury from any untoward accident or from any wrong done to him unless he permit it to break into his self-sufficience and mar his inner harmony. It matters little what happens to a man, for all depends upon the way he takes it.[1]  "'For my part, unless I conceive my hurt to be such, I have no hurt at all,' boasts the would-be apathetic emperor, 'and how I care to conceive of the thing rests with me.' Yet when his children fall sick or die, this pretence breaks down, and he is broken-hearted."

At the gladiatorial show with its spectacle of suffering and bloodshed that sweeps the amphitheatre with mad frenzy and shouts of applause, Marius sees Marcus averting his eyes, reading or writing, or " perhaps revolving that old Stoic paradox of the *Imperceptibility of pain*." As emperor he is tolerant of the people's pleasures. Yet " there was something in a tolerance such as this, in the bare fact that he could sit patiently through a scene like this, which seemed to Marius to mark Aurelius as his inferior now and for ever on the question of righteousness, to set them on opposite sides in some great conflict." Marius is aware of a crisis in life. Apathy at such cruel sights is the " sin of blindness, of deadness." Beware of falsifying your impressions. " Surely evil was a real thing, and the wise man wanting in the sense of it, where, not to have been by instinctive selection on the right side, was to have failed in life."

A discourse on Morals by the aged rhetorician Fronto, the emperor's early instructor, induces in Marius an inquiry after " some principle of conduct which might give unity of motive to an actual rectitude, a cleanness and probity of life," with tenderness for every sentient creature as having its rights. The orator proceeds to expound Humanism and the Platonic idea that we are all fellow-citizens in a supreme

[1] "Stoicism is fundamentally the psychological doctrine of apperception, carried over and applied to the field of the personal life,—the doctrine, namely, that no external thing alone can affect us for good or evil, until we have taken it into the texture of our mental life . . . and stamped it with the approval of our will " (Hyde, " The Five Great Philosophies of Life," p. 70).

City on High, *Urbs Beata*, in which all men should learn their place and their duty from an aristocracy of elect souls. As he listens, it dawns upon Marius that, in his Cyrenaic philosophy of life, in his pursuit of perfection in all that is " fair " and in exquisite capacities of feeling, there was something narrow, " the perfection of but one part of his nature." Something greater is wanted in a wider humanity.

In a memorable interview with Marcus Aurelius, when the emperor, to raise funds for the war, is having the treasures of the Imperial palace sold at public auction and is finding an austere joy in such a costly sacrifice, Marius comes to see that the renunciation of the things of purest beauty and delight may bring a deeper, simpler joy and satisfaction than the personal enjoyment of them. Renunciation, then, is the next stadium in his spiritual pilgrimage. As amanuensis he is given some papers of the emperor's, a sort of private journal, full of self-communings, which reveal to him that the emperor, despite his cheerful demeanour and " forced and facile optimism," lay under a heavy melancholy—*Tristitia* ; he was carrying the burden of a sad heart, with too much of a " complacent acquiescence in the world as it is," amounting to " a tolerance of evil." In spite of his belief in a universal Reason, he has no happy faith creative of spontaneous joy. When his little son lies dying Marius sees him " carry the child away . . . pressed close to his bosom, as if he yearned just then for one thing only, to be united, to be absolutely one with it, in its obscure distress."

Walter Pater is not setting up Marius to find faults in the character of Marcus Aurelius ; the emperor as portrayed in these chapters is a noble gentleman, the benignant father of his people, the unpretentious pattern of virtue, hard on himself but generous to others, loyal to his wife Faustina, whose marital fidelity, despite the mutterings of scandal, he never questioned, magnanimous to his brother co-regent, the vain and vicious Lucius Verus, " with his strange capacity for misusing the adornments of life," and to the ill-starred Avidius Cassius, who fell in his attempted revolt. True, he was what is called superstitious, or at least he lent countenance to the practice of all varieties of foreign and native superstitious ceremonies for the purification of Rome in time of public peril; he was a Stoic fatalist; he took counsel from dreams, and sanctioned suicide as a man's right on due occasion. But on the whole he appears a man of *fides et religio*—religion that is half-Pantheist, half-Polytheist—single-minded in his public service, amiable, meditative, and tender.

The author's purpose in bringing out the emperor's defects and inner melancholy is to show how Stoicism, represented at its best in Marcus, fails to cover the realities of life and sustain the heart in a victorious joy (see further *infra*, p. 303), and in this particular instance fails to satisfy the mind of Marius in his quest for truth and grace. The late Dean Church wrote : " No one can read the wonderful sayings of Seneca, Epictetus, or Marcus Aurelius without being impressed, abashed perhaps, by their grandeur. No one can read them without wondering the next moment why they fell so dead—how little response they seem to have awakened round them." In Matthew Arnold's words, in his " Meditations," we see the emperor " wise, just, self-governed, tender, thankful, blameless ; yet with all this, agitated, stretching out his arms for something beyond—*tendentemque manus ripæ ulterioris amore.*"

Marius goes out from the great Stoic to the hill-side and with a strange uplifting of spirit wonders whether, if (as Marcus taught) " it is in thy power to think as thou wilt," he might not deliberately choose to cherish the cheerful restorative beliefs which sustain life : for instance, the belief in " an eternal friend to man, just hidden behind the veil of a mechanical and material order, but only just behind it, ready perhaps even now to break through." He is feeling after the Great Companion beside him, no occasional wayfarer, but rather " the unfailing ' assistant ' without whose inspiration and concurrence he could not breathe or see." It is (in St. Augustine's phrase) " one moment of understanding." For once " to have apprehended the *Great Ideal*, so palpably that it defined personal gratitude and the sense of a friendly hand laid upon him amid the shadows of the world, left this one particular hour a marked point in life never to be forgotten." If he does not yet absolutely believe, he shows a willingness to believe.

Old things that failed him are fading in the dawn of new things which are waiting to break upon him.

The dawn comes clear through the person of the young knight, Cornelius, with whom he had journeyed to Rome. Occasionally, in their meetings he had found in that soldier " some inward standard of distinction, selection, refusal, amid the various elements of the period and its corrupt life. . . . There was a breeze of hopefulness—freshness and hopefulness—as of new morning, about him."

Then the secret comes out: Cornelius is a Christian! After a conversation with the celebrated Apuleius, who unfolds a theory of a hierarchy of beings mediating between men and the Deity, and whose fantasies make him yearn the more for the manifestation of Divine presences, Marius accompanies Cornelius along the Appian Way to a doorway in the wall of a villa near Rome : it is the entrance to Cecilia's house, a meeting-place of Christians " under the cross." Cornelius holds the door open in pause for his companion to decide whether he will cross this threshold, as if saying, " Are you prepared to take this step, and see that which may define the critical turning-point in your days ? " They enter together : the step is taken beyond recall, and it seems as if a door were closed behind Marius upon the past. Much care is spent on a description of the characteristic orderliness, noble taste, industry, and bland peace of this Christian interior, like a vesture expressive of the spirit that has fashioned its comeliness.

Marius first catches the sound of singing, the singing of children, singing a " new kind " of song, expressing a " new world of poetic song. . . . the blithe self-expansion of a joyful soul in people upon whom some all-subduing experience had wrought heroically, and who still remembered the hour of a great deliverance." He finds the virginal beauty of chaste women and children in a cheerful family life after some rare model. The place is as a bride adorned for her husband.

Across an old flower-garden at the rear he is conducted through a narrow cut in a low hill into a crypt which is the family burying-place. It is the centre of the peculiar sanctity of the whole scene, which blends the Greek and

the Christian at their best. Along the subterranean gal-
leries of this catacomb are the berths where the dear dead
are carefully laid. Significant to Marius this burial instead
of burning of the dead, suggesting a peculiarly sacred conception of the body and a feeling of hope entertained concerning it. (Here, however irrelevant scientifically and
even theologically, the question occurs to the reader whether
cremation of the dead does in fact affect the Christian
sentiment towards the " sure and certain hope " of things
to come.) Here are signs of departed infants (with toys
beside them in their narrow bed), and of martyrs, defining
some new and weighty motive of action, by which they
" had not loved their lives unto the death." Graven on
the walls are designs symbolic of succour and regeneration—
the Good Shepherd carrying the sick lamb upon His shoulder,
Hercules wrestling with death for the possession of Alcestis,
etc.—and the benediction, " Peace ! Pax tecum." Then
" Marius finds himself emerging again, like a later mystic
traveller [Dante, of course] through similar dark places,
' quieted by hope,' into the daylight."

As evening descends he hears the voice of singers in
solemn antistrophe chanting the " candle " hymn :

> " Hail ! Heavenly Light, from His pure glory poured,
> Who is the Almighty Father, heavenly, blest :—
> Worthiest art Thou at all times to be sung
> With undefilèd tongue."

Cecilia, widow of a " Confessor and Saint," gives greeting,
and in her temperate beauty reminds Marius of " the best
female statuary of Greece," with an expression no Greek
knew of maternal care as she carries a little child at rest
in her arms.

It all alike seems " determined by that transporting
discovery of some fact or series of facts, in which the old
puzzle of life had found its solution," in contrast with the
jaded aspect, the malign enchantment and the suffocating
atmosphere of passing paganism. Here, it might be, was
the solace of sorrow and the healing of the " disease of the
spirit." At the same time, Marius is aware that if (as in
the myth already retold of Cupid and Psyche) he gazes
candidly into the face of this new love, it will lay on him

some penalties, untried responsibilities, "a demand for
something from him in return." At any rate he suspects
that, after beholding it, "he can never again be altogether
as he had been before."

In this Christian home of the Early Church, Marius discovers that "regenerate type of humanity" which will
later be embodied in the art of Giotto and Raphael. He
feels there, "amid the stirring of some wonderful new hope
within himself, the genius, the unique power of Christianity."
He sees, in the "immeasurable divine condescension in a
certain historic fact," its influence in the demand for "some
sacrifice of one's self for the weak, the aged, little children,
and even the dead." Marcus Aurelius had taken a blithe
pleasure in selling his treasures for the progress of the war,
and pagans had cared for the sick. But Christianity is
doing, not tardily and in burdened sadness, but almost
without thinking about it, all that humane charity, and all
that chastity, require, doing it, not *as* sacrifice, but with all
the joy and "liberal enterprise of youth." Even common
labour is beautified under the workman of Galilee. "Such
aspect of the divine character of Christ, rightly understood,
is indeed the final consummation of the bold and brilliant
hopefulness in man's nature." Along with this aspect of
it, this sacrificial *ascesis* or discipline, Marius the former
Epicurean observes that other aspect of Christianity, the
harmonious culture of human nature, the cheerful liberty
of heart, the "beauty of holiness," the "regeneration of
the earth and the body in the dignity of a man's entire
personal being," which give æsthetic perfection to the
sacrificial spirit in fullness of life. In this sense he appre-
ciates "the naturalness of Christianity." What appeals
to him in Christianity is "its humanity, or even its
humanism, its generous hopes for man, its common sense
and alacrity of cheerful service, its sympathy with all
creatures, its appreciation of beauty and daylight." It
seems to say to paganism at its best, "You fail to realize
your own good intentions: here is your fulfilment."

The æsthetic charm or grace of Christianity is presented
visually and audibly to Marius at a celebration of the Holy
Communion in the Cecilian domestic sanctuary suitably

adorned for the sacrament. Seen for the first time, this
wonderful spectacle comes to him in " wonderful evidential
power over himself." Here are great varieties of rank, of
age, of personal type. " The Roman *ingenuus*, with the
white toga and gold ring, stands side by side with his slave."
In the profound silence of this assembly, so entirely united
for purposes unknown to him, Marius feels for a moment as
if he had stumbled upon some great conspiracy. But in
the various expressions of those countenances he detects
human sorrow assuaged, the fulfilment of desire among the
aged and the poor, and in those young men, who have faced
life and are glad, the light of knowledge without parallel
in the older world. Was some credible message from
beyond " the flaming rampart of the world "—a message
of hope, regarding the place of men's souls and their interest
in the sum of things—already moulding anew their very
bodies, and looks, and voices, now and here? At least
there was a cleansing and kindling flame at work in them,
which seemed to make everything else Marius had ever
known comparatively vulgar and mean.

The ritual of the Holy Sacrament, after a very high liturgical type, is described in sensuous beauty and splendour
to the point of excess, reflecting the ceremonial preoccupa-
tion of Walter Pater's own mind. It is said (Wright, II,
84 f.) to be an exact description of the Eucharistic service
in St. Austin's, South London, which Pater frequently
attended. After the impressive symbolic acts comes " a
narrative which, with a thousand tender memories, every
one appeared to know by heart, displaying, in all the
vividness of a picture for the eye, the figure of Him towards
whom this whole act of worship consistently turned—a
figure which seemed to have absorbed, like some rich tinc-
ture in His garment, all that was deep-felt and impassioned
in the experiences of the past. In the ceremonial mystery,
the pure wheaten bread and the pure white wine consecrated seem to signify the consecration of earth's gifts, and
of all we touch and see, in strong contrast with ascetic
renunciation of all such things. *Adoramus te Christe,
quia per crucem tuam redemisti mundum !*—they cry together. So deep is the emotion that at moments it seems

to Marius as if some there present apprehend that prayer prevails, that the very object of this pathetic crying Himself draws near."

The action of the closing chapters must be hastened. The denouement is almost within sight, though it is not such as we could foresee. We must pass over a rather irrelevant or at least distracting conversation of the satirist Lucian, tending to damp or perhaps intended to test the young man's wistful aspirations. Pass over also Marius' pensive glimpses, given in vignettes, of the fond and poignant things in the phantasmagoria of the human world, the *motif* being to show the need for a generous charity and humanity, and the power of sympathy. In such heartful sympathy he seems to " touch the eternal " and transcend the appearance of kindness in the soul of things. " Dared one hope that there is a heart, even as ours, in that divine ' Assistant ' of one's thoughts—a heart even as mine, behind this vain show of things ? " Here he seems to take up and re-knit himself to well-remembered hours in his early pieties, and feels the power of an unseen person in controversy wrestling with him.

In Cecilia's household again, at the burial of a little child, in contrast with " the hard contempt of one's own and others' pain " enforced by the Stoic emperor, the pain, the sorrow, is felt with stifled sobbing, but faced with a wonderful hope, the comforting words of the psalter carrying the potency of the *Alleluia* of Easter morning. An Epistle is read aloud from the Churches of Lyons and Vienne, reporting the recent martyrdoms in Gaul under persecution, the wonderful new heroism of Blandina, Ponticus, and others, under cruel tortures and in death, " which sent them like conquerors to the great King, with joy at the end as to a marriage feast." For " there is nothing fearful where the love of the Father overcomes."

Marius sees the triumphal return of the emperor from the war, with a train of chained captives in the procession, turning the show to tinsel. " Aurelius himself seemed to have undergone the world's coinage, and fallen to the level of his reward, in a mediocrity no longer golden." Marius revisits his old country home, solemnized before the ancestral mausoleum, touched with tenderness for his beloved dead, having forebodings that he is to be " the last of his race," and he resolves to bury all their remains deep in the ground : he will never come back.  In this dramatic act he is, about the midway of life (cf. Dante), decisively cutting himself from his past—for what ?

Cornelius finds Marius at White-Nights, who welcomes him as " more than brother."  They set out for Rome.  But the plague is abroad, combining with earthquake to excite the suspicions and superstitions of the people.  A group of Christians at prayer before the tomb of the martyr Hyacinthus is attacked by the mob as though calamities were due to Christian neglect of the protecting gods.  Cornelius and Marius are arrested—it is known that one of them is a Christian, which of them is not clear.  Marius privately bribes the guards to liberate Cornelius on the plea that he will go and procure the means of legal defence. He is at first touched with gratification that he, who had suspected himself of lacking the heroic element, can thus put his life at stake for the life of a friend ; but dark depression overtakes his spirit, as he thinks how he will endure the fate of a common felon without the consolations of a Christian martyr.  On the march he is stricken with fever, is left behind, and in closing crises enjoys moments of vision and peace with the remembered image of Jesus, and the expressive faces of the Christians at worship.  " Again the sense of gratitude seems to bring with it the sense also of a living person at his side."  He awaits death now with keen curiosity as opening a door to an ampler vision, taking up a " lost epic " and disclosing " the house ready for the possible guest."

Marius has not declared himself a Christian ; but the Christians of the country village have heard what he did to save the life of Cornelius.  In his fast-failing strength he hears them, as they minister to him, praying fervently round his bed—*Abi ! Abi ! Christiana !* " Depart, O Christian soul ! "  The mystic bread is placed between his lips, without sign of protest on his part ; the anointing with oil completes the last tender offices.  " It was the same people who, in the grey austere evening of that day, took up his remains, and buried them secretly, with their accustomed prayers; but with joy also, holding his death, according to their generous view in this matter, to have been of the nature of a martyrdom; and martyrdom, as the Church had always said, a kind of sacrament with plenary grace."

On this note the book ends. It is characteristic of Walter Pater, whose eye preferred half-lights to noonday sunshine, whose mind appreciated suggestive implications more than determinate conclusions. To Marius, he says, " perpetual twilight came in close identity with its moral or intellectual counterpart as the welcome requisite for that part of the soul which loves twilight, and is, in truth, never quite at rest out of it, through some congenital uneasiness or distress, perhaps, in its processes of vision." This reserve in clear utterance was natural to him. His intimate friend, Lionel Johnson, in his ultimate poem entitled " Walter Pater," wrote :

> " Half of a passionately pensive soul
> He showed us, not the whole;
> Who loved him best, they best, they only, knew
> The deeps they might not view;
> That which was private between God and him;
> To others justly dim."

He was " enamoured of the difficult mountain air," and knew " how deep within the liturgies lie hid the mysteries." The good, the beautiful, and the true carried larger meanings than could be cast in final terms when touched with mystical elements. " Scholarship's constant saint, he kept her light in him divinely white." Like Amiel, and with something of Amiel's lack of vital energy, he saw such various aspects of truth that he expressed his mind in balanced and qualified statements. Dr. Gosse says, " He was not all for Apollo, nor all for Christ."

Marius' spiritual development is left incomplete, his attitude to Christianity indeterminate. His life is closed with no express avowal of belief in it; yet he is on the very threshold, *tending inwards*. Hitherto, like Pater himself, he had been a spectator of life; in the closing scene by a single sacrificial deed he became an actor, and the act was an implicit decision which, had he survived, would presumably have issued in adhesion to the Christian faith. His part in the play ended with the third act ; we may infer the next step which he would have taken in subsequent scenes.

Walter Pater progressed further in the nine years that followed the completion of " Marius." Asked what his object was in writing that book, he replied, " To show the need of religion." In those later years it was the Christian religion that increasingly brought him the long-desired fullness of life. To the influence of stately ritual he was keenly sensitive.[1] According to his sympathetic friend, Dr. F. W. Bussell, vice-president of Brasenose College, " his interests centred more and more on the liturgy and fabrics of the Catholic Church ; on the truth of the creed from a High Church standard ; on the education of the young in the faith of their fathers . . . the cardinal mysteries of the Faith." At the same time it was the beauty and holiness of the Christian ideal rather than theological theories that subdued him to devotion.

In his case, as in some measure in the case of Marcus Aurelius, philosophic thought had discovered the inadequacy of its resources in the natural reason ; we see the mystic wrestling for the mastery with the scholastic, and finding in a great historical organization of religious life a dynamic manifestation of grace and truth, of " gracious reality." The words of Plato in the " Phædo " were fulfilled in his experience : " If we cannot of our own effort discover the truth, then it behoves us to choose among the opinions of men that which may seem to be the best and the most assured, and, clinging to it as to a raft, to make our adventure across the sea of life—unless, indeed, we may find a stouter barque to entrust ourselves to, viz. a *divine word*, which may carry us in safety to the end of the voyage." Walter Pater—much more, " Marius "—never overtook

---

[1] In Mallock's " New Republic," a clever skit which we read long ago when " æsthetic " extravagances were attributed unjustly to Walter Pater, he figures as Mr. Rose, who, it is said, attended Ritualistic churches " when in the weary mood for it. . . . The dim religious twilight, fragrant with the smoke of incense . . . the tapers, the high altar, and the strange intonation of the priests, all produce a curious old-world effect." But this dilettante representation was a caricature of the serious piety of his mature years.

the triumphant joy, the creative energy and glorious freedom of the sons of God that characterized the early Christian Church ; but he won serenity, purity of motive and human sympathy as well as vision of perfection through unison with Him in " whose will is our peace." He represents Humanism seeking and experiencing God.

Marius expressed the desire for companionship, for some one to whom he might tell his secret for his relief, with whom he might share his joy and so double their pleasure. Walter Pater, though he does not speak the language of most people's experience, has a goodly company of men and women, most of them as reticent, as fastidious in self-expression, as himself, who have an understanding touch with him along the avenue by which he reached his true home in God.

# Rabindranath Tagore's " Song Offerings " and " Meditations " : And his Indian Precursors

FROM India, that most religious country, have come authentic voices of the spiritual mind in lyric expression which have no equal outside the sphere of Christendom. It is impossible here to deal with the older Indian classics in hymns and epics ; for our present purpose we need only consider those of recent times which have caught the impact of the modern mind and the Christian atmosphere. They are lacking in some characteristic features of Christian experience, while yet their distinctive effusions have been deeply tinctured by the purifying ideals of the Christian ethic. One of the early Fathers said suggestively, God is not so poor as to have a Church only in Sardinia. In the interest of comprehensiveness, we may well include in these studies a representative seer from regions beyond the organized Church who yet abides in the City of God.

Dostoievsky, speaking as a Russian of " the vast impending contribution to civilization whereby we shall awaken the European people," said that " Russia must reveal to the world her own Russian Christ, whom as yet the people know not." And Tolstoy thought to produce a " new religion " after the true mind of Jesus. Each race may be expected to see Jesus from its own angle and evolve its own type of spiritual life, with due. regard to something normative disclosed in the original Christian documents. Whatever type may be expected to emerge ultimately in Russia, we have more reason to anticipate a distinctive Indian Christ.

When the new-born Church of India is mature enough to construe its own experience after its own cast of mind, its conception of Him is likely to be deeply impressed by independent Indian seers, as the early Gospel was impressed in its interpretation by Greek thought. Meanwhile, in the Indian literature here surveyed we mark certain tendencies and ascertain certain elements likely to be infused into Indian Christianity.

Rabindranath Tagore (1861–) has given us a new and enchanting order of mystic vision and spiritual utterance in the accent of modern India. In his poetic and prose writings—chief among them being *Gitanjali*: " Song Offerings," and *Sādhanā* (Meditations) : " The Realization of Life "—he has transfigured his religious inheritance and the genius of his race. His mind is deeply rooted in Indian philosophy and civilization; his compositions glow with Oriental intensity and colour, and abound in Oriental imagery and spiritual symbolism; his thought is often marked by such delicacy, elusiveness and universality as to outrange the compass of our Western grasp. At the same time the West has found in him " the refreshment that comes from another order of mind," while his words of fire often touch something primitive in us like an old, haunting memory. He has done more perhaps than any other to bring the Indian mind and the Anglo-Saxon mind to meet understandingly. His recognition in the Western world was marked in 1913 when he received the Nobel Prize for Idealist Literature. At the same time the fact that in connexion with the Great War and in his peaceful support of Indian autonomy he renounced his British honours—we may no longer entitle him " Sir "—warns us that he lives and thinks decisively in terms of India. He has been claimed as a supporter of Indian nationalism, but it is not a political nation that he has in view ; it is rather, in his own words, India as a spiritual area that he seeks to conserve. " Nationalism is the training of a whole people for a narrow ideal," stands for selfishness, and " leads to moral degeneracy and intellectual blindness " (" Creative Unity," 143). As against any new public organization, his demand is for freedom of the individual spirit among peoples of all lands.

Tagore's immediate spiritual ancestry casts interpreting light upon his own mind and writings. The renascence of Indian thought was promoted, if not originated, by impact from the West during the past century. The educational policy of the British governors and the education provided by Christian Missions bred a large educated class, who were taught English as a second language and introduced to English literature, for better or for worse. The Press, including journalism, popularized Western knowledge. As part of the general influence of Christian Missions, medical missions, medical education, the care of the suffering, the famine-stricken and the outcasts, the work done for girls and women, especially youthful widows, awakened a new social conscience and a new humane ethical ideal animated by the Christian spirit. Oriental study, assisted by the translation and publication of Sacred Books of the East, led educated Indians to the re-discovery of their own early religious classics. These influences and other contacts between India and the West caused a deep ferment in the Indian mind and wrought powerfully in diverse directions. Some crude and evil customs were discredited. Religious reform in the line of a spiritual theism was undertaken by some liberal leaders ; later, in the rise of nationalism, counter-reform movements have become strong, discarding idolatry and caste, but seeking the revival of the pure ancient religion of India, comparable to the attempted reconstruction of pagan faiths in the Roman Empire in the third century in reaction against the growth of Christianity. On these and other diverse developments Farquhar's " Modern Religious Movements in India " is invaluable (cf. *infra*, p. 305 f.).

Tagore entered into an inheritance from the Theistic movement crystallized in the Brāhma Samāj (Society of Believers in God). It was founded by Ram Mohan Rai, the pioneer and powerful leader in all living progress, religious, educational and social, among the Hindu people. Tagore calls him " one of the immortal personalities of modern time." While regarding Jesus as a Theist misinterpreted by theologians, he confessed that Christ's " simple code of religion and of moral principles is admirably calculated to elevate men's ideas to high and liberal notions of the one God . . . and well fitted to regulate the conduct of the human race in the discharge of their various duties to God, to themselves and to society." He discarded transmigration —fundamental in Hinduism—and taught that (in his own words) " worship is the communion of the soul with God ; on the part of man, it is the opening of his soul, the outpouring of his aspirations, the acknowledgment of his failures and transgressions and the consecration of his life and work to God as his Lord, Refuge and Guide ; and on the part of God, the communication of His light, strength and inspiration and blessing unto the longing soul." At the same time India could gain nothing by adopting Western things unchanged ; they must be naturalized in the soil.

Debendra Nath Tagore, father of our Bengali poet-seer, member of an influential princely family, was emancipated from Hindu paganism in a " spontaneous awakening." The story of his new birth in a mystical experience, after desperate and often despairing struggles to find a spiritual God as a new centre of loyalty, is given in his " Autobiography," amply summarized in Pratt's book on " The Religious Consciousness." The awakening began when he was only twenty, evidently suffering from the youthful malady of sensibility and reflection. He had been very wretched, not from the sense of sin (which never greatly troubled him), but from the barrenness, vanity and dreary darkness of life (outwardly plentiful in luxuries) in a world like a graveyard. His Confession reads like that of St. Augustine or of Tolstoy, though he could not know of either of these. " I found happiness in nothing, peace in nothing. The temptations of the world had ceased, but the sense of God was no nearer. . . . I was dead to all happiness, earthly or divine."

The crisis lasted through four years. Some help came from memories of Ram Mohan Rai and from English books. The light of a new life reached him almost accidentally when he picked up a loose page fluttering past him from a Sanscrit book which proclaimed the universal Divine presence and its close unity with the human spirit. The vision burst on him of the " Friend of the sinner, protector of the helpless, who in

His infinite mercy appeared in my corrupt heart to heal and chasten me." He exclaims : " A divine voice had descended from heaven to respond to my heart of hearts. I wanted to see God everywhere, and I found just what I wanted. . . . The very mercy of God descended into my heart. Enjoy that which He has given unto thee ! What is it that He has given ? He has given Himself. Leave everything else and enjoy that supreme pleasure. It was not the dictum of my own poor intellect, it was the word of God Himself. My faith in Him took deep root ; in lieu of world pleasure I tasted divine joy." His saying, " I was satisfied with getting so much, but He was not content with giving so little," might have come from St. Augustine.

He joined and rejuvenated the Brāhma Samāj, maintained a life (closed in 1905) of constant communion with God, though giving less homage to Christ than Ram Mohan Rai, and reading chiefly Vedānta scriptures. He was honoured with the title of " Maharshi," " great rishi or seer," as the patriarch of the Theistic movement. Such was the father of our famous Indian poet.

Before passing on to the younger Tagore, mention must be made of Keshab Chandra Sen, who succeeded Debendra as the dominant leader of the Theistic community. His spiritual history and work [1] show that he absorbed much more of the mind of Christ and put a much higher valuation upon Him than others who figure in this chapter, though his later course was somewhat deflected. India was asking— Who is Christ ? Sen's answer varies in form of expression, but usually in terms of experience, not harmonized in any consistent system.

To condense his " confession " (in his " Oriental Christ ") : " Twenty years ago, my troubles, studies and circumstances forced upon me the question of personal relationship to Christ. . . . As the sense of sin grew upon me, and with it a deep miserable restlessness, a necessity of reconciliation between aspiration and practice, I was mysteriously led to feel a personal affinity to the spirit of Christ. . . . Often

[1] See T. E. Slater's " Keshab Chandra Sen and the Brāhma Samāj, with Selections from his Works " (Madras : S.P.C.K., London : James Clarke & Co.).

discouraged and ridiculed, I persisted in according to Christ a tenderness of honour which arose in my heart unbidden. I prayed, I fasted, I secretly hunted the book-shops of Calcutta to gather the so-called likenesses of Christ. I did not know, I cared not to think, whither all this would lead. . . .

"About the year 1867 my inward travails had reached a crisis. It was a week-day evening; gloomy shades had thickened into darkness. I sat near the large lake in the Hindu College compound. A sobbing, gusty wind swam over the water's surface. I was meditating on the state of my soul, on the cure of all spiritual wretchedness, the brightness and peace unknown to me which was the lot of God's children. I besought heaven; I cried and shed hot tears. . . . Suddenly it seemed to me, let me own it was revealed to me, that close to me there was a holier, more blessed, most loving personality upon which I might repose my troubled head. Jesus lay discovered in my heart as a strange, human, kindred love, as a repose, a sympathetic consolation, an unpurchased treasure to which I was freely invited. The response of my nature was unhesitating and immediate. Jesus, from that day, became a reality whereon I might lean. It was an impulse then, a flood of light and love. It is no longer an impulse now. It is a faith and principle, it is an experience verified by a thousand trials . . . a character, a holy, sacrificed, exalted self, whom I recognize as the true Son of God. My aspiration has been, not to speculate on Christ, but to be what Jesus tells us all to be. In the midst of the crumbling system of Hindu error and superstition, of the cold, spectral shadows of secularism and Agnostic doubt, to me Christ has been like the meat and drink of my soul."

Such a high personal valuation of Christ led to a lofty yet somewhat indefinite conception of His inner being and status, sufficiently indicated here in a few selected statements. " Christ was nothing but a manifestation on earth, in human form, of certain ideas and sentiments which lay before in the Godhead." " The Spirit of the Lord filled Him, and everything was thus divine within Him." " Divinity coming down into humanity is the Son; Divinity carrying up humanity to heaven is the Holy Ghost." " As soon as the soul is emptied of self, Divinity fills the void." Thus Christ " always felt that the root of His being was in God."

The " Theologia Germanica " was one of the books— Seeley's " Ecce Homo," F. W. Robertson's " Sermons," etc.—that deeply influenced his mind. He reflects it, and indeed much in William Law, when he says, " The crucified Christ does not belong to him who (though accepting the outward fact or the dogma) is not prepared daily to crucify himself." Or again, " Christ reigns in some as the spirit of trustful, speechless suffering ; in others as the spirit of agony for others' sins . . . ; as the recognizer of divine humanity in the fallen and despicable, the healer of the unhappy and the unclean and sore diseased ; in the sweet humanity that goes forth to find and save its kin in every land and clime." Social reform for him, as for others, was " an accessory to men's progress in spiritual life." The one was proportionate to the other.

He emphatically and repeatedly urged that the people of India must not be expected to renounce their nationality in becoming Christian. " It seems as if the Christ that has come to us is an Englishman, with English manners, the English spirit. Hence it is that the Hindu people shrink back and say—who is this revolutionary reformer who is trying to sap the very foundations of native society, and establish here an outlandish faith and civilization incompatible with Oriental instincts and ideas ? . . . Is not Christ's native land nearer to India than England ? Are not He and his apostles more akin to Indian nationality than Englishmen ? . . . Was not Jesus Christ an Asiatic, His disciples Asiatics ? . . . When I reflect on this, I feel Him nearer my heart, and deeper in my national sympathies. . . . If you say we must renounce our nationality, all the devotion of our Eastern faith, we shall say most emphatically, No ! It is *our* Christ, *Asia's* Christ, you have come to return to us. The East gratefully and lovingly welcomes back her Christ." His protestation was pertinent in the circumstances ; and doubtless there is much in the New Testament that can be evaluated better by the Eastern than by the Western mind. But he failed to penetrate to the deeper ground for the universal appeal of the Christian gospel, the common need of all mankind, the infinite value of every individual soul, and the love of God for all men without distinction of race, Greek or Jew, Oriental or Occidental.

Here we can see that Indian nationalism is deeply rooted in religion, as we can see clearly in Rabindranath Tagore.

## II

Rabindranath Tagore, while of the stock of the Brāhma Samāj, returns to earlier Indian founts, and with poetic idealism transfigures all that is central in his heritage.

He was, to use his own words, " brought up in a family where texts of the Upanishads were used in daily worship ; and he had before him the example of his father, who lived his long life in the closest communion with God, while not neglecting his duties to the world or allowing his keen interest in all human affairs to suffer any abatement." In the frequent absence of his father, and especially after the early death of his mother, he was very lonely as a boy and suffered from harsh discipline in his schooling. With his innate craving for open-air contact with nature, he was jubilant when at the age of eleven his father took him on a long journey up the great rivers and over the plains to the foothills of the Himalayas, where his soul was suffused with the wealth of colour and majestic grandeur and his imagination enraptured with sylvan mysteries in nature. After further education in Calcutta he was dispatched to London to study for the bar ; but he revolted against compulsory study and soon returned to Bengal. Indeed, as he avowed in a much later visit to Europe and America, the aggressive, grinding strife and crass discords of Western civilization struck harshly on his Indian instinct for a life of harmony. In an early letter describing the joy of evening in " golden Bengal," playing upon the Hindu idea of re-birth, he exclaimed : " I am always afraid that I may be born in different environments . . . afraid most of all that I may be born in Europe ! For there . . . I may have to drudge in a factory, in a bank, or in a parliament. As the streets in the European cities are made of hard stone, brick and mortar, to be made fit for commerce and transportation, so the human heart becomes hardened and best suited for business." He has Ruskin's distaste for industrial mechanism. But this is to anticipate.

Meanwhile disorder had invaded his own nature and marred the music of his mystical simplicity. The strong wine of passion, love and romance intoxicated him ; for a time he indulged in fashionable dress and the pleasures of an epicure and *bon-vivant*, while composing love-songs, novels and plays. Looking back from his fiftieth year, he confesses, " At the dawn of youth revolt against nature, so characteristic of that time, also captured my hauteur-filled heart. I had no connexion with the usual spiritual life of our family. . . . The period of my life between the age of sixteen and twenty-three was one of extreme wildness and irregularity." And he compares the gigantic forms of his inner longings roaming in a pathless wilderness to huge, strange-looking creatures roving in the primitive forests before land and water were separated. " So these longings did not know themselves, nor the purpose of their existence." As with Tolstoy the two sides in his dual nature, sensuous and spiritual, are at war with each other, and he knows Tolstoy's alternations between thrills of ecstacy and the gloom of disappointment in the depths of darkness. In " The Gardener," with its artistic love-lyrics, we have the pictorial drama of the surge of sense in conflict with native spirituality.

He had married at the age of twenty-three, and been sent to manage his father's country estate near the Ganges, where for long years he lived in a house-boat on the Padma and came close to the peasant people whose helpless poverty and sorrows he was moved to depict in tales and parables. Then, as a biographer says, " death came and looked him in the face ; he lost first his beloved wife ; then, within a very few months, the daughter who took her place ; and then his youngest son." He confessed, " this death-time was a blessing to me. I had through it all such a sense of fulfilment, as if nothing were lost." It was felt as a solemn preparation for some vast change, for some better work of life.

Illumination came to him in the very mid-years of life,

a mystic experience after the mode of his father's. One morning in Calcutta, when looking out from his veranda upon the tree tops of the Free School grounds and gazing at the sunrise, " suddenly a covering seemed to fall away from my eyes, and I found the world bathed in a wonderful radiance, with waves of beauty and joy swelling on every side. This radiance pierced in a moment through the folds of sadness and despondency which had accumulated over my heart, and flooded it with this universal light. Every one, even those who bored me, seemed to lose their outer barrier of personality ; and I was full of gladness, full of love for every person and every tiniest thing. . . . That morning in the Free School street was one of the first things that gave me the inner vision, and I have tried to explain it in my poems. I have felt ever since that this is my goal in life : to explain the fullness of life, in its beauty, as perfection." This change, so true to India in its ethereal mode, made him a deeper and more penetrating thinker, and brought him an access of spiritual power.

In his *Gitanjali,* " Song Offerings," we have the poetic product of his awakening and intensified vision, expanded and somewhat hardened in *Sādhanā* (Meditations) : " The Realization of Life," as an orderly statement in prose of his philosophic outlook, in " Personality," and later in " Creative Unity." It is with his " Song Offerings " that we are primarily engaged, adding expository matter from the other books. His English in its diction and cadence is as pure, lambent and expressive as that of our own literary masters, and the original Bengali, from which he has made his own English version, has, we are told, a subtlety of rhythm and delicacies of colour which are lost even in his translation, and indeed are untranslatable.

Tagore heard " deep calling unto deep," the deep within and the Deep beyond us calling in a sacred antiphony. In his own way of putting it : " Something inexplicable has happened, my whole being is aching with an awakening, and I hear at a distance the call of the Great Ocean. Yes, it calls ! the Great Ocean calls. And yet, at this moment, why all these walls around me ! " Break the walls of bondage. " I come, I come—where is He, and where is

His country ? " [1] Boutroux's phrase, " The Beyond that is Within," indicates the way he took.

His spirit is emancipated when he discovers that the Beyond and the Within are the same, that one soul animates all, that " the stream of life which runs through my veins night and day runs through the world and dances in rhythmic measure." Everything in the universe is enveloped in God. In our Western phrase, He " descends to us in all things seen." Tagore leans far towards a naturistic mysticism. But the unity in all is not mere cosmic consciousness ; it is spiritual ; and when we open our whole being to this universal Presence, then it becomes a radiant joy, an overspreading love. Then is the soul free, in harmony with all creation, and knows itself to be immortal. Its gift, its love-token, is joy.

" He it is, the innermost one, who awakens my being with his deep hidden touches." " At the immortal touch of thy hands my little heart loses its limits in joy and gives birth to utterance ineffable. Thy infinite gifts come to me only on these small hands of mine. Thou hast made me endless, such is thy pleasure. This frail vessel thou emptiest again and again, and fillest it ever with fresh life. Ages pass, and still thou pourest, and still there is room to fill." Often, as we say, we are found of God when we are not consciously seeking Him. " The day was when I did not keep myself in readiness for thee ; and entering my heart unbidden even as one of the common crowd, unknown to me, my king, thou didst press the signet of eternity upon many a fleeting moment of my life."

The spiritual nature of true worship is emphasized in these lyrics, which recognize " the law of the spirit of life," and religion in the open spaces. " They come with their laws and their codes to bind me fast ; but I evade them ever, for I am only waiting for love to give myself at last into his hands." " Leave this chanting and singing and telling of beads ! Whom dost thou worship in this lonely corner of a temple with doors all shut ? Open thine eyes and see thy God is not before Thee ! He is there where the tiller is tilling the

---

[1] The works here quoted are the copyright of Messrs. Macmillan and The Macmillan Co.

hard ground and where the pathmaker is breaking stones. He is with them in sun and in shower, and his garment is covered with dust. Put off thy holy mantle and even like him come down on the dusty soil! . . . Leave aside thy flowers and thy incense! What harm is there if thy clothes become tattered and stained? Meet him and stand by him in toil and in sweat of thy brow." For pictorial commentary we might here introduce Millet's "Angelus," which exhibits three fundamentals of life, reverence for labour and the very soil in which the two peasants work, the sanctity of human affection as between the man and the woman in common toil, and piety expressed by their bowed heads at the call of the Church bell. Tagore, like Tolstoy, had learnt something from his contact with peasant people. But he did not learn this principle of purely spiritual worship from Hinduism, even from the early Vedānta, which represents ritual prayer as a divine power in itself when performed by Brahmin priests according to prescribed procedure in which they alone were adepts. He derived it, directly or indirectly, from Christ who taught, "God is Spirit, and they that worship Him must worship Him in spirit and in truth."

Tagore did not, according to Hindu wont in such a case, turn to an ascetic life, but continued to find pure delight in the wonderful world of Nature as ever new to him, and in the love of humankind. "Deliverance is not in renunciation . . . I will never shut the door of my senses to the delights of sight and hearing" in the beauty and music of the world. Contrast this with St. Bernard who covered his eyes that they might not dwell upon the lakes of Switzerland, unlike Jesus who found delight in lilies and the play of children.

But does not Nature include passionate desire, craving for every form of natural satisfaction, that desire which has ever been the misunderstood bogy of Indian religion? It is, however, in its moral sense that Tagore sings: "When desire blinds the mind with delusion and dust, O thou holy one, come with thy light and thy thunder. . . . Desire puts out the light from the lamp it touches with its breath. It is unholy—take not thy gifts through its unclean hands. Accept only what is offered by sacred love."

In this ethical spirit Tagore cries: " Life of my life, I shall ever try to keep my body pure, knowing that thy living touch is upon all my limbs.  I shall ever try to keep all untruths out from my thoughts, knowing that thou art that truth which has kindled the light of reason in my mind.  I shall ever try to drive all evils away from my heart and keep my love in flower, knowing that thou hast thy seat in the inmost shrine of my heart.  And it shall be my endeavour to reveal thee in my actions, knowing it is thy strength gives me strength to act."[1]

Tagore has been keenly interested in social and educational reform, demanding selfless love for the stricken millions of India.  Alas ! " Thou art the Brother amongst my brothers, but I heed them not, I divide not my earnings.  In pleasure and in pain I stand not by the side of men and thus stand not by thee."  This is a distinctively Christian idea (cf. St. Matt. xxv. 40).

Do we recognize (cf. Ps. cxxxix.) the Presence that everywhere besets us ?  " Day after day, O Lord of my life, shall I stand before thee face to face ?  With folded hands, O lord of all worlds, shall I stand before thee face to face ? Under thy great sky in solitude and silence, with humble heart shall I stand before thee face to face ?  In this laborious world of thine, tumultuous with toil and with struggle, among hurrying crowds shall I stand before thee face to face ? And when my work shall be done in this world, O King of

[1] Compare George MacDonald's " Noontide Hymn " :

" I love thy skies, thy sunny mists,
    Thy fields, thy mountains hoar,
Thy wind that bloweth where it lists—
    Thy will, I love it more.

I love thy hidden truth to seek
    All round, in sea, on shore ;
The arts whereby like gods we speak—
    Thy will to me is more.

I love thy men and women, Lord,
    The children round thy door ;
Calm thoughts that inward strength afford—
    Thy will than these is more.

But when thy will my life doth hold
    Thine to the very core,
The world, which that same will doth mould,
    I love, then, ten times more."

kings, alone and speechless shall I stand before thee face to face ? "

Our deeper loves, we of the Western world say, involve deeper anguish at our lasting separations, and the essence of all melancholy (according to Neil Munro) lies in the sentiment of final farewells. Conversely, according to Tagore, this overspreading pain deepens into loves and joys in human homes. Does he imply, what is so true, that death has intensified human affection ? When I first crossed the threshold of this life unaware of the moment, " I felt I was no stranger in this world, that the inscrutable without name and form had taken me in its arms in the form of my own mother. Even so, in death the same unknown will appear as ever known to me. And because I love this life, I know I shall love death as well." Hence, in better terms than the Roman gladiators' hail, " morituri salutamus," the departing one can say : " Bid me farewell, my brothers. I give you back the keys of my door. The day has dawned. I only ask for last kind words from you."

Meanwhile, though " time is endless in thy hands, my lord," and " thy centuries follow each other perfecting a small wild flower, we have no time to lose . . . we are too poor to be late. . . . At the end of the day I hasten in fear lest thy gate be shut ; but I find that yet there is time." It is the note of the parable of the Ten Virgins, with a glint of other vistas.

The nostalgia of St. Augustine—" Thou hast made us for Thyself, and our hearts are restless till they rest in Thee " —is expressed more picturesquely in the closing sentence of the " Song Offerings " : " Like a flock of homesick cranes flying night and day back to their mountain nests, let all my life take its voyage to its eternal home in one salutation to thee."

From this lofty outlook we recall his appropriate prayer. " This is my prayer to thee, my lord—strike, strike at the root of penury in my heart. Give me the strength lightly to bear my joys and sorrows. Give me the strength to make my love fruitful in service. Give me the strength never to disown the poor or bend my knees before insolent might. Give me the strength to raise my mind high above daily trifles. And give me the strength to surrender my strength to thy will with love." There is much here in these Indian lyrics to remind us of the " Imitatio Christi," with much deeper difference. In Thomas à Kempis sanctity is set in the closed cell, while in Tagore the scene is the open temple under encompassing skies.

" *Sādhanā* (Meditations) : The Realization of Life "—its chapters being lectures or addresses delivered in England and the United States—elucidates the general principles in his philosophy of life. Here his self-expression seems to be somewhat stiffened into academic form under the consciousness of an unfamiliar audience looking to him as a new teacher. It has literary charm, with many utterances of Emersonian positiveness that are pregnant of suggestion for thought ; yet its process is quite theoretic, above the region of actual experience, and lacks the spontaneity and effectiveness of his lyrics. We cannot in this chapter attempt a summary of its contents, and must merely indicate some of its characteristic notes. It elaborates germinal ideas in his " Song Offerings " as above.

The vision and the attainment of the soul's unity with the whole of life in the universe, in harmony with universal nature, is the fundamental need. This, according to Tagore, is less instinctive for the Western mind which has been developed within restrictive city walls than for the Indian mind which was bred within the forests close to the mystery of things. He transcends Hindu pantheism when, recognizing the all-pervading Spirit, he yet recognizes the differences of value in different things. " The universal is ever seeking its consummation in the unique." Yet we must " knock at every door," for in all things we must seek something that is truly our own. And the discovery of it makes us glad. Did not St. Paul indicate something of the same kind in saying, " all things are for your sake " ? This discovery, this vision of the Supreme One in as well as beyond ourselves, is not based on reasoning and demonstration, but is a direct and immediate intuition. It is through our heart, a river moving ever to the sea of God, that we know God ; our intellect *is* but a bridge that spans the river only at one point.

But evil—what of evil under this idealist optimism? His solution is only partial, not profoundly moral, nor Christian, though some Christian thinkers adopted it. " It could not be otherwise," says Tagore. But if evil is a necessity, it is not really immoral. " Creation, being gradual, must be imperfect," he says. But imperfection as only a lack of being is not the same as moral evil which lies in a perverse will. And for the same reason sin is not mere ignorance, needing nothing but enlightenment. He is speaking of its effects rather than its real nature when he says, " sin is the blurring of truth which clouds the purity of our consciousness." It is doubtless a misdirected effort after a delusion as to what is good. " In sin we lust after pleasures, not because they are truly desirable, but because the red light of our passion makes them appear desirable " and great, falsifying the perspective and proportion of things. " Pain is not a fixture in our life " ; " the essence of evil is its impermanence, for it cannot accord with the whole." True, evil is disorder, like disease, and in a world in which order ultimately rules it tends towards self-destruction. But the essence of evil lies not there but in the moral will. In a world which is ever moving forward evil belongs to a passing stage. But it is not true that " evil has to grow into good." No really moral evil ever grew into good, though the moral ordeal, by free personal conquest, does eventuate in good. If evil had the latent potentiality of good, it would not be absolute evil, as moral èvil is. " We feel that good is the positive element in man's nature." Yes, as truth is the positive affirmation and error the negation of reality. Yet moral evil while it lasts is a violent actuality in human experience. While perhaps in " confessions " we harp too much on sin and hesitate to affirm the essential holiness of human nature, on the other hand the Hindu mind, from the very nature of its conception of the universe and its deficient measure of personality, has never adequately grasped the problem of moral evil, its seat in the free will, and the possibility that evil may become settled in the personal will ; it never realized the need of regeneration and redemption by a Divine act of grace. It looks to constituent nature, as when in another book, " Personality,"

Tagore speaks of a " second birth " out of " Nature's womb into the world of spirit."

In the problem of Self, Tagore departs from Hindu tradition in recognizing human freedom as the gift of God in which He limits His control. In line with the teaching of Jesus Christ he observes that " it is the function of religion not to destroy our nature but to fulfil it." We are free to disown our proper King. Here " our God must win his entrance. Here he comes as a guest, not as a king, and therefore he has to wait till he is invited." He comes not with armed force, but with beauty to court our love. And, as said in the " Song Offerings," " if I call not on thee in my prayers, if I keep not thee in my heart, thy love for me still waits for my love." Freedom, however, is not an abstract and natural possession of man. Self-will is not true freedom. In line with St. Augustine, it is (in practical fact) only in perfect love that we find freedom in our self through freedom from self.

Insistence upon self after our narrow impulse means severance from all else, and obscures our true well-being. " Pleasure is for one's own self, but goodness is concerned with the happiness of all humanity and for all time. To live the life of goodness is to live the life of all." " Whatever we treasure for ourselves separates us from others." " Pride of self interferes with the proper function of the soul, which is to realize itself by perfecting its union with the world and with the world's God." And " this we can do by winning mastery over self, by rising above all pride and greed and fear, by knowing that worldly losses and physical death can take nothing from the soul." Buddha saw that, for the release of mankind from the misery of natural cravings, a man " attains his highest end by merging the individual in the Universal," so becoming free from thraldom to pain. And " this is the vision of the heavenly kingdom of Christ. When we attain to that universal life, which is the moral life, we become freed from the bonds of pleasure and pain, and the place vacated by ourself becomes filled with the unspeakable joy which springs from measureless love."

We enlarge our region and adjust our burden when we extend our interest beyond our own possessions. " The tragedy of life lies in our vain attempts to stretch the limits of things which can never become unlimited. . . . Man's abiding happiness is not in getting anything, but in giving himself to what is greater than himself." What, then, shall be our appropriate prayer ? " O God, my Father, the world of sins remove from me. When this life of self wants to get everything for itself, it gets knocked and knocked because it is unnatural, hurting its wings against the prison cage. . . . From this comes our suffering, and we say, ' Break open this prison. I do not want this self. Break all the sins, cravings of self, and own me as your child—your child, not the child of this world of death.' " (" Personality," 196.)

Human life, according to Tagore, is a pilgrimage. " Man's history is the history of his journey in quest of the realization of his immortal self—his soul." And individually the history of " the human soul is only its journey from the law to love, from discipline to liberation, from the moral plane to the spiritual."

God and love are one and the same. " From love the world is born, by love it is sustained, towards love it moves " —which recalls the last line in Dante's Vision, " the love which moves the sun and other stars." Love finds the meaning of everything. " We do not love because we do not comprehend, or rather we do not comprehend because we do not love." Our relationships are perfected only in love. " Because we find in love the infinite satisfaction of our personality, we have come to know that our relationship to the Infinite Personality is that of love. And in this way man has learned to say ' Our Father,' not merely King, or Master, but Father." For there is something kin and common between that Eternal Person and one's little finite person. " Our heart ever changes its place till it finds love, and then it is at rest."

In action as well as in love lies the realization of life. The Hindu goal of hope in the past, we know, was rest in quiescence ; the Western disposition was that of striving. The Northmen of Europe, fighting the dangers of the sea, learnt to fight all tyranny of matter. Indians, bred in level tracts of forest, learnt unity and harmony in all things. But

Tagore imports the action of striving into his scheme of things. The joy of life lies in creative action (as Bergson has likewise said), and not in detached meditation or the negation of asceticism. Renunciation is the law of life, the soul saying of things, " I do not want it for I am above it," but only in the interest of a deeper joy in full unison with the eternal joy which is ever active in creation.

Tagore, we may add, has not seen the world of action " in deep disdain, and plunged in thought again." He has been busy in editing magazines, in social reform and (by peaceful methods) in the cause of Indian nationality, and in the Feminist movement. His chief undertaking has been that of a keen educationalist, especially in his Boarding School at Bolpur, Bengal, where two hundred boys receive a sound modern education. It has been called a " boy's republic, a schoolhouse without a taskmaster." Teachers and taught live in a community of equals, who largely rule themselves in an atmosphere of freedom and joyousness. The boys study in the open under the trees, in close touch with nature, do much of their own house-work, pass from games, the practice of song and dramatic plays, to the exercise of simple daily worship, with occasional addresses from Tagore himself. The aim of all is, not mere practical efficiency, but the culture of wholesome life and of the religious nature.

In his latest book in English, " Creative Unity," reiterating the need of harmony between the soul and all nature and races under a creative ideal, he demurs to Kipling's " East is East and West is West, and never the twain shall meet," and declares that " the East and the West are ever in search of each other, and that they must meet not merely in the fullness of physical strength, but in fullness of truth. Yes, the East did once meet the West profoundly in the growth of her life. Such union became possible, because the East came to the West with the ideal that is creative." He does not seem to agree with Keshab Chandra Sen in welcoming back from the West the " creative ideal " which in Christ came from the East.

Tagore owes much to Western influences and to Christian inspiration. He and his admirers have not sufficiently acknowledged the extent to which he has absorbed characteristic ideas and more particularly moral and social ideals from the West. His thought and writings are by no means the undiluted outcome of Hindu tradition and other Indian sources, though their Eastern cast is apt to conceal the transformation and transfiguration which his inheritance from the Vedānta has undergone. He often quotes from the Upanishads as the basis of his message. These quotations, however, are sifted selections from the mass of religious and speculative literature of a very mixed and generally a much lower quality, and are not representative of the whole context and Hindu system. When Jews have insisted that all of Christ's moral teaching had already been taught by the Rabbis and had parallels in the Talmud, Christians have answered, as Wellhausen put it, " Yes, all, and a great deal more ! " — much that is inferior and even trifling. Tagore has lifted fine penetrating expressions out of old texts and charged them with more spiritual values and given them other bearings than those they had in the original. He has largely modified, rationalized, and sometimes even sublimated Hindu doctrines. In his own words, " to me the verses of the Upanishads and the teachings of Buddha have ever been things of the spirit, and therefore endowed with boundless vital growth." This true insight must be welcome to his own people as it is to us. We are not by any means disposed to challenge him in making a selective use of traditional scriptures and in giving to the best therein their finest interpretation and their widest significance. New Testament writers and early Fathers did the same with Hebrew prophets and other Old Testament documents. Enough if it be commonly acknowledged that he is selecting materials and translating ancient forms of Hindu thought into freer expressions of the life of the spirit.

Tagore's scheme of thought is eclectic, and, while attractive in its facile use of disparate material in the effort to find universal truth, it loses force from its indefiniteness. The two sources of inspiration, Oriental and Occidental, are brought together, but the diverse ideas thus derived are not fused into a fresh creation. This is not the place for a critical estimate of his philosophical thought (for that see Urquhart's " Pantheism and the Value of Life," chapter xvii.) We may note, however, that the Western and Christian inspiration has had a refining, ethical and consequently spiritual effect on his mind, while that mind is fundamentally determined by Neo-Hinduism. And, indeed, he has said, rightly or questionably, that " the regeneration of India will come through gradual change within the body of Hinduism itself rather than from the action of any detached society like the Brāhma Samāj." Pantheistic concepts cling to his view of the universe—as when he says, using God and Brahma as interchangeable terms, " there is no question of searching for him in one thing in preference to another," and again, " we would pray thee, O maker of the universe, to let the irresistible current of thy universal energy come like the impetuous south wind in spring." Christ proclaimed His oneness with his Father, and yet, Tagore protests, Christians in the West, except some mystics, " condemn as a piece of blasphemy any implication of man's becoming God "; but in Christianity the original idea of man's unity with God is a moral unity of persons, and not, as in India, a unity or identity of constituent being. Again, in writing as a Feminist upon " Woman," he says : " I believe that to love is to worship the mysterious one. Only we do it unconsciously. Every kind of love is the direct outcome of the universal force that tries to express itself through the human heart." Whatever aspect of truth is in his own mind, the last sentence might lend support to the morally perilous Hindu idea that a " universal force " in " every kind of love " or even passion has a sacred significance. The East, and now to-day the West, have to guard against the assumption that every natural force in man has its sanction in itself as good.

As to our deliverance or redemption : " Where is this deliverance to be found ? Our master himself has joyfully taken upon himself the bonds of creation ; he is bound with us all for ever," and " God has bound himself to man." It appears thus to be a naturistic, cosmic process ; the activity of the Divine as universally given in eternal creation by its constitution is the source of deliverance. Christianity pledges and effects deliverance in a definite, signal Personal manifestation of God, and by a great act of sacrificial love in the midst of human history. Hindu religion has always been lacking in historical actuality in experience and authentic events, has relied upon universal theoretic concepts, so losing much redemptive dynamic. Tagore has an illuminating message for those already enlightened and healed; has he an efficient message of recovery for the multitudes of men of evil taste and habit and the multitudes of burdened consciences? The spiritual experience consequent upon the above teaching cannot compass the full measure of Christian experience.

But our aim here is, not to find churlish fault or defects, but to observe with discrimination and appreciation the vast and comprehensive range of his vision and his gift to us in suggestiveness and insight into the spiritual structure and meaning of the world. It is doubtless easier for the Indian mind than for ours to pass from the confines of sensible nature to the supernatural zone of spirit; with his fertile imagination and mystic ideality he helps to lift us above material forces to the unseen and eternal. It is in his " Song Offerings," a rare treasure of superb lyrics some of which he has set to music, with delicate touch and swift glances into the empyrean, that he makes universal appeal. No wonder that, though not representative of common song among the mass of Hindus, they are sung by millions widely over India, and that he has received garlands from his own people as the king of Bengali literature.

### III

Brief notice may here be added of Sadhu Sundar Singh, whose exodus from Indian religion and whose type of Christian experience and faith differ from any in the above survey. It is too early to say much now of one, born so late as 1889, whose record is incomplete. He has not produced any written " confession " or manifesto, and we are dependent upon others for reports of his career and utterances (cf. " The Sadhu," or " The Message of Sundar Singh," by Street and Appasamy). A Sikh by parentage, reared in luxury at Rampur in North India, he was early familiar with the sacred books of the Sikhs (the Granth) and the Hindus and had shared in their religious practices, but he failed to find spiritual satisfaction therein, and in his despair wished for death even by his own hand.

In the pride of his race and religion, he was repelled by the Bible when he first encountered it; he criticized it, though sometimes feeling its power; he tore it up or burnt it when he had a chance, and threw stones at Christian preachers. He cried to God in desperation, " Show me the right way, or I will kill myself." In 1904, while praying at early dawn, he saw a great light in his room as if it were on fire, yet on looking round he could find nothing. " Then the thought came to me that this might be an answer God had sent me. Then as I prayed and looked into the light, I saw the form of the Lord Jesus Christ, whom I had been insulting a few days before. It had such an appearance of glory and love. I felt that a vision like this could not have come out of my own imagination. I heard a voice saying in Hindustani, ' How long will you persecute me? I have come to save you; you were praying to know the right way; why do you not take it? ' Then the thought came to me, ' Jesus Christ is not dead but living and it must be He Himself.' So I fell at His feet and got this wonderful Peace which I could not get anywhere else. This is the Joy I was wishing to get. This was heaven itself. When I got up the vision had disappeared; but the Peace and Joy have remained with me ever since." He told his incredulous father (in later years himself to become a Christian), " I have discovered now that Jesus Christ is alive, and have determined to be His follower." He is unable to explain psychologically the visions he has had, but he is very sure of the Divine call and message of grace. His family used every means to dissuade the lad of fifteen from adopting the Christian religion—promises of wealth, reminders of the dishonour he would bring on his home, indignities, persecution—but all in vain. After nine months he was disowned and bidden depart for ever. The story reads like a new version of the case of Gautama the Buddha. The first night he spent shivering under a tree, but (he says) " I held the New Testament in my hand ; I remember the wonderful joy in my heart, the presence of my Saviour, who changed the suffering into peace." On his sixteenth birthday in 1905 he was baptized in the Church of England in Simla, and made the decision, still maintained, to don the habit and adopt the way of life of an Indian professed " holy man " or Sadhu.

For years to follow he wandered from place to place, with only his robe, his blanket, and his New Testament, living upon food offered him, or on roots or leaves, and, where hospitality was withheld, sleeping in caves or under trees. He travelled in his mission through the Punjab, Kashmir, Afghanistan and Tibet. In Tibet he was arrested, his life at stake, but the prison was opened for him by an invisible hand. For two years he worked among lepers. In more recent years he has become widely known in Great Britain and America, although disliking notoriety and taking his own detached pilgrim way. The ideals and manner of life of St. Francis of Assisi have always strongly appealed to him.

He early came across Thomas à Kempis' " Imitatio Christi," which, more than any other book except the New Testament, has left its mark on him, on his " philosophy of the Cross," and on his enthusiasm for suffering, not for its ascetic value or merit, but as a bond with Christ. The saying in the " Imitatio," " Bear the Cross and it will bear thee," is clearly reflected in his confession, " From my fourteen years' experience of life as a sadhu for Jesus Christ I can say with confidence that the Cross will bear those who bear the Cross until it lifts them up to Heaven into the presence of the Saviour."

The Sadhu is characteristically a mystic, and has found green pastures by still waters in Jacob Behmen, Sta. Teresa and Madame Guyon. The personal Christ is central in his mystical experiences, including his moments of ecstatic vision. He has spoken of the feeling of " the recognition of Christ as one known long ago. I felt when first I saw Him as if there were some old and forgotten connexion between us, as though He had said but not in words, ' I am He through whom you were created.' All sinners have within themselves a battered image of their Divine Creator, and so when converted they recognize and worship Him." Again, " when God speaks to the soul we have an immediate apprehension of His meaning, somewhat like what occasionally happens in conversation when you know what the other man is going to say before he says it. His thoughts are put directly into our minds without words, and very often they are thoughts which are not expressible in words." He knows by experience the " dark night of the soul," the sense of desolation and eclipse, but he soon emerges into light clearer than before. In his moments of ecstasy he has the "feeling of being at home," surrounded with a wonderful atmosphere, and sees reality in pictures. And Christ is always the centre of the scene.

Wonder and mystery pervade the world as his eyes see it. The supernatural is never far away and waits upon him : not the miraculous as a physical portent, but the presence and action of supersensible potencies. The atmosphere for him is charged, and spiritual signs are not wanting. In his long journeys, with beasts of prey at hand, "never to this day has any wild animal done me harm." In prison Peace and Joy sang in his heart.

Here, one may venture to say, we find something very close akin to the atmosphere, the outlook, the sensitized consciousness, the wonder-elements in the New Testament. The case of the Sadhu enables us the better to understand the sense of brooding presences, the enlargement of psychic powers, the authority of the spirit over evil agencies, the inspirations, and intuitive insights, the signs and wonders which meet us in the Gospels and in the Apostolic Church. Such spiritual phenomena, no strange thing in India, were at home and not surprising in the region and circle where Jesus "manifested forth His glory."

Baron von Hügel is able from personal interviews to say, " The Sadhu most rightly does not, by a specific Indian Christianity, mean a Christianity so much adapted to Indian thought as to cease to be a living Christianity. . . . He is rightly proud of being an Indian, and is anxious to remain as Indian as deep Christianity allows." He does

not pretend to be a philosopher ; his gift is of another order.
What he has sought and knows by experience is, not metaphysical comprehension of the Infinite but personal
devotion, not the vision of Reality but the love of One
who saves.

## XV

# The Significance of the Same:

## COMPARISONS—STOICS, OMAR KHAYYÁM—AND THE DISTINCTIVENESS OF CHRISTIAN EXPERIENCE

THE spiritual documents brought under review in these chapters are not a mere miscellany of singular cases, much less excrescences upon the living growth of human experience; they belong integrally to a large body of authentic literature and to a continuous movement of life. They are, indeed, select writings of outstanding eminence, more or less exceptional in literary expression as well as in the personal ordeal of which they are creations. But they are not abnormal, and are neither casual nor artificial by-products. They are the flowering of perennial life in the recurring vernal rejuvenescence of the soul. They rise like wave-crests out of broad tides and currents of the Spirit. The very fact that they have continuously evoked an appreciative response from multitudes in succeeding ages and in most diverse communities certifies that they are representative of the human soul in its higher reach and potential grasp.

The perusal of this literature calls forth some general questions, comparisons and reflections.

1. Why, it is asked, have we in modern times no great classics of Christian experience which can be ranked with those produced in past generations? The corresponding question might be raised, Why have we apparently been unable to build great cathedrals? We might first contest the assumption involved in the

question. We have not been entirely without contemporary writings entitled to be counted among classics of the soul, such as Tolstoy's " Confessions," Amiel's " Journal," and Pater's " Marius the Epicurean." Yet we have to admit that they do not, equally with older documents, fully compass the four dimensions of the Christian life, the depth of its spiritual experi nces and convictions, the breadth of its interests and sympathies, the height of its divine relationships and contacts, the length of its ideal goal of effort.

Why this shortage, in so far as it is a fact ?   Probably it is due, not to any single cause, but to a complex of causes.

Is it traceable to the multitudinous affairs which distract our minds, disperse our interests, and preclude deep continuous meditation ?  Yet some of the greatest books of this kind, as we have seen, were composed in the midst of public tumult, social unrest, wars, religious controversies, and other distractions.  Is it due to the spirit of questioning which is in the air we breathe, and specifically to critical problems concerning the scriptural sources of Christian knowledge ?  These have doubtless been disconcerting to some minds in the transitional movement from the literal and forensic to the historical and estimative way of treating the traditional sources of belief ; but many earnest Christians have not been disturbed by these problems or have surmounted them and subdued them to a sure enlightened faith.

On a wide scale there is a new outlook upon religion itself, another order of values for life as God wills it in the world here and now.  There is a somewhat different conception of what it means for a man to be a Christian, of what Jesus Christ signifies for the relation of man to his universe.  The emphasis has increasingly been laid on the teaching of our Lord in the Synoptic Gospels, especially upon the Kingdom of God.  This adjustment of orientation may produce a different emphasis in religious experience.

As a further answer to the question posed, much of the religious spirit which formerly found expression in confessional and devotional writings, and otherwise in the building of great cathedrals, has run into other channels, especially into social redemptive enterprise and into missionary service. The call of the community or the common weal has caught the ear of many a faithful " listener to God." The " City of God," set forth by St. Augustine under a division of the world into two realms sacred and secular, and also by Dante in " De Monarchia," has been recapturing in new modes the imagination of " public souls," and has become a charge laid upon their conscience. As Walter Pater says of " Urbs Beata " in " Marius the Epicurean," the ideal had grown up in the Church " in a somewhat false alienation from the light and beauty of the kingdom of nature, of the natural man, with a partly mistaken tradition concerning it, and an incapacity at times for an eventual reconciliation thereto." But it is no longer merely the " City on High " which haunted the mind of Marcus Aurelius as well as the seer of the Apocalypse. It was humanized in fantasies like More's " Utopia," Bacon's " New Atlantis," Campanella's " City of the Sun." It has become the vision of " a reasonable and divine order in the condition of human affairs, in which a consciousness of the Divine will is everywhere realized." Royce accordingly interprets the Christian religion as " loyalty to the Beloved Community." [1]

This social construction of Christianity is partial and one-sided, and it is liable to incur personal loss for lack of experimental religion in its regenerative and sanctifying power. But at any rate it stands for a long-neglected feature of the gospel of the Kingdom ; it stands for community of human life and welfare. A distinct type of religious life is likely to be developed from this way of looking at the Christian religion and of translating the gospel into action. We may, accordingly, anticipate future documents of Christian experience shaped in this social matrix and inspired by this devotion to the City of God.

Much of our spiritual devotion, again, has run into channels of Missionary activity. From the new ground thus brought under cultivation we may look for spiritual records of a fresh character—indeed, we have already had,

---

[1] It was said of the prodigy Randolph Bourne, that " he was the child of some nation yet unborn, smitten with an unappeasable nostalgia for the Beloved Community on the far side of socialism."

as in India, some firstfruits thereof. There are peoples who are passing through a transition from paganism such as we observed in Augustine and " Marius," and are starting their separate career within the Christian era. From the heart of races just awakened to the new Light of day, from an elect few enabled to report the progress of their pilgrim souls and the aspects of " that One Face " as they have come to see it, we may hope for a new series of confessions and spiritual testaments.

We cannot expect a reduplication of religious classics after the old mode when conditions within and without have changed, even if Christian experience is as deep as ever it was. Classics, like Creeds, spring out of fresh movements of the Spirit, and out of reformations and revolutions in the corporate life of men.

2. These and kindred classics, distinctive in spiritual literature, exhibit the distinctiveness of Christian experience.

Spiritual writings born of other great religions disclose kindred needs, conflicts, cravings for " a Friend behind phenomena," for a harmonious state of self-being and superiority to the world and death. The support and nourishment they gave to generations of men cannot be fully measured by us. But there is a manifest difference between the type of personality and the process prescribed for its attainment which they set forth and that which is specifically Christian.

(a) In the writings of the Roman STOICS, Seneca, Epictetus and Marcus Aurelius, aphoristic instructions for the conduct of life express a magnanimous ideal of manhood and an heroic method of self-conquest, contributory to the culture of Christian character. But their world-view, their deficient conception of the Supreme Being as personal and graciously active in human life, involved a loss of resources for the achievement of vital godliness. As already indicated in the chapter on Marcus Aurelius, the Stoic recognized the *animus mundi*, the divine principle permeating all things, the universe as divine in all its parts, and viewed as Nature, Reason and Destiny.

The Stoic problem is one of circumstance, the balanced

adjustment of personal life to circumstance.   The strength of life lies in individual self-sufficiency and imperturbability. The independent soul, by its native powers and Roman discipline, can dauntlessly repudiate the power of fortune or of fate to hurt it.   We can endure, with inward freedom, whatever happens to us, encased in the coat of mail of inward indifference :  as Henley put it mordantly :

"In the fell clutch of circumstance
I have not winced nor cried aloud,
Under the bludgeonings of chance
My head is bloody but unbowed."

The Christian does not regard man as a creature of chance or subject of fate, but, through all the seeming confusion of incidents, as a free spirit set in a world where nature and circumstance can be made to serve his highest ends, not by his own effort alone but in conscious alliance with the Lord over all things.   He seeks, not to suppress emotion as discomposing, but to engage it and so consume it as energy in great tasks.   He has deeper heart-searchings than the Stoic, who utters no cry *de profundis* for Divine grace to recreate the soul.   Both win peace, the Stoic the peace of detachment and of contentment with his fate, the Christian the peace of working together with God in the endless task of love and perfection.   Both have love for man, even for those who do wrong ;  the Stoic is pitiful under consideration that men are what Nature makes them ;  the Christian sees the infinite value of every soul as capable of redemption and potentially a son of God.   For the former, virtuous character is elaborated by specific self-management ;  the Christian life transcends the limits of nature under inspiration of a personal attachment, and gives the fullest scope for high adventure, with guarantees that all prayer, endeavour and sacrifice will have their personal values eternally conserved.

The Christian graces, faith, hope and love, are not merely moral virtues ;  they are spiritual energies.   And Christian experience accordingly manifests a dynamic for measureless life.

Both Stoic and Christian practise renunciation of selfish aims and pleasures as the way to peace.   But, in the words of F. W. H. Myers (on Marcus Aurelius in " Classical

Essays "), " the difference lies in the light in which they regard it. To the Stoic in the West, as to the Buddhist in the East, it presented itself as a renunciation which became a deliverance, a tranquillity which passed into an annihilation. The Christian, too, recognized in the renunciation a deliverance from its evil. But his spirit in those early days was occupied less with what he was resigning than with what he gained ; the love of Christ constrained him ; he died to self to find, even here on earth, that he had passed, not into nothingness but into heaven. . . . His only objection to the Stoic manner of facing the reality of the universe was that the reality of the universe was so infinitely better than the Stoic supposed. If, then, the Stoic love beside the Christian was ' as moonlight unto sunlight and as water unto wine,' it was not only because the Stoic philosophy prescribed the curbing and checking of those natural emotions which Christianity at once guided and intensified by her new ideal. It was because the love of Christ which the Christian felt was not a laborious duty, but a self-renewing, self-intensifying force ; a feeling offered as to one whose triumphant immortality had brought His disciples' immortality to light."

(b) The great classics of the historical religions of INDIA, often remarkable for their spacious intellectual range and their emotional reaction upon invisible Presences, are generally engrossed with the relation between the finite and the Infinite, between the individual and Absolute Being, ever seeking the One under the multiplicity of things. They usually move in a sphere of abstract thought, or come from minds afflicted with the illusory nature of the world (maya), and seeking the Something permanent in the continuous process of birth and death, of emanation and dissolution, " the Self seated at the heart of things." Owing to their Pantheistic philosophy, they are lacking in their grasp of personality both Divine and human, and in their measure of human need.

The " Bhagavad Gita " (Song of the Adorable One), the popular devotional classic, glorifies Krishna as representative of Supreme Being, an object of worship and trust, saving helper and guide in the search for emancipation. Yet, as a mythological figure, he has no coherent personal history and consistent moral character. All things, even the basest, are woven of his being; and all religious cults are ways of worshipping him. He is represented as saying, " As often as there is a decline of virtue or an increase of vice in the world, I create myself anew; and thus I appear from age to age for the preservation of the just, the destruction of the wicked, and establishment of virtue." The Gita enjoins purity of heart, renunciation, compassion for all things, and in its charm of expression it touches noble sentiments. Yet it sanctions the system of caste, and rests upon *karma* (the entail of action) in the transmigration of souls through countless lives. It is blind to the real evil of sin, and offers no Divine grace by which the guilt and power of sin may be removed, the soul renewed and sanctified. Other Indian classics are poetic, romantic myths meant to account for phases of nature, forms of life, suffering and death, or devotional formulæ for ritual offices having inherent virtue for purification and securing identity of being with the All.

Indian poetry of later times follows more ardently " the way of devotion " (*bhakti*), transcends formal doctrine, and appeals to the heart and to subjective experience such as all religious natures can share. Its outcry for God, who is believed to be able to help if only He would, is intense. " O God, my cry comes up to Thee—How sad a cry is it! What is this tragic destiny, That Fate for me has writ? " But, while it comprises notes of praise and attainment (though less than the Hebrew Psalter), it displays more desire than satisfaction. It is haunted by the traditional idea that the " Formless " cannot really be known, and by the sadness that arises from *karma* and the endless " wheel " of birth and death. Sometimes it breaks bounds and indulges in extravagant religious raptures such as may be found among some mystics of the West.[1] Unable to understand, the devout will strive still to love Him and at least win the beatific rest of sacred contemplation. " He lights the lamp of knowledge in the heart of holy men."

[1] Cf. " Hibbert Journal," Oct., 1917, " The Indian Poetry of Devotion," by Dr. N. Macnicol.

Yet the note of joyous triumph is absent. And, it must be added, this sacred poetry contains no prayer for others, for mankind. The Hindu religion, bedded in the divisive system of caste and in individual isolation in the process of emancipation from the illusory world, lacked the social consciousness, the sense of universal commonweal in a divine community.

The writers of Christian classics attest experience of the living Lord whose message was conveyed mainly by His personality in word and deed, through moral insights rather than theoretic conceptions, so securing fellowship. They are more particularly engaged with inward personal states, with character and duty, with human delinquency and Divine grace in recovery and service. Their problem is, not (as in India) finitude and suffering as essential ills, but the perversity of the human will, and suffering only as incidental or as potentially fruitful of good. Evil is not in the constitution of the universe or the illusion of existence, but in the human heart. And, as it can be cured by a change of heart, pessimism is excluded. The means by which this end is gained is, not mere renunciation nor " seeing through " appearances in contemplation, but a signal act of God in history, a Personal Life whose sacrificial love is reconciling and vitalizing, under the conjoint action of the ever-present Spirit. The goal of all endeavour is, not escape from illusion and from desire of individual life, the absorption of the stream in the Ocean of the All, but " life more abundant," fullness and power of personality, the fellowship of love and service in a spiritual common-wealth.

(c) The *Rubá'iyát* of OMAR KHAYYÁM, in Edward Fitz-gerald's free rendering, is one of the popular and cherished classics of the soul. Its fascination is partly due to its literary excellence, the polished flashing jewels of its imagery, the haunting music of its quaint quatrain (*rubá'i*). It acquires a glamour also as the fusion of Oriental reflections eight hundred years old with modern Western criticism of life. And its genial dalliance with the baffling mystery of human fortunes, its sly or audacious thrusts at the ironies of Providence, and its cult of social enjoyment forgetful of sinister fate and of responsibility, make appeal to some naughty pleasure common to men, especially when bearing the sanction of refined taste and artistic charm. Fitzgerald wrote, " You will find a sort of *triste plaisir* in it, as others besides myself have felt. It is a desperate sort of thing, unfortunately at the bottom of all thinking men's minds, but made music of." The touch of melancholy upon its jocund philosophy of life adds relish to the cunning gaiety it cultivates amidst falling rose-leaves.

The Persian poet, Omar—Khayyám, " tent-maker," being his pen-name—lived at Nishapur through the last half of the eleventh and the first quarter of the twelfth century. By profession a learned astronomer, addicted to philosophy and the study of medicine, he had brought a scientific mind to bear critically upon the conventional Moslem doctrine of his people, upon all pious make-belief and the mystic pantheism of the Sufis. He calls himself " a slave in revolt "; he is often defiant and satirical, while haunted by the grand curiosity as to the Secret of the " spangle of Existence." His epigrammatic poetic estimates of life were written, as Fitzgerald says, " not all at one period of his life, but from time to time, just as circumstances and mood suggested, and under the influence of thoughts, passions and desires which happened to be uppermost at the moment." The quatrains accordingly were not consistent in tone, now irreligious and Epicurean, again devotional. When collected they were placed in alphabetical order without logical sequence. But Fitzgerald in his reconstruction arranged them in a certain progressive series, following vaguely the stages in a soul's history. Selecting and recombining passages he produced a tesselated mosaic from the " Rubá'iyát," a poetic transfusion rather than a literal translation of the quatrains. His mind was one with Omar's, and his version is " the re-delivery of a poetic inspiration." In some of the touches and settings which he imposed, he occasionally defaced the spiritual content of stanzas in the original, pointing them with sharp flicks of gay insolence. The product is Omar wrought over by Fitzgerald.

Edward Fitzgerald (1809-83),[1] Cambridge graduate, beloved among friends like Tennyson, Suffolk recluse, steeped in the wistful sentiment of Persian poetry, had leisure and inclination for a sedentary literary life of gentle philosophical reflection. A lover of poetry and music, a man of simple tastes scornful of self-indulgence, with an eccentric turn and a vein of misanthropy, he was sensitive to the impress of a world of beauty flowering only to die, and lived in pensive, melancholy regret at the fleeting years and the fugitive efforts that failed to achieve lasting satisfactions in life. He was *Le Penseur*, a spectator of life, afflicted with a tender sadness in reflecting on the irrevocable past and the passing away of all that is much to be desired. It is often the bystander of highly refined sensibilities, rather than the worker and sufferer, who is liable to become a caustic critic of the Providential "Scheme of Things." His humorous jests at life with a cynical accent betray a painful tenderness. He could and did indulge imaginative sympathy with Omar Khayyám in his attitude to life.

Omar, according to Fitzgerald, " having failed (however mistakenly) of finding any Providence but Destiny, and any world but this, set about making the most of it; preferring with a humorous or perverse pleasure rather to soothe the soul through the senses into acquiescence with things as they are than to perplex it with vain disquietude after what *might* be." What afflicts him is the elemental fact of the transitoriness and vanity of life rather than any unbearable wrongs endured under the inverted bowl of the sky. "'Come, fill the bowl " in the wine-party, and drink, for " the bird of Time has but a little way to flutter, and the bird is on the wing." Time is the enemy. " In this batter'd caravanserai whose portals are alternate night and day " each in turn has his destined hour (xvii., xlviii.) :

> " A moment's halt—a momentary taste
>    Of BEING from the well amid the waste—
>       And lo !—the phantom caravan has reach'd
>    The NOTHING it set out from—Oh, make haste ! "

---

[1] Cf. Batson and Ross, The " Rubá'iyát " of Omar Khayyám translated by Edward Fitzgerald (Methuen) ; Translations of the " Rubá'iyát " by Fizgerald, E. H. Whinfield, and J. H. McCarthy, with Introduction by J. B. Rittenhouse (Little, Brown) ; Sell, " The Faith of Islam," pp. 139 ff. ; Benson (A. C.), Edward Fitzgerald (" English Men of Letters ").

To-morrow, like ourselves, will soon be with " yesterday's seven thousand years." We have but to-day ; we have a little hour ; " let us waste it well." We have a jug of wine, tulip-cheek'd women beside us in the wilderness, the melodies of song and lute—such wilderness were paradise enow. Take the roses of the hours in the flush of spring as they bloom and drop. Some set their hearts upon the glories of this world that turn to ashes ; and some

> " Sigh for the prophet's paradise to come ;
>    Ah, take the cash and let the credit go,
> Nor heed the rumble of a distant drum."

Take the moment's " ready money " of enjoyment—present values alone are sure. Saints and sages have perplexed their minds with discussions of the tangle of two worlds human and divine : " their words to scorn are scattered, and their mouths are stopp'd with dust." We come into this world " *why* not knowing, nor *whence*, like water willy-nilly flowing," nor *whither* like wind, willy-nilly blowing. We grope in thought for the meaning of it all, but come out by the same door we entered in by. " Me " and " Thee " are shadows passing on a lantern. " Many a cup of this forbidden wine must drown the memory of such insolence." In the tent of the day, in the social tavern, enjoy the draught, " for once dead, you never shall return." Man is helpless under inevitable law, and is wise to accept the standpoint of fatalism. We are moved by fate like pieces in the game of chess. " Past regrets and future fears " are vain.

> " The moving finger writes ; and, having writ,
> Moves on : nor all your piety nor wit
>    Shall lure it back to cancel half a line,
> Nor all your tears wash out a word of it."

Omar does not see that, while what is done remains as fact, much that has been done amiss may be repaired or at any rate cleansed of its guilt and stain through repentance and the forgiveness of sins, to the transformation of the personal life ; with his world-view he has " no place for repentance " and for the doctrine, " I believe in the forgiveness of sins." Indeed, " repentance oft before I swore—but was I sober

when I swore ? " Spring and roses came, and " my thread-
bare penitence apieces tore." So his mood changes, and
with a jest he returns to his merry inn. As to penitence,
was not man enmeshed in predestined evil, and how then
impute his fall to sin ? Was not a snake devised for Paradise ? Hence the impious address to the Deity (lxxxi.) :

> " For all the sin wherewith the face of man
>    Is blackened—man's forgiveness give—and take ! "

This gesture—man's offer of forgiveness to God—is due
entirely to Fitzgerald, and is an inversion of what Omar
wrote, accurately translated thus :

> " O Thou who knowest the secret of every one's mind,
>    Who graspest every one's hand in the hour of weakness,
>    O God, give me repentance and accept my excuses,
>    O Thou who givest repentance and acceptest the excuses of every one."

Strange that the English versifier, on learning of his
misapprehension of the Persian, declined to amend the
lines !

Omar is indeed a moral sceptic, and an Epicurean. But,
as in Tennyson's " Two Voices " and Browning's " Bishop
Blougram's Apology," he suffers from a duality of mind,
and doubts his doubts, in the oscillation of his moods.
Estranged from the effete orthodox Moslem creed and the
false esoteric mysticism of the Sufis of his day, he has
moments of Agnosticism, and dissuades men from appealing
to Heaven which is as helpless as they. He sarcastically
criticizes the Master of life ; yet again, with a touch of
mysticism, he recognizes God and the need of Him, more
than appears in the English version. As in another version
he cries :

> " I cannot reach the Road to join with Thee ;
>    I cannot bear one breath apart from Thee ;
>    I dare not tell this grief to any man ;
>    Ah hard ! Ah strange ! Ah longing sweet for Thee."

Again (lxx.), " And He that toss'd you down into the field,
*He* knows about it all—He knows—HE knows." He had
sent his soul through the Invisible, " Some letter of that

after-life to spell." And, before Dante and Milton said it, he said :

> " By and by my soul returned to me
> And answered, ' I myself am Heaven and Hell.' "

At times he cannot be content to make his dwelling in " this plot of earth," and bids his heart become free from dust and soar naked to a seat beside the throne of God (xliv.). Questioning, he still inquires ; he has a wish to believe. The wine he brags of drinking is not the " booze " of the Western sot but the seal of the jocund party. As might be said also of Fitzgerald, " it requires little discernment to see that he talked far more than he acted, and that his arraignment of the Deity is largely bravado to conceal his misgiving and unrest." The popular cult of Omar to-day is likewise largely playful bravado, though liable to infect his devotees with the ironic spirit and a lightened sense of personal responsibility. But he ends in a supervening note of irony and prudent hedonism.

> " Ah Love! could you and I with Him conspire
> To grasp this sorry Scheme of Things entire,
> Would we not shatter it to bits—and then
> Remould it nearer to the Heart's Desire."

Agreed ; but according to the Christian view it is not the world in itself, but the world familiar to us as the companion of " the flesh and the devil," aye, and " the heart's desire," that need remoulding.

His better mind never leads him to renunciation, to which Tolstoy was led. He does not even attain a positive principle of life and effort, such as we have in the kindred book of Ecclesiastes—" Fear God and keep His commandments, for this is the whole of man." An air of softened melancholy hovers over his horizon. The sad sense of youth gone and natural forces abated overtakes us all with the presentiment of last farewells. But Omar, like Tolstoy, experiences a deeper sadness, though he does not express it, due to the decay of sense in palate and passion and the loss of the capacity for enjoyment. " Marius the Epicurean " was quickened to renounce the lesser for the greater satisfactions of life and to enjoy the " new song."

3. Christian experience, in its four dimensions, is the most significant thing in history for a true understanding of the ultimate meaning of life and as a pathway to Eternal Reality. It is vastly more extensive and manifold than these select studies unfold; but they disclose what is characteristic of it and touch its core. Divine manifestations encompass us on all sides, in the universe and human history, in all that is sincerely felt and truly known; and there are countless manuscripts of the Divine Spirit and classics of the human quest for the infinitely Good, Beautiful and True, in the disclosures of science, in works of art, in Greek and modern dramas, and in heroic lives. "There are, it may be, so many kinds of voices in the world, and none of them is without signification" (1 Cor. xiv. 10).

(a) But, when we inquire into the intensive, qualitative power and permanent values of human life, we must search for them in spiritual experience as giving us the closest contact with the Eternal; we must seek them in Christian experience, distinguished by its profoundly moral quality creative of character, and consummated in love which is the perfection of goodness. Our primary need is not that of conceptual truth, needful as it comes to be, but that of reality, the discernment of spiritual reality, which is reported to us through insight given in religious experience. God as apprehended in Jesus Christ by the power of the Spirit "ceases to be an object and becomes an experience." The promise "He will guide you into all truth" means, "He will guide you into all authentic experience of reality."

Christianity, wrote Amiel ("Journal," 121), "is above all religious, and religion is not a method, it is a life, a higher and supernatural life, mystical in its root and practical in its fruits, a communion with God, a calm and deep enthusiasm, a love which radiates, a force which acts, a happiness which overflows." It is a potency of salvation, which is new life in friendship with God and new strength in the joy of forgiveness, overcoming sin and self in endeavours after goodness and the welfare of men. The forgiveness of burdensome sins pierces to the core of the moral situation in man; and the sacramental experience of being absolutely forgiven at the cost of suffering love stirs springs of vital renewal and measureless energy. And, in Herrmann's words, " to anyone who really experiences it, forgiveness comes, not as a matter of course, but as an astounding revelation of love." It is a revelation or a discovery of the supreme reality, of " gracious reality " (which is the meaning of " grace and truth "). Touching bottom, this experience and others germane to it are accordingly the most significant for an authentic apprehension of God among all diversities of human experience and investigation.

(b) Christian experience calls for and still awaits adequate interpretation. When a man makes confession, "*I have felt* this and thus," it does not follow that the opinion or the doctrine which he forms is thereby certified as true. It may seem as if the vivid impression made on the soul in an hour of spiritual quickening or elevation seals or justifies the beliefs or inferences of the person therein engaged ; but this is a mistake. A Quaker and a Ritualist may receive a kindred influx of gracious power or illumination ; but they draw very different conclusions therefrom. The mystic in that " one moment of understanding " when he seems to himself to gain direct perception of the Eternal is apt to suppose that divine knowledge has been communicated to him or that his existing views have been confirmed. But, while the vision or insight may be quite authentic, definite truth is not conveyed to him in the process. His spiritual consciousness has been intensified ; but the ideas in his mind are not guaranteed.

Christian, or any genuine religious, experience is significant of reality and provides data for a judgment of what is truth ; but the experience in itself does not declare its meaning. It gives us a sense of immediacy, assures us of veritable values, and invests our faith and practice with sanctity ; but the beliefs entertained or derived therefrom are not immediately given in the act. Critical and reflective thought is required to purify emotions, to sift impressions, and to find their significance in forms of general intelligence. Religious experience is necessary, and is the basis of religious belief, the material of doctrine ; yet it must await sane and enlightened interpretation in the light of the rest of our knowledge. Every experient reads into his experience much that he brings with him to it. He must test it and set it in the light of a wider body of experience.

What in defined doctrinal form Christian experience signifies does not, of course, come within our present task. A book starting from and working directly upon the evidence of Christian experience on a wide base, without undue regard to scholastic theology, is much to be desired. The great book on the subject has yet to be written. James's " Varieties of Religious Experience," a promiscuous treasury of suggestive material, is engrossed with psychological analysis, often with eccentric and even neurotic cases, does not explore the wealth of distinctively Christian experience, and still less does it pretend to construe such experience in positive judgments of what is the truth from the Christian standpoint. Professor T. R. Glover's title for his book, " Jesus in the Experience of Men," is too wide for its contents. It is engaged with the experience of the Apostolic Church, with historical origins and parallels. Illuminating within its special field, it does not attempt to cover the whole ground. Stearns' " Evidence of Christian Experience " discusses vital material with a full estimate of its value, but it is mainly apologetic in its aim, and, having appeared so long ago as 1890, it does not contain the results of modern critical and psychological analysis of the documents.

Possibly no one man is capable of comprehending and expounding the whole subject-matter to general satisfaction. We may have to wait for what we want until research and reflection have brought us nearer a solution of initial problems at present in the crucible, and until some constructive thinker has arisen who has power to see the proportions of the Christian faith and to express in universal terms the spiritual contents of vital experience in the light of the Living Word Himself and the Apostolic norm.

(c) The creative initiative of the Spirit of God is recognized as the primary condition of the Christian life. In saying this we are not committed to any theory of human capacities—of latent evil or potential good; but we do observe the stupor of nature in man at the outset. His native powers may be fully alive and competent, while yet his soul sleeps or is unborn. He needs more than self-realization; he needs spiritual quickening—not a new religious faculty (there is no peculiar religious faculty), but a new power of life which shall bring the redirection of his finest powers to the highest ends. It is not a gift of nature; it comes to birth in a fresh experience. It vitalizes the whole man, and gives a unity to his manifold interests by subduing them all to a central governing motive.

Benjamin Jowett (" Theological Essays," 55) emphasizes the importance of this radical activity. " Easier to change many things than one, is the common saying. Easier, we may add, in religion and morality, to change the whole than the part. Easier because more natural, more agreeable to the voice of conscience and the promises of Scripture. . . . Take care of the little things of life and the great things will take care of themselves, is the maxim of the trader. But more true is it in religion that we should take care of the great things, and the trifles of life will take care of themselves. Christianity is not an art acquired by long practice; it does not carve and polish human nature with a graving tool; it makes the whole man : first pouring out his soul before God, and then casting him in a mould."

This creative life is commonly ascribed to " supernatural grace," and rightly if we do not take such in a superstitious sense. The spiritual is the true supernatural. At the same time the Divine action operates through the use of agencies and through the psychic processes proper to man's nature. Biographies and books on the Psychology of Religion[1] exhibit the infinite variety in the processes, the phases, the stages gradual or concentrated in a day, the influence of the pre-formed type due to Church tradition, through which spiritual life emerges. To compare and estimate them in all the diversity of operation would take

[1] Cf. Pratt, " The Religious Consciousness "; Steven, " The Psychology of the Christian Soul "; James, " Varieties of Religious Experience "; Granger, "The Soul of a Christian "; Pym, " Psychology and the Christian Life," and books (of very diverse value) by Coe, Ames, Leuba, Stratten.

us too far afield. Cases of remarkable religious revolution figure prominently in Christian records : being vivid or dramatic, they were capable of observation and definite description. In most instances the new life of the kingdom comes without observation. There is no fundamental difference between the gradual and the apparently sudden in such awakenings. The factor of time is not an element in causation. The short and swift change had antecedent preparation, and only condensed the movement of the soul, which in most others proceeds by steps. But, whether observed or not, there was some critical decision or repetition of decisions ; determinate choice was made, determining the soul's attitude ; and attitude, when definitely taken, is potential destiny.

The guarantee of the Divine presence and grace does not lie in remarkable phenomena as " signs " or in the mode of experience, but in the abiding consciousness of a new energy of life in friendly relations with God and His Saviour-Son.

The experience of such awakenings or reversals, when viewed as a psychic process, is not confined to Christianity, or even to religion. As William James and others have shown, there have been counter-revolutions away from religion. There have been intellectual new-births, as in John Stuart Mill's " Autobiography." Gautama, afterwards the Buddha, experienced a religious renewal as real after its separate kind as that of Saul of Tarsus. Among Mohammedans, especially among mediæval mystical Sufis, such inward revolutions occurred. Both Devendranath Tagore and his poet son Rabindranath Tagore (see earlier pages) passed through a similar change in keeping with the renascence of India. Carlyle related in " Sartor Resartus " his mental travail and deliverance ; all else in the book, he wrote afterwards (Froude's " Early Life of Carlyle," cap. vii.), is symbolical myth, but this experience " occurred quite literally to myself in Leith Walk, Edinburgh, during three weeks of total sleeplessness. . . . I remember it well, and could go straight to about the spot."

With these might be compared the outstanding cases cited above in this book, as well as those of Pascal, George Fox (see his " Autobiography "), and others recounted in books on the subject (see Appendix).

We have to note here that what distinguishes a Christian awakening or conversion is, not the process or the psychic modes through which it comes, but the type of spiritual life generated, the direction of faith and endeavour, the contents of the new acquisition, all corresponding to the rich clear conception of God the Father as known to us in Jesus Christ, and as at work in His kingdom among men.  Its vital ideas actualized and made magnetic and dynamic in the person of Jesus Christ through the Spirit, guaranteeing God to the soul and unselfing our life in a larger community of life, give a distinctive quality and range to our experience of the " new creation " in Christ.

Carlyle in his " Sartor " is entitled to say (subject to the modification of a phrase or two) in the light of Christian experience : " Blame not the word (conversion) ; rejoice rather that such a word, signifying such a thing, has come to light in our modern era, though hidden from the wisest ancients.  The Old World knew nothing of conversion ; instead of an *Ecce Homo*, they had only some *Choice of Hercules*.  It was a new-attained progress in the moral development of man : hereby has the Highest come to the bosom of the most limited ; what to Plato was but a hallucination, and to Socrates a chimera, is now clear and certain to your Zinzendorfs, your Wesleys, and the poorest of their Pietists and Methodists."

This Divine initiative, in a critical decision, continues in the progress of the Christian life.  " The perseverance of the saints consists in ever-new beginnings."  In the words of the Psalm (lxxx.), " turn us again . . . again . . . again, and cause Thy face to shine and we shall be saved." In George Macdonald's words :

> " But he who would be born again indeed
>      Must wake his soul unnumbered times a day,
>   And urge himself to life with holy greed ;
>      Now ope his bosom to the Wind's free play
>   And now with patience forceful, hard, lie still,
>   Submiss and ready to the making Will,
>   Athirst and empty for God's Breath to fill."

The spiritual forces released in creative moments go to work in the evaluation of material given in our early instruction and in our personal history, and in the adjustment of our life to the enlarged spiritual world into which we have been initiated.    The Divine *gift* has called us to a *task*.   We have to " work out " the saving grace which was given us. Our general task individually is to unify our " divided self," making " one whole man," and to harmonize the forces in our complex nature and our environment with the new spiritual interest which has become predominant.    " The expulsive power of a new affection " (in Dr. Chalmers' words) meets with opposition from old propensities.    The fight for freedom in national life has been a long, long fight, and has to be renewed in successive generations.    Personally we have still a fight for it—for that freedom which is won when we have subdued all that is beneath us in sense and the world, below the level of our best mind, to the service of that which in spirit we acknowledge to be our rightful lord. But, in this long strife, the verdict of Christian experience declares that God by His Spirit is our invisible " Assistant," not only working with us but working in us astonishingly to accomplish His " good pleasure."    " All that we have He takes—all that He is He gives," as Ruysbroek wrote, and what we are is raised to a higher power.

This Christian endeavour has taken and may take two distinct directions towards two centres of interest.   Both involve the moral discipline of our life.   In one of these the ruling interest may be our relation to God, our personal holiness, involving a course of spiritual self-culture, as in the " Imitatio Christi " and Jeremy Taylor's " Holy Living." This cultivation of saintliness is liable, often though not necessarily, to run into excessive self-abnegation, as in the " Theologia Germanica," and even into unnatural pagan asceticism.   In another direction the centre of spiritual interest may lie in the human community in which the kingdom of God is to be planted.   This social consciousness in Christianity has recently gained ascendancy in Christian teaching.   Jesus Christ evidently was keenly sympathetic with common humanity, and He refused in His temptations and in His life-work to claim any benefits which could not be shared with the community of devout men.  Yet this sense of the social well-being was related intimately to the fatherly love of God to all men, and to the redemption of men from sin through His Son, Jesus Christ, who gave His life for all men.

These two directions of Christian service are found ultimately to be identical.  God has identified Himself with human life.  The service of God is one with the service of man.  In the service of man, our aim is to share the mind of God.  The ultimate reference of our social service must be to unison with the heart of God, and social service apart from inspiration from the loving purpose of God for all men is liable to be coldly dry and ineffective.

4. The historical Jesus Christ is the indispensable source and constant prerequisite of Christian experience.  For most men this might be taken for granted.  Yet it is left in doubt or called in question in some influential quarters.  We are asked whether our spiritual contact with God is really dependent upon a specific person in a particular time and place, and may not be immediate between Spirit and spirit.  This question comes to us from two different quarters or standpoints.

(a) Mystics, in seeking immediate touch with God through intuitive vision, have sometimes appeared to dispense with all mediation, whether that of the Jesus of history or that of the Holy Scriptures.  It is said that they attempt union with God independently of any single objective medium.  This may be true of some mediæval mystics of the speculative type of mind ; they may use Christ as a stepping-stone at an intermediate stage in the instruction of their souls during the ascent towards God, but they pass beyond Him in the higher range of attainment to undivided consciousness of the Absolute.  These, however, are more Neo-Platonist than Christian.  In our own day Maeterlinck as in " The Treasure of the Humble " represents a mode of mysticism which, however ideally lofty and suggestive, lacks the distinctive content of Christian experience.

Other mystics, like Thomas à Kempis, transcend all organized agencies and ceremonies in their highest moments, and speak of being " alone with the Alone." But we must not restrict them to single utterances expressing the uncritical ardour of an exalted hour; the context of such language shows that it is in virtue of having the mind of Christ, of being " in Christ," that they are enabled to rise above all " things " of sense and " see God " in the uppermost heaven of the spirit.

William Law laid emphasis mainly on the Christ who is within, and he was accused of neglecting the incarnation and the atonement as objective grounds of faith and sources of life. But, as his chief biographer says, " Law over and over again affirms, as Behmen affirmed before him, that the doctrine of the Christ within in no wise weakened his belief in the historical Christ who was born of the Virgin Mary, suffered under Pontius Pilate; and all the more moderate mystics affirm the same."

The Friends (Quakers) have given a primary place to the Inner Light and regarded it as the judge of the written Word. According to Barclay (" Apology," 67) " Scripture is only a declaration of the fountain, not the fountain itself," and only a " secondary rule." We need not here inquire how far we have come to adopt his principle when stated in a more discriminating form. The witness within acts conjointly with the witness without; and authority in religion lies in the constraining appeal which the Divine light in its highest Personal and Scriptural embodiments makes to the kindred light in the responsive human spirit. Yet even the response of the human spirit to such appeal is largely the product of training within the religious community and of the historic Christian revelation. The Friends have been far from neglecting the central place and function of Jesus Christ. George Fox, the founder of Quakerism, while revolting against the mechanical authority of external ecclesiasticism and book-religion, declared, " I knew not God but by revelation "; and his inward deliverance came to him chiefly through an " opening " which brought him a new insight into the possibility of a perfect moral life through the help of Christ.[1]  A modern Friend, Caroline Mason, has

[1] Cf. Rufus M. Jones' edition of George Fox's " Autobiography," I, 68–85, etc.; Caroline Mason's " Light Arising," 45.

said : " Too often the Light Within seems to be understood as meaning such light as is contained within my or thy individual experience, rather than as the innermost Central Light whether of the individual or of all life.   The teaching of inwardness seems to require, to make it either safe or adequate, the recognition of the *concentric structure* not only of human beings but of humanity and consciousness."   This recognition of a Central Light and of a corporate body of human experience correcting and completing anyone's private insight surmounts the individualism of the Quaker's appeal to the Inner Light ; and it provides a place for the central Light of the World.

While some religious mystics within the Church have used language which seems to eliminate Jesus Christ from the uppermost room of communion with God, this is not true of Christian mystics as a class.   They have attained unison and union with God through identification with Christ by faith ; and, even when in high moments they are conscious of God alone, it is in terms of Christ and His gospel that they think of God, and it is because of being " one " with His Son, " clothed " with Him, that they have the most intimate fellowship with the Father.

(b) In a very different quarter, it is sometimes said that spiritual truth and Christian values are independent of historical fact and the person of Jesus Christ.  Spinoza held that the function of the Scriptures is, not to teach doctrines regarding God and man, but to foster piety and the practice of justice and love ; they have a cultural value, no matter what opinions we entertain concerning God. Matthew Arnold, taking the Scriptures merely as literature, reiterated the same view after his own manner.   And to-day we are told that Christian documents would retain their spiritual value as instruments of soul-culture, no matter what the historical facts really were in the story of Jesus Christ, no matter what His rank and nature, no matter even whether He ever lived.   The story has set afloat great religious ideas and erected noble ideals, which now hold possession in virtue of their inherent truth and practical value. All that is required of us is that we adopt a specific mode of life inspired by the *ideal* of Jesus as depicted in the tale.

It is a specious and seductive theory. It seems to deliver us from anxiety about the results of historical criticism, and give us a religion of the spirit free from doctrine and from doubt. But it cuts at the very root of Christian experience. It is the great heresy dealt with in the New Testament. The First Epistle of St. John vehemently controverts it, saying, " Every spirit that confesseth not that Jesus Christ is come in the flesh is not of God—this is the spirit of antichrist " ; the word of life " was manifested, we have seen it, our hands have handled it." Further, the Christian Church was founded and built up upon the historicity and memoranda of Jesus Christ. The great religious ideas and spiritual values which obtain among us were derived therefrom. And the continued maintenance of these ideas and values depends largely upon historical actuality in the life, teaching and unique Person of Jesus Christ, and upon the authenticity of the Apostolic witness in its central content. The New Testament is not preoccupied with an -*ism* called Christianity—the term does not occur in the documents ; it is engrossed with the personal Jesus Christ and whatever flows from Him. Christian experience has, from first to last, been generated in conscious relations with the Supreme Being taken as objectively real, and with Jesus Christ as central and vital in historical experience.

Renan, in his " Life of Jesus," pointed out that, when Jesus Himself was asked what His doctrine was, what exact dogmatic truth He had to declare, He could give no direct answer. He could not produce a series of doctrinal texts. He could only say, " Follow me." We may go further and say that Christianity is the most personal of religions. It is a religion of personal relations. It is summed up in a Personal Word ; it is inspired by personal devotion ; it operates in inner personal experience ; and it has for its end fullness of personality in wealth of being and expansion of life in an " ecclesia " or blessed community of God's folk. " What happened at Pentecost " (see Prof. Anderson Scott's book under that title) comprised a new intensity and quality of personal fellowship in which the Spirit witnessed to the continued presence of the living Christ in a common experience.

This claim does not require that everything in the records, every report or individual view or theory found in the documents, must be adopted as indispensable for the great ideas and for the vital moral values which we desire to conserve for the enhancement of life. But it does demand that we are in contact with historical actuality, with a life lived unto the uttermost in verity and sacrifice, with an ideal that had its personal embodiment, with a spiritual society which originated from the creative spirit of Him who " dwelt among us."

True, the Classics of the Soul which we have studied can be and have been used for their cultural value irrespective of their historical basis. But they could never have come into being had they not drawn abundantly upon the historical material certified in Christian origins. Fiction, or myth, however admirable in its expression and implicit ideas, cannot wield the same redemptive and inspiring force in the making of character as fact and especially as a supreme Personality incarnating both truth and love. The ideal of Jesus viewed only as a symbol would undoubtedly still make its appeal and challenge, and would summon men to live in the same spirit, no matter who or what He was. But, if only an ideal, its missionary efficiency would be lost. It would still animate many people who had been nourished in the Christian faith and atmosphere; but, even among them, its significance and its life-value would tend to decline, as it has done in the past in such circumstances.

This does not mean that any particular traditional body of dogmas is necessary for the creation and continuance of Christian experience. Doctrine can rightly be only the interpretation of experience. And Christian experience springs up out of life, out of life given creatively in Christ Jesus and ministered through the " Beloved Community " which is the " mother of us all."

The spiritual magnitude required for fullness of life is not Christ regarded as a solitary absolute, apart from all before and after Him, but the Christ who has constituted by His self-imparting presence a " body " of spiritual consciousness and energy, a *lebenssystem*, which mediates contact with Himself and generates Christian experience continuous with the

Apostolic norm. This spiritual magnitude reappears in every vital epoch of faith in new modes and adjustments, and takes fresh expression in language and in action. Yet every great rejuvenescence of Christian faith and life has been accompanied by a return to the original founts in Holy Scripture. From every stage in the progress of the pilgrim church, from every point in the compass of our diverse standpoints, there is constant reference to Jesus Christ as " Head over all." He is the contemporary of every generation.

\* \* \* \* \*

The literature of Christian experience, whether in hymns and prayers or in confessional writings, is the literature of the Spirit ever causing new meanings to break forth out of old Scriptures with the " eternal voice of prophecy." It is never complete and cannot fully compass or exhaust the significance of the Living Word. As Dr. T. R. Glover has said, " one element of Christian happiness is that there is always more in Jesus Christ than we supposed." He Himself *means* more to us than anything He ever said. No attenuated form of Christianity, reduced to its lowest conceivable terms, can account for, generate or guarantee Christian experience in its wealth and power. Our heritage of grace and truth is great ; the cost at which it was procured and conserved none of us can ever estimate :

> " None of the ransomed ever knew
> How deep were the waters crossed."

Ours is the privilege to make use of it, as much of it as with sincerity and insight we can assimilate, that thereby we may attain fullness of life and be " meet for the Master's use."

# Appendix I

## KINDRED CLASSICS IN BRIEF

ON some kindred classics, selected from the extensive literature of the subject, chapters were in hand which, under limitations of space, are reluctantly set aside. They are briefly characterized and compared with others in the Introductory Survey, some of them also referred to in other chapters. Here a few guiding notes, indicating special lines of interest and relevant books, are appended for the use of those who desire to pursue the study further. Some of these writings, without regard to chronological order, are placed together because of their spiritual affinities.

### PASCAL'S " THOUGHTS " AND AMIEL'S " JOURNAL "

Pascal and Amiel may for our present purpose be considered together in that they endured a kindred mental travail as " God-seekers " (to use the Russian term) ; both were oppressed with the immensities of the universe and afflicted with the sense of human responsibilities and disabilities and the " fear of things "; and both sought certainty of soul through the insights of faith or intuitions of the heart penetrating and informing the processes of reason. In his essays on the two, Walter Pater, though from a different temperamental interest, revealed a sympathetic understanding of both in their quest for a spiritual home in the universe. According to Pater, Amiel " said some things in Pascal's vein not unworthy of Pascal."

(1) In the " Pensées " of Blaise Pascal (d. 1662 aged only 39)—conversations with himself, like those of Marcus Aurelius—are collected occasional and often fragmentary memoranda, scribbled (after prayer) on scraps of paper in frail health, drafted for a later but unwritten Apologetic work, and afterwards arranged by editors variously in orderly sequence. French in their lucidity and precision, often epigrammatic, vast in their sweep of vision, aglow with a sacred passion for a faith that is as reasonable as it is experimental, these " Thoughts "

have been germinal of subsequent impulse and reflection. He speaks of himself, and we must estimate him, in his triple capacity of geometrician, sceptic and Christian: these subsist together, though Christian faith predominates. Any account of Pascal would note his early scientific discoveries and inventions, his first theoretic conversion (so-called), his relapse into the worldly enjoyments of the refined Parisian society in which he had been bred, the sardonic infection derived from Montaigne, his " definitive conversion " in which eternal things were stamped on his heart and his eyeballs, certified by the memorial parchment he afterwards wore on his breast, full of the illuminating fire received and of his tearful joy and vital certainty through the grace of Jesus Christ. Yet his mental problems as to the incongruities of life persist: the ideal greatness of man and his littleness and infirmities, " the infirmities of a discrowned king," both recognized in Christianity; the incompetency of the philosophic reason to comprehend the immeasurable universe, and the need of refined perceptions and experimental action as the practical attestation of faith. " The heart has reasons which the reason does not know." Our search for God is due to the Divine initiative—" Thou wouldst not have sought Me unless thou hadst already found Me." Christ gives a practical solution of the ruling problems of our life. Then follow arguments in favour of Christianity.

See English versions of the " Pensées," by C. Kegan Paul, and by W. F. Trotter; Biographical and general works by Viscount St. Cyres, E. Boutroux, W. Clark, " Encyclopædia of Religion and Ethics," IX ; Studies, in Stewart's Hulsean Lectures on " The Holiness of Pascal," by Dean Church in St. James' Lectures, I, " Companions of the Devout Life," by Vinet in " Études sur Blaise Pascal," and by Pater in " Miscellaneous Studies."

(2) The " Journal Intime " of Amiel (d. 1881) presents the itinerary of his soul through thirty-three years, the " confidences of a solitary thinker " in whose complex nature several minds maintain a controversy without a unified conclusion. There is no personal history behind it—beyond the somewhat sterile occupancy of a university chair in Geneva—to cast light upon it. Yet, according to Mr. J. Middleton Murry, " he sounded in his soul the whole octave of the nineteenth century consciousness, and left a record of his experiences which has become a minor classic of the century." There appears no single crisis in his spiritual career, rather a continuous crisis in the ordeal of an inquiring religious mind that sees life from all points of

view in turn yet attains no unity of conviction, rejoices in nature's beauty and dreams of achievement yet sits brooding at his window an ailing and detached spectator of life without living. The sad ecstasy of the ideal restrains him from putting it to the proof through fear of failure or mistake. He would willingly give himself wholly to some noble end, but responsibility is his nightmare weakening him for action ; he is intimidated by the fatality of unforeseen consequences of action. Inward purity promotes intuition, but active endeavour also is a solvent of misgivings. " Faith is a certitude without proofs, and is an energetic principle of action," and " faith is made a dull poor thing by attempts to reduce it to a simple moral psychology," by " the transference of Christianity from the region of history to the region of psychology." " To win true peace, a man needs to feel himself directed, pardoned, and sustained by a supreme power, to feel himself in the right road, at the point where God would have him be—in order with God and the universe. This faith gives strength and calm. I have not got it." Though faith fails him with failing health, yet his heart's sympathies cry out in these words : " The Gospel proclaims the ineffable consolation, the good news, which disarms all earthly griefs, and robs even death of its terrors—the news of irrevocable pardon, that is to say, of eternal life. The Cross is the guarantee of the Gospel. Therefore it has been its standard."

See Mrs. Humphry Ward's translation, with Introduction ; Walter Pater's " Essays from the Guardian " ; J. Middleton Murry's " Countries of the Mind " ; J. A. Hutton's " Pilgrims in the Region of Faith."

### STA. TERESA, QUIETISTS, MADAME GUYON, AND QUAKERS

(1) The well-born Spanish lady, Sta. Teresa (d. 1582), pre-disposed to the allurements of the world, her precipitate entrance into a convent under a romantic disappointment being the start rather than the culmination of her inward contentions, carried passional womanly humanity, recurrent gaiety of spirit and a fine intelligence into her ardent religious devotion. In St. Augustine's " Confessions " she found herself described (see above, chap. I, par. 4). She displayed adventurous chivalry, organizing and executive ability in the extension and reform of Religious Houses, and shrewd sagacity—with the beak of the eagle no less than the coo of the dove—in her dealings with superiors and nuns and her penetration into human nature. Thus, apart from incidental visions and voices, the essential characteristics of this " Lady of the Lamp " have a parallel

in the real Florence Nightingale rather than in Madame Guyon. Of her Quietist moments something will be said immediately. Of her insight into the soul's revulsions let this example suffice. "Let no one ever say: If I fall into sin, I cannot then pray. In this the devil turned his most dreadful batteries against me, saying it shewed very little shame in me if I could have the face to pray, who had just been so wicked. And under that snare of Satan I actually as good as gave up all prayer for a year and a half. . . . What folly to the stumbler to run away from the light! When I was shunning prayer because I was so bad, my badness became more abandoned than ever it had been before. Rely on the waiting and abounding goodness of God, which is infinitely greater than all the evil you can do. . . . I grew weary of sinning before God grew weary of forgiving my sin."

Of her writings see her " Life " (not a full autobiography, rather a confession of " The Mercies of God " as she designated it), her " Foundations " (of historical value, with shrewd human vignettes), her " Way of Perfection " (to which William Law's " Christian Perfection " was much indebted), and her " Letters." See Mrs. Cunninghame Graham's ample work, " Sta. Teresa, her Life and Times "; Father Coleridge's " Life of Teresa," based on her " Letters "; Alex. Whyte's " Sta. Teresa: An Appreciation, with Selections from her Writings." Vaughan in " Hours with the Mystics," II, is antipathetic and unjust. In Huysman's novel, " En Route," a Parisian Pilgrim's Progress, Sta. Teresa is allotted a vital part in the return of the prodigal to his father's house.

(2) Quietism, at its best in a widespread movement, did not signify torpid inaction and sheer passivity, but a specific way of initiating activity. The Quietist relied, not on " creaturely " efforts of the human reason and will, but on the " direct invasion of God," the incursion of " supernatural " motions, operations and manifestations. The soul, carefully stilled in the repose of all its powers, awaits spontaneous quickenings, " openings," or " stoppings," and spiritual fecundity begetting directed action. Outwardly " the bush is bare," but psychologically there is keen action in the limitation of interest under the repression of " nature " and self-will, with consequent susceptibility to the subconscious and the " supernatural." In Prof. Rufus M. Jones' words, " the soul is unified, intensified, penetrated, *stands absolutely on attention* . . . and becomes a living centre of receptivity."

Baron von Hügel (" The Mystical Element of Religion," II, 133) shows that this unified consciousness, oblivious of self and all else, " is truly characteristic of the deepest, most creative moments," not only in the seers, but " in Nelson at Trafalgar, Napoleon at Waterloo, St. Ignatius in the amphitheatre, and Savonarola at the stake."

Sta. Teresa described this equilibrium. " It is a gathering together of the faculties of the soul within itself. . . . But the faculties are not lost, neither are they asleep; the will alone is occupied in such a way that, without knowing how it has become a captive, it gives a simple consent to be the prisoner of God." While in the first ordinary stage of prayer we are aware of our laborious endeavours after God, " in pure supernatural, transcendental prayer we do nothing at all. His Divine Majesty it is who does it all." We see extremes of Quietism conducing to self-sufficient unfruitful isolation, with psychic illusions and occasional vagaries. After other modes and theories of Being the quietist method is being employed to-day for the evaluation of resident psychic powers through the imagination directed by the personal will. Will it serve for the cure of sin or the perverse and devitalized moral nature without redemptive religion, as well as for the cure of natural ills ?

(3) Upon Madame Guyon (d. 1717) condemned by Bossuet, and imprisoned as a Quietist, see her " Autobiography " (translated by T. Allen); her " Method of Prayer " with Notes by D. Macfadyen; the " Life " by T. C. Upham; Vaughan's " Hours with the Mystics," II. See also Fénelon's " Spiritual Letters," and Life of him by Viscount St. Cyres. In spite of common sentiments, Madame Guyon and Fenelon were not robust enough to please William Law; the former's revelations and amatory language in relation to Jesus Christ were alien to his wholesome mysticism.

(4) English Quakers, the " Friends " of George Fox, were kindred with Madame Guyon in general idea and attitude, as also in inward reactions and in persecutions. Mr. Rendel Harris, who (he has confessed) " owed to her more help and guidance in the things of God than to any other," has noted that her " Method of Prayer " and " Autobiography " were among the chief causes which transformed militant Quakerism into Quietism. Fresh spiritual experience (see above, chap. I. par. 2) came to George Fox when, human help and even the reading of Scripture having failed him, his " heart did leap for joy " as an individual " revelation " or " Voice " said to him, " there is One, even Christ Jesus, who can speak to thy condition." The " opening " came to him that " every man

was enlightened by the Divine Light of Christ "; and this came to him without external help, though afterwards he found it in the Scriptures (cf. " Journal "). This Inner Light is held to be primary as " the fountain itself," the Scriptures being " secondary and subordinate to the Spirit, from whom they have received all their excellency and certainty," and to " the inward testimony of the Spirit " (Barclay's " Apology "). The need of correctives of untested individual inspirations from the light of all other human knowledge is now enforced. The distaste of Bunyan and others for early Quaker ways was to be expected. Quaker Quietism has been united with social reforming activity.

Quakers, watchful of inner " operations " have run to the production of Journals. After that by George Fox as primary (Barclay's " Apology " being expository), the classic is John Woolman's " Journal." Of that illiterate tailor (d. 1772). the " consummate flower of American Quakerism," who recorded his inward motions with unconscious grace, Charles Lamb said, " Get the writings of John Woolman by heart." To this add " Some Fruits of Solitude " by William Penn, which tinctured the heart and philosophy of R. L. Stevenson. See William C. Braithwaite's " Beginnings of Quakerism " and article in the " Encyclopædia of Religion and Ethics," VI ; works by Rufus M. Jones ; Teignmouth Shore's " John Woolman, his Life and our Times."

### JEREMY TAYLOR'S " HOLY LIVING " AND " HOLY DYING "

These twin books, while condensing the experience of Jeremy Taylor (d. 1667), as regulative directories of the religious life (see above, chap. I, 2) need little comment. Chaplain to Archbishop Laud and again to Charles I, attached to the Royalist troops during the Civil War, deprived of his living, captured by the Parliamentary Party, he found shelter for eleven years as chaplain to Lord Carbery at Golden Grove, South Wales. His public ministry silenced, he betook himself to the ministry of the pen, like his contemporaries John Bunyan and Samuel Rutherford, and wrote his classic of spiritual wisdom, abounding in pictorial imagery, pithy phrase and practical counsel with prayers attached. The principle of religious toleration announced in his " Liberty of Prophesying "—unfortunately assailed by Samuel Rutherford—he found it difficult to observe when later he became Bishop of Down and Connor and of Dromore. Of his spiritual kindred may be named Bishop Lancelot Andrewes, Archbishop Leighton and Bishop Thomas Wilson. See the

"Life" by Bishop Heber revised by Eden; another by Wilmott, especially that by Edmund Gosse in "English Men of Letters."

## Samuel Rutherford's "Letters"

John Wesley, after visits to Scotland which bore little fruit, wrote of the Scots: "They *hear* much, they *know* everything, and they *feel* nothing." The last count in the witty indictment would be disputed by any one acquainted with Scottish songs and ballads, deeply tinctured with covert emotion, and with the "Letters" of Samuel Rutherford (d. 1661), so tense with both natural and spiritual feeling. When under the Royal Supremacy Archbishop Laud imposed the English Church polity and worship upon the Scottish (Presbyterian) Church, Rutherford was removed on a charge of nonconformity from his beloved parish of Anworth near the Solway, and confined to Aberdeen and to "dumb Sabbaths." Of the 365 Letters preserved, 220 were written when an exile in "Christ's palace in Aberdeen," and they have a rightful place, if not in prison literature, in the literature of exiles, along with Dante's "Vision," Jeremy Taylor, and many others. On his release he was ere long appointed Regent, Professor, in St. Andrews University, and later a commissioner to the Westminster Assembly which produced the Confession of Faith and Catechisms. At the Restoration, when near death, he was summoned on a charge of high treason. In "Lex Rex" he had prophetically declared that "the power of creating a man a king is from the people," that "the law is not the king's own, but given him in trust." He answered the summons, "Tell them I have got a summons already from a Superior Court and Judicatory." On his last words, "Glory shineth in Immanuel's land," is based Mrs. Cusin's hymn, "The sands of time are sinking." A very gladiator, hot controversialist, learned theologian, he was yet a seraphic man of God, though he wrote, "My white side comes out on paper—but at home there is much black work. All the challenges that come to me are true." "I am made up of extremes," as he wrote, now in joyous transport and anon in sore "downcastings." Much consulted in things of the soul, he ministered in his Letters to the lesser nobility and to farmer folk consolation, correction and cheer. His sentences are often like lances, original in their metaphors—"we live far from the well, and complain but dryly of our dryness," "dry rather than thirsty,"—and luxuriant (sometimes drawing too much on the language of espousals) in his expressions towards Christ—"Christ is as full a feast as you have to hunger for."

See edition with Introduction by Dr. A. Bonar ; Selections for daily read'ng in Miss Soulsby's "Christ and His Cross" ; Alex. Whyte's "Samuel Rutherford and some of his Correspondents."

### NEWMAN'S "APOLOGIA PRO VITA SUA"

The narrative of the steps in his transition from the Anglican to the Roman communion given by John Henry Newman (d. 1890) in the "Apologia" lies outside our field of interest here ; yet under the controversial self-vindication there is found a rare confidential disclosure of a pure soul, in distrust of private judgment and liberalism, and in fear of the perils of personal responsibility, reasoning his way to religious certainty above reason and guaranteed by ecclesiastical authority. Early grounded in dogma, superstitious (he confesses), owing almost his soul to the evangelical commentator Thomas Scott, deeply impressed by William Law's "Serious Call" in an opposite direction as also by Sir Walter Scott's historical romances, he became enamoured of romantic mediæval ideals and of antiquity. His give and take in the Oxford Movement cannot here be recounted. Conscious of unseen guidance in his search for a secure fold—witness his hymn, "Lead, Kindly Light"—he groped his way, tortuous and enigmatic it may seem to us, to a position and destiny implicit in the early direction of his mind. The "Apologia" was called forth (see above, p. 226) on his entering the Roman Church by Charles Kingsley's reflections on the "economy" of truth of the Roman clergy and Newman. He put his sincerity and honour beyond suspicion. With all his purity of motive, he builds specious arguments on carefully selected premises, dexterous in cornering critics. " His subtlety misled himself as well as others. Like Pascal, he was by the natural turn of his intellect, next to a believer, a sceptic" (Cornish, "The English Church," I, 297). His humility touched with a silent pride, his freedom from earthly aims and his remoteness, his credulity and lack of critical scholarship, his stringency in virtue and holiness are features in his lofty, complex personality.

See Oxford edition of the "Apologia" (with earliest and later versions) ; biographies by W. Ward, by R. H. Hutton, Letters and Correspondence, edited by Miss Mozley ; "Characteristics from Newman," by W. S. Lilly ; Studies by J. A. Hutton, and G. G. Atkins.

# Appendix II

## SELECT LIST OF BOOKS

CHAPTER II.  ST. AUGUSTINE'S "CONFESSIONS"

*Text (Latin)* :
>   Gibb and Montgomery, with Introduction and Annotations
>       (Cambridge Patristic Texts).
>   Loeb (Latin and English).

*Translations* :
>   Bigg (C.), with Introduction (Methuen), occassionally quoted
>       in this chapter.
>   Smellie (A.), with Introduction (Melrose).
>   Pusey (E. B.), in Dent's "Everyman Library."
>   Nicene and Post-Nicene Fathers.

*Biographies* :
>   Farrar (F. W.), "Lives of the Fathers," II.
>   Bertrand (Louis), "St. Augustin," translated from the
>       French (Appleton).
>   Cunningham, "St. Austin and his place in the History of
>       Christian Thought."
>   "Dictionary of Christian Biography" (art. by Pressense).

*General Studies* :
>   Montgomery (W.), "St. Augustine : Aspects of his Life and
>       Thought."
>   Ottley (R. L.), "Studies in the Confessions of St. Augustine."
>   Harnack, "Monasticism and the Confessions of St. Augus-
>       tine."
>   "Encyclopædia of Religion and Ethics" (art. by B. B.
>       Warfield), Vol. II.
>   Atkins (G. G.), "Pilgrims of the Lonely Road," II.
>   "St. James's Lectures : Companions for the Devout Life,"
>       1st Series, V.

CHAPTERS III-VI. DANTE'S " VISION ": THE
" DIVINE COMEDY "

*Translations*—in verse: by Longfellow; Cary; Plumptre;
M. B. Anderson (new). In prose: by Norton;
" Inferno," by J. A. Carlyle.

*Aids and Interpretations:*
  Gardner (E. G.), Dante (Dent's Temple Series): brief
    summary.
  Wicksteed (P. H.), " Six Sermons on Dante."
  Dean Church, " Dante."
  Carroll (J. S.), 3 vols.: " Exiles of Eternity " ("Inferno");
    " Prisoners of Hope " ("Purgatorio"); " In Patria "
    ("Paradiso"): general full exposition.
  " Villani's Chronicle," edited by Selfe: historical.
  Sedgwick (H. D.), " Dante."
  Federn (K.), " Dante and His Times."
  Witte (K.), " Essays on Dante."
  Moore, " Studies in Dante," 3 series.
  Butler (A. J.), " Dante."
  Gardner (E. G.), " Dante and the Mystics "; " Dante's Ten
    Heavens "; article in " Encyclopædia of Religion and
    Ethics," Vol. IV.
  Wicksteed (P. H.), " Dante and Aquinas."
  Rossetti (M.), " Shadow of Dante."
  Boyd Carpenter, " Spiritual Message of Dante."
  Vernon, " Readings from the ' Purgatorio'."
  Carlyle, " Heroes and Hero Worship."
  Harris (W. T.), " Spiritual Sense of ' Divina Commedia'."
  Symonds (J. A.), " Introduction to the Study of Dante."
  Toynbee (Paget), " Studies in Dante "; " Dante Diction-
    ary "; " Dante in English Literature."
  Wright (Payling), " Dante and the ' Divine Comedy'."
  Oelsner, " Influence of Dante on Modern Thought."

CHAPTERS VII, VIII. TAULER'S " SERMONS," AND THE
" THEOLOGIA GERMANICA "

  Winkworth (C.), " Life and Sermons of John Tauler," with
    Preface by Charles Kingsley.
  Winkworth (C.), " Theologia Germanica," with Historical
    Introduction, and Preface by Charles Kingsley (Golden
    Treasury Series).

Jones (Rufus M.), " Studies in Mystical Religion."
Inge (W. R.), " Christian Mysticism."
Ditto, " Faith and Knowledge," chap. XIX (" Theologia
    Germanica.").
Ullmann, " Reformers before the Reformation," Vol. II.
Maeterlinck (M.), " Ruysbroeck and the Mystics," translated
    by J. T. Stoddart.
Kettlewell, and Montmorency, in their books on Thomas à
    Kempis (cf. chap. IX).

CHAPTER IX.   THOMAS À KEMPIS' " IMITATIO CHRISTI "

*Translations :*
    Liddon (H. P.), " Musica Ecclesiastica " (Scott).
    Bigg (C.), with Introduction.
    " Everyman Library " (early archaic version).
*Biographical and Historical :*
    Kettlewell (S.), " Thomas à Kempis and the Brothers of
        the Common Life," 2 vols.
    Montmorency (J. E. G. De), " Thomas à Kempis, his Age and
        Book."
    Butler (D.), " Thomas à Kempis: A Religious Study."
    " Encyclopædia Brit.," art by T. M. Lindsay, Vol. XIV.
    Wheatley (L. A.), " The Story of the ' Imitatio Christi.' "
    Fitzgerald (P.), " The World's Own Book."
    Ullmann, " Reformers before the Reformation," Vol. II.
*General Studies :*
    " St. James's Lectures : Companions for the Devout Life,"
        1st Series, I.
    Atkins (G. G.), " Pilgrims of the Lonely Road," III.

CHAPTER X.   BUNYAN'S " GRACE ABOUNDING," AND
        " PILGRIM'S PROGRESS "

*Texts :*
    " Grace Abounding," edition by Dr. John Brown (Cambridge
        University Press).
    " Pilgrim's Progress," ditto.
*Biographical :*
    Brown, " Life of John Bunyan."
    Mark Rutherford (Hale White), ditto (Literary Lives.)
    Froude, Bunyan (English Men of Letters).
    " Encyclopædia of Religion and Ethics " (art. by J. M. E.
        Ross), Vol. II.

*Studies :*
Whyte (Alex.), " Bunyan Characters " : Vol. IV, " Bunyan Himself."
Macaulay's " Essays."
Glover (T. R.), " Poets and Puritans " : chapter on Bunyan.
Royce, " Studies in Good and Evil : The Case of John Bunyan."
" St. James's Lectures : Companions for the Devout Life," Second Series, VI.
Atkins (G. G.), " Pilgrims of the Lonely Road," V.
*Expositions of the Pilgrim's Progress :*
Whyte (Alex.), " Bunyan Characters."
Kelman (J.), " The Road."
Kerr Bain, " People of the Pilgrimage."


CHAPTER XI.   WILLIAM LAW'S " SERIOUS CALL " :   JACOB BEHMEN TO JOHN WESLEY

*Works of William Law :*
" Christian Perfection."
" The Serious Call."
" The Spirit of Prayer."
" The Spirit of Love."
*Biography and Studies of William Law :*
Overton (J. H.), " William Law : Nonjuror and Mystic."
Inge (W. R.), " Studies of English Mystics " : IV.   William Law.
Whyte (Alex.), " Characters and Characteristics of William Law " (with introductory biography and ample quotations from Law's works).
*Jacob Behmen :*
Martensen (H. L.), " Jacob Boehme : His Life and Teaching."
Vaughan (R. A.), " Hours with the Mystics," Vol. II.
*John Wesley :*
Wesley's " Journal."
Winchester (C. T.), " Life of John Wesley "; Tyerman's.


CHAPTER XII.   TOLSTOY'S " CONFESSIONS "

*Tolstoy's Works.*
" My Confession."
" My Religion."
" Anna Karenina," " Resurrection," and other works of fiction.

*Biographies and Studies :*
  Maude (Aylmer), " Life of Tolstoy."
  Noyes (G. P.), " Tolstoy " (Master Spirits of Literature).
  Rolland, " Life of Tolstoy."
  Winstanley (L.), " Tolstoy " (People's Books),
  Lloyd (J. A. T.), " Two Russian Reformers."
  " Tolstoy (Count Ilya), Reminiscences," by Tolstoy's son.
  Phelps (W. L.), " Essays on Russian Novelists," V.
  Arnold (Matthew), " Essays in Criticism," 2nd Series.
  Attins (G. G.), " Pilgrims of the Lonely Road," VII.


CHAPTER XIII.  MARCUS AURELIUS IN WALTER PATER'S
" MARIUS THE EPICUREAN "


I

*Marcus Aurelius :*
  *Translations* of the " Meditations " (with Introduction) by
    G. H. Rendall in " Marcus Aurelius Antoninus to Him-
    self " ; by C. R. Haines (in the Loeb Classical Library,
    with Greek text) ; and (older) Collier (revised by
    Zimmern), Long, Casaubon (1634) in " Everyman
    Library."
  *Historical :*
    Dill, " Roman Society from Nero to Marcus Aurelius."
    Bussell, " Marcus Aurelius and the Later Stoics."
    Sedgwick, " Marcus Aurelius."
    Hicks, " Stoic and Epicurean."
    Davidson, " The Stoic Creed."
    Alston, " Stoic and Christian in the Second Century."
    Myers, F. W. H., " Classical Essays " (Marcus Aurelius).


II

*Walter Pater's " Marius the Epicurean " :*
  Wright, " Life of Walter Pater," two vols.
  Benson, " Walter Pater " (English Men of Letters).
  Edmund Gosse, " Critical Kit-Kats."
  Greenslet, " Walter Pater " (Contemporary Men of Letters).
  Kelman, " Among Famous Books."

CHAPTER XIV.    RABINDRANATH TAGORE'S " SONG OFFERINGS "
AND " MEDITATIONS "

Rabindranath Tagore, *Gitanjali* : "Song Offerings."
*Sādhanā* (Meditations) :    " The
Realization of Life."
" Personality."
" The Gardener."
" My Reminiscences."
" Creative Unity."

Rhys (Ernest), " Rabindranath Tagore : a Biographical
Study."

Roy (Basanta Koomar), " Rabindranath Tagore : the Man
and his Poetry."

Farquhar (J. N.), " Modern Religious Movements in India,"
chapters I, II, VII.

Urquhart (W. S.), " Pantheism and the Value of Life,"
with special reference to Indian Philosophy, chapters
XVI, XVII.

# Index

*Printed in Great Britain by* Butler & Tanner, *Frome and London*

Printed in the United States
1004300001B